SYMBOL AND MYTH IN ANCIENT POETRY

The Acts of the Pagan Martyrs: Acta Alexandrinorum (Oxford 1954)

St. Methodius: The Symposium, Translation in Ancient Christian Writers 27 (London and Westminster, Md. 1958)

ΚΤΗΜΑ ΕΙΣ ΑΙΕΙ

SYMBOL

AND MYTH

IN ANCIENT POETRY

𐃀𐃀𐃀𐃀𐃀𐃀𐃀𐃀𐃀𐃀𐃀𐃀𐃀𐃀𐃀𐃀𐃀𐃀𐃀𐃀

HERBERT MUSURILLO, S.J.

FORDHAM UNIVERSITY PRESS. NEW YORK

To John and Mildred

and

Jack and Jill

Acknowledgments

The Classical World for permission to use a reworked version of my article "Horace's Journey to Brundisium," *CW* 48 (1955)159ff.

The Macmillan Company for the two poems quoted from F. L. Lucas, *Greek Poetry for Everyman*, copyright 1951.

The Johns Hopkins Press for permission to use a reworked version of my article "Sunken Imagery in Sophocles' *Oedipus*," *AJP* 78 (1957)36ff.

The University of Chicago Press for permission to use a reworked version of my article "Dream Symbolism in Petronius," *CP* 53 (1958)108ff.

The University of Michigan Press for the quotation from F. O. Copley, *Catullus: The Complete Poems*, 1957.

CONTENTS

POETRY AND SYMBOLIC COMMUNICATION

It has often been wondered what impression the modern world would make upon the ancient Greek or Roman, if, by some miracle of time, he were suddenly brought back from the past. According to one version of the story, Thucydides would become a news reporter, and Herodotus would join a conservative historical association; Plato would feel quite at home in the company of modern philosophers, but he would be quite chagrined that philosophy had advanced so little since his own day; Aristotle, Hippocrates, and Ptolemy would be quite mystified by the unbelievable progress of science and medicine, but Pericles, Alexander, and Caesar would see little change in the world of power politics, and Cicero would be willing to stay and settle for a modest Cabinet post. One group has been left out of the story, and I think they are the ones who would feel most at home in the modern world: the ancient poets and artists.

For Homer, Vergil, Sophocles, and Horace would surely be aware that, apart from the differences of time and place, all poets fundamentally speak the same language. It is not that national traditions do not develop their own poetic conventions and artistic problems. But all poetry—and all art—no matter what the language or culture, must revolve about two stable foci: the essential mystery of man in the world, and the symbolic mode by which the poet attempts to express and explore it. Herein lies the foundation for the continuity of western art and literature, even though we may trace a vital, organic growth through the centuries. It is the purpose of this study to throw some light on the ancient poet's use of image and symbol, and to show how close, in craft and imagination, the Greek and Roman poets are to the psychological and artistic awareness of today. It is the ancient poet's imagination which especially reveals how integral a part of the western literary tradition is the poetic achievement of the ancient world.

It may be said in general that symbols are objects or events which are considered to have, in addition to their original, objective function, another deeper reference or relationship. I have found it useful to distinguish three types of symbol; the gestural symbol, the symbol-artefact, and the verbal or linguistic symbol. All of these are analogous, and it would perhaps be impossible to formulate a definition which would fit all of them; but they have this much in common, that in every case there is a manipulation of the spatio-temporal, the sensuous, for the purpose of conveying an intelligent or spiritual experience — an idea, a desire, a conflict, a decision. Although in more recent times symbolic expression has served as a vehicle of thought and self-exploration, it would appear that primitively, at least, all symbols were dialogic and interpersonal. Man has used symbols to communicate with other men as well as with the forces beyond the visible universe; and the world in turn was felt to be a "forest of symbols," as Baudelaire called it, by which the otherworldly powers communicate with men.

It should, however, be noted that a distinction should be made between the terms image and symbol, although they are sometimes used synonomously. Any manipulation of the sensuous in literature may, in general, be called symbolic, and when the term "symbol" is used, what is uppermost in one's mind is the further dimension or meaning implied, especially if it be of a philosophical or theological sort. The term "image," however, usually stresses the aspect of sensuous picture; at the same time, since in poetry images most often have a further reference (the *vehicle* is said to carry a *tenor*, in the terminology of I. A. Richards) it is easy to see how an image might be said to be symbolic. Again, symbols tend to be more explicit, whereas imagery may be "sunken" and barely suggested. The actual persons portrayed in a piece of poetry or literature are not correctly discussed under the heading of imagery; they may, however, be symbolic. What is most important in this discussion is not the terminology, but the analysis of the various levels of meaning that human communication can and does have, especially in the very complex area of literature. These levels of meaning are, it would seem, indefinite in extent. This is the true function of literary criticism, to comprehend the depth and complexity of the artistic message.

Symbols occur in all human activities, and before enumerating the broad categories, I should like to discuss the conditions of the "sign-situation" according to the viewpoint of modern communication theory.[1] In all communication we may distinguish the sender or encoder, the message, and the interpreter or decoder. The sender selects from a vast "set" or area of possibilities; the receiver or decoder interprets the information, despite the "noise" or obstacles in the circuit, in accordance with certain mathematical formulae. From the scientific point of view, the message is considered as consisting of so many "bits" of information. But here we are primarily interested in the role symbols play in conveying meaning.

In discussing the meaning of the symbol, we may usefully distinguish between the sign-type and the sign-token. The sign-type, as it is called, is the sign (symbol, word, or whatever) as explained, for example, in a dictionary or manual; it is a universal and not a concrete; it is what the sign may be expected to mean from previous occurrences. The sign-token, on the other hand, is the actual use of the sign in the concrete communication. Further, the meaning of the sign may be considered as a continuum, at each end of which are two important poles, denotation and connotation. The sign may be primarily denotative, conveying definite information, or it may be primarily expressive, as, for example, in a purely emotional manifestation; but in human communication both elements are usually interrelated. For this phenomenon Allen Tate has, in another context, used the term "tension" to express the equilibrium which exists between "extension" (or denotation) and "intension" (or connotation).

There must invariably exist a gap between man's inner awareness and its outward, symbolic expression. Hence the meaning or tenor of the symbol (sign-token) will always involve a certain degree of ambiguity. There is, first of all, the ambiguity of self-description. The ability to become aware of oneself and to express oneself to others has had a long, progressive growth; and many of the interrelated problems have been discussed by the German phenomenologist, Georg Misch in his *History of Autobiography in Antiquity*.[2] In this area, as in others, it is not only the expression that causes difficulty: it is also the problem of knowing ourselves—a problem all the more acute because it appears so easy

4

of solution. This problem will recur from time to time in our analysis of ancient poetic expression. For even in literature which pretends to be an accurate transcription of the poet's own feelings or his immediate experience, there is always the tension between *Dichtung und Wahrheit*, as Goethe called it, imaginative creativity and factual truth.

A similar symbolic tension exists, indeed, in the expression of any historical phenomenon; once again there is the unbridgeable gulf between the bare, pragmatic linguistic symbol and the infinite complexity of the historical facts, especially when they are interwoven with the feelings and motivations of men. Thus it may perhaps be said that there is no area of written human history that has been definitively expressed without the possibility of further revision. Written history—not to be confused with History as such—is constantly subject to sharper focussing, clarification and correction. The problem of history is intimately connected with the discussion of the ambiguity of symbolic expression; we cannot, however, attempt to cover it in this book.

The chief area of our concern here is the employment of signs in a work of literature and, specifically, in ancient poetry. William Empson has advanced the problem with his *Seven Types of Ambiguity*;[3] indeed, the number seven might here be taken in the ancient Semitic sense of "manifold," and "indefinitely many." For there is not only the difficulty of literary craftsmanship as such in the expression of complex emotional or ideational states; as Empson has reminded us, a large area of ambiguity arises in the very transition from the spoken to the written word. Now this sort of ambiguity can become very acute in our study of ancient literature, be it Greek or Latin, Hebrew or Sanskrit. For, to restrict ourselves to the poetry alone, there was the whole dimension of performance, oral communication, often with the accompaniment of music and the dance. Thus many of our problems of comprehension arise merely from the appearance of the words on the printed page—an eventuality which the ancient poet did not always foresee. The difficulty is perhaps more extensive than some would at first suppose. The Temple-performance of ancient Hebrew psalms, the song-dance enactment of the Greek choral lyric on festive occasions, the historic context even of Latin poetry such as Vergil's *Eclogues*—the loss of all these concrete circumstances in the performance of ancient poetry renders us seriously liable to misinterpret it. It is the concrete context which makes the communication more intelligible. In any case, it is a fact that the spoken word may be quite unambiguous in a dialogue between two persons immersed in the sign-situation; yet once consigned to the printed page and removed from the original context in time and space, the word can give rise to serious misinterpretations. As theorists in communication would say, the written message does not have a sufficient degree of "redundancy;" the "noise," or interference in the channel, is too great for us to comprehend the original message. Thus, for various reasons, symbols are said to be ambiguous and plurisignificant; they may have many levels of meaning, and the area of correct interpretation must depend upon the complexities of the concrete relationship between sender and receiver linked in the sign situation.

Although we are here primarily concerned with the linguistic sign, it will be useful for us to enumerate some of the various types of symbols and discuss some of their implications. Of the three basic types of sign which we have mentioned earlier, the gestural, the artificial and the verbal, the gestural is perhaps the most primitive and at the origin of all the others. The gestural symbol is at the root of all human communication. Among the most common of these are the so-called "natural" semantic gestures in use within various linguistic communities: there are gestures to indicate

joy and disgust, love and sorrow; there are gestures to indicate direction and distance, praise and blame, as well as
various other nuances of human communication. There are
a vast number of these—there is so much variety from community to community—and they are now being catalogued
and correlated in the comparatively new science of kinemics
or kinesics. A second type of gestural symbol is the dramatic. It would seem instinctive to man to make-believe, to
play-act, to enact a role; and it is impossible to give an ade-
quate definition of what we mean by acting. We can only
define it ostensively, by demonstrating how it is done. Whether
the prehistoric origins of drama are to be connected with
religious ritual or with man's play instinct or, as I feel, with
both, is not relevant to our present discussion. We are here
simply considering the dramatic gesture as one type of human
symbol.

For the history of religions, the most important symbol
is the third type, the ritual gesture, which scholars today
tend to break down into many kinds, as, for example, the
magical, the therapeutic, the sacramental, and the sacrificial.
Here we have all the various types of prayer-gestures, rituals for curse or cure, acts which help to bring man in
contact with the transcendent or manipulate otherworldly
powers for man's own benefit. Whether the dance should be
listed as a dramatic or a religious gesture is open to controversy, and it would be best perhaps to consider it as a separate type. Dancing is, fundamentally, the movement of the
human body and limbs to rhythm; it is another vehicle of
human expression and communication.

The artificial symbol or symbol-artefact need not detain
us long. It is the use of shape or design for communication.
We see its primitive form in fetishes, amulets, and charms;
it is at the basis of pictographic design, and thus at the heart
of all written language as well as the plastic arts.

Finally, we have the verbal or linguistic symbol, and this may be considered on various levels. The primary linguistic symbol is the word, that is, the spoken or phonated word (or message) in the concrete context of communication. The pictographic or written word is, in the various languages, merely an artificial design used to represent the flow of speech. It is often said by some extremists that the spoken word is ultimately untranslatable from language to language; although this an exaggeration, there is an important truth in the statement. But so much the more untranslatable is the *written* word; but nonetheless it is to the written word that we are of necessity condemned for the bulk of our philosophy and literature; the invention of civilised man, the written word is also his curse. The written text, even apart from all the possible errors of transmission, the farther it moves in time and space, must inevitably give rise to greater difficulty and ambiguity.

It was the primitive use of the linguistic symbol in folktale and in poetry which brought about the development of the various literatures. On the one hand we find gifted writers (or speakers) using very complicated symbols to produce permanent records of events, celestial phenomena or medical experiments; on the other hand, some engage in the symbolic verbal play associated with community or family song and dancing. Poetry and the dance become the regular accompaniment to harvest festivals, religious rituals or purifications, marriages and deaths, work and play. In very primitive literature it was not always important that a song or narrative be recognized as an individual creation; very often the original author or authors would have been forgotten. The symbolic importance of a poem or a narrative would be the fact that it served as a community vehicle, to embody the feelings and attitude of the entire audience; later, perhaps, the literary work would express the more complicated emotion or experience of an individual poet; it would be the vehicle by which he could communicate to an audience his personal awareness of the meaning of life and death and of the power of the gods. So too, within the body of the narrative or poem, the poet would make use of various images, objects, or events to symbolize meanings which he found otherwise difficult to express.

So much then by way of a preliminary on the nature of the symbol. Though it is a difficult concept and covers an extremely wide range, we have not, at the moment, a substitute for it equally as good. "Symbol" refers to the whole realm of meanings which we give to man's concrete gestures and acts of communication. Man, as Ernst Cassirer has said, is *animal symbolicum*. In dealing with the symbol we are touching the deepest part of man; and in the sign-situation we are at the heart of man's dialogic relationship with the universe. The symbol is man's vehicle for the exploration of the self and of the cosmos; though expressive of his emerging awareness, it is always incomplete and ambiguous, ever entailing further search, and further penetration into the infinite depths of reality.

What this poetic exploration meant for the ancients I shall try to discuss in the course of the following chapters. But one final remark is perhaps in order. I do not intend to assert that all the best of ancient poetry was allegorical, or even in the strict sense didactic. In a day when didactic poetry has fallen into disrepute and somehow requires an apology, it is important to recall that poems like Vergil's *Georgics* were among the finest pieces of poetic craftsmanship of the ancient world. Indeed, if generalizations can be made, the Latins, who had a more practical concept of the role of the poet than the Greeks of the classical age, (cf. Horace, *Ep.* 2.1.126ff.) were far more successful in producing truly great didactic poetry. But much of the modern aversion for ancient

Greek and Latin poetry is, I think, based on a misconception of Horace's notion that a poem should combine the *utile* and the *dulce*, the useful and the pleasant. The entire passage in the *Art of Poetry*, where the line occurs, is stressing the importance of content and meaning in poetry as opposed to empty technique (295ff.)

Poetry should not consist of mere tuneful pleasantries (*nugae canorae*), but have a further dimension to hold the mind. Great poetry should have the intuitive vision and the wisdom of Socrates which Horace so commends in the earlier lines.

How the ancient Greek and Latin poet used imagery to convey this further dimension in poetry will be the subject of this book. Our method is admittedly of its nature a limited one; the area of the ancient imagination is one in which much more work remains to be done. In any case, our effort will perhaps throw some light on the origins of that orphan child, as Horace calls her (*Ars* 377),

> Born and found
> Only to give delight to the souls of men.

THE CRITICISM OF ANCIENT LITERATURE

THAT THE ANCIENT POETIC SYMBOL HAS BEEN FOR THE most part neglected is nothing to be wondered at.[1] And yet, until this avenue is fully explored we can never be said really to understand ancient Greek and Latin poetry. We must then enter, so far as we can, into the ancient poet's creative imagination. Though modern literary criticism has provided us with a wide variety of techniques, these still remain to be fully exploited in the field of ancient poetry.

Our chief problem in criticizing ancient poetry has been intimated in our first chapter: it is now almost impossible to bridge the time-gap, to recreate the original concrete terms of communication, to eliminate all the "noise" or interference which renders interpretation difficult. The more ancient a poet is, the more removed in cultural and linguistic background, the more difficult will it be to penetrate his poetry and to comprehend the relationship which he enjoyed with his prospective audience. The poet's job is to make his message capture the sympathy of his audience; he is hardly to be blamed for being unaware of the peculiar sort of imagery or poetic logic which might appeal to later generations of critics. That the message of so many Greek and Roman poets does "involve" a modern trained reader is, indeed, a sign of special power; but when his tone, poetic texture, and meaning-sequences sometimes escape our grasp, this should hardly cause us to wonder.

In the criticism of ancient poetry translation is only a tool, never a goal. The degree of inadequacy of a translation apart from a translator's technical competence, will usually be a function of the originality and aesthetic complexity of the original. In an age distinguished by its "little Latin and less Greek," we are fortunate in possessing whole libraries of competent translations. But in the case of ancient poetry at least, we must not lose sight of the fact that the translation has a relative, not an absolute, value.

Translation is, of course, an indispensable tool. But it is only the beginning. In the past, perhaps too much emphasis was placed on mere translation as an approach to our ancient authors. Rather, once the preliminary work of philology has been done, we must attempt to probe the poetry by internal analysis. For this purpose, I shall discuss a number of useful headings which are designed to create the proper psychological threshold for the analysis and appreciation of the Latin and Greek poets.

I. PERSONA AND VOX: THE POET'S VOICE

In our criticism of ancient poetry, it is of prime importance to grasp the *tone* of the poem. To do this adequately we may ask ourselves a series of questions, or consider the poet's achievement according to certain limited categories, Voice, Setting, Sense, Feeling, Tone, Symbol, Mythology, Landscape, and so on. Each of these considerations, however, will invariably involve all the others; the poem is always a totality, and it can be dangerous to treat any element in isolation. One of the first questions to be asked is: in what character, in what voice, is the poet speaking? Most often in Greek and Latin lyric poetry, he speaks in his own person: it is Archilochus, Sappho, Catullus, and so on, speaking from their limited vantage point, addressing a particular audience or even a particular individual.

Greek choral odes here raise a delicate problem. The Chorus has, indeed, several voices: at times it is the voice of the particular character—maiden, woman, sailor, old man—which they represent. Here the remarks will be in character, limited and sometimes stereotyped. This is the attitude assumed by the Chorus-leader when he speaks the dialogue portions of the play. Here the vision of the Chorus as well as its action is severely restricted; they may not normally initiate anything nor take sides in a conflict. At other times, and especially in the choral odes, the Chorus seems to doff the character-mask and assume a prophetic air: they may have knowledge of distant places; they dispense advice of a deeply theological sort. Here most often it is the dramatist himself speaking through a very thin disguise. In its third role, the Chorus simply sings a hymn or a poem, related to the action at least as a kind of arabesque or a lyric comment on the drama. Here the Chorus offers little more than a pause, an interlude between the episodes. It is the Chorus functioning as Choir. There are then three voices: the Chorus-Actor, the Chorus-Prophet (often the voice of the poet himself), and the Chorus-Choir. It is important to distinguish these three levels if we are to recapture the dramatic significance of the Chorus' role. For it is only as Chorus-Prophet and Choir that it may penetrate the fourth wall of the theatre, acting as a link between the audience and the world of fantasy of the stage. Again, the Greeks experienced no difficulty in reconciling the flat comments of the Chorus-Actor with the more profound analyses of the Prophet. It was precisely this tension which lends the Chorus a profound and moving quality within the total tragic rhythm.

In some of the most effective of ancient poetry the poet may speak through the mouth of another person or even by personification (the Greek προσωποποιία) in the guise of an inanimate object. The ancient funeral elegy or lament was presented as sung over the dead *by the living*—like the mourning of Priam, Helen and Andromache over the death of Hector. And care would be taken to make the poetic expression fit or suit the person who uttered the lament, by a device often called ἠθοποιία, or character adaptation. The epitaph or sepulchral epigram was, however, quite different. This was represented as being spoken by the grave, the tomb-stone, or by the shade of the dead person himself. These inscriptions were ultimately intended as identification; hence the epitaph would usually contain some reference to the identity of the person buried, the cause of death, and so on. Some of the extant epigrams are dull, commissioned work; but others reflect an inspiration and a depth that is quite moving. An early example of the first sort of composition is Martial's lovely lament for the baby Erotion (5.34):

> I pray that she may be playing carefree
> Among guardians so much older than she,
> And that her baby lips may lisp my name.

An early example of the formal tomb inscription is the song of the bronze maiden over the grave of Midas, a composition attributed to Cleobulus.[2] In the delightful version of Lucas, it runs:

Here, a maiden of bronze, I stand on Midas' grave,
And as long as runs the water, as long as tall trees wave,
As long as the sun, to light us, and the bright moon mount
the sky,
As the rivers flow, and the breakers along their beaches cry,
Beside this tomb of sorrow my shape its vigil keeps,
To tell the traveller passing that here King Midas sleeps.

In these pieces the very restrictions of the form have helped shape the total symbol.

Much of the charm of the ancient lyric poet lay in his ability to change the Voice of his poem dramatically. In epic narrative this would be common enough. It is in the subjective lyric where the technique becomes more difficult and challenging. In the lyric, it should be noted, the poet does not attempt to change the style completely as he might were he writing epic. He must keep within the total mood and tone of his poem. In Alcman's *Maiden Song*, we are aware of the poet's ability to move from one team to the other as the girls compete among themselves. We notice a similar skill in Catullus' *Epithalamia* 61 and 62; Horace's *Carmen saeculare* is quite heavy-handed by comparison. Dramatic sections in ancient lyric poetry are not always successful from this point of view; but the theophany and speech of Aphrodite in Sappho's famous hymn form the real focus of the poem;[3] and the plaintive prayer of Danae in Simonides' famous fragment[4] is surely one of the most beautiful pieces in ancient literature. The technique, of course, tends to become a mere trick in later Hellenistic poetry; statues, paintings, doors, animals, and streams all speak in character and the Greek Anthology offers full evidence of the extremes to which writers could go.

In ancient poetry, then, it would seem that the poetic voice is not as important as it was later to become in medieval and modern literature. But we must not, for all that, completely neglect it. For example, in Catullus' *Carm.* 4, the poet partly lets his yacht speak for him and boast of its origins and achievements. We may, of course, prescind from the controversy whether Catullus is speaking of a real yacht or a miniature model or an ex-voto. Poetically we see a yacht, magically transformed from virgin forest to a flying ship bearing her master back to Italy. Emotionally the yacht is almost human, as she passes from the "violent swells," *impotentia freta*, of the sea to the calm of Sirmione's "limpid lake;" there is an almost unconscious identification of the yacht with the poet himself, as he makes his imaginative trip from Asia Minor back to his home. And now, too, like the little boat, he "grows old in peace" (*senet quiete*)—now that he has seen his brother's grave, and has finally broken with Lesbia. The suggestion is a bold one, but the identity of poet and ship recalls the theme of Rimbaud's *Drunken Boat* (*Bateau Ivre*). Rimbaud, too, a young man like Catullus, sees himself transported over wild seas and exotic lands until, at the end, he cries, *Je ne puis plus*, "I can go no further." A vast difference in poetic talent separates Catullus and Rimbaud but the bond that unites them is their childlike view of the world of the imagination which both shared.

2. SCAENA: THE SETTING

Once we have established the Voice of the poem, we should attempt to discover whether it has a particular setting. Sometimes the setting will be obvious—as, for example, in Horace's *Odes* 1. 5 *Quis multa gracilis*, and *Odes* 1. 9 *Vides ut alta*. In many ancient lyrics, it is true, setting is either unimportant or non-existent. But there are others where an exact understanding of the *scaena* would immeasurably clarify the meaning of the poem. Such a poem is Catullus' *Carm.* 4, for example: we are not sure how the yacht, *phaselus*, is being exhibited, nor are we sure that guests, *hospites*, refers to Catullus' house-guests; they may merely be the ξένοι, or passersby, and in this case the poem would have the tone of a dedicatory inscription.

Setting is an important factor in Catullus' *Carm.* 51, *Ille mi par*,[5] and the poem of Sappho's from which it is derived, Sappho LP 31. Sappho's fragment is apparently concerned with one of the young girls who has begun to move out of Sappho's protective orbit; she sits opposite a young man, and Sappho, almost with a tinge of jealousy, thinks that he surely has reached the pinnacle of happiness while she herself undergoes all the fierce pangs of love and despair and sensuous attraction. It is a curious poem, and the frank expression of passion raises a psychological problem which modern scholars have found difficult to solve. Further, what is the poem's concrete setting? It would appear that the only occasion on which two young people would be sitting together conversing, as Sappho's poem suggests, would be in connection with betrothal or actual marriage; this indeed would give a somewhat ironic tone to the expression of Sappho's love.

Now when we shift to Catullus' poem and the environment of Rome, the setting is completely different. Any man is divinely happy, says Catullus (and he need not be thinking of any man in particular), who sits conversing with Lesbia, and the sight of her arouses the various symptoms of passion which Catullus borrows from the Sapphic fragment, including even the *tenuis flamma* which courses through his limbs.[6] But what are we to think of the final strophe, "Leisure is bad for you, Catullus," *Otium, Catulle, tibi molestum est*, which all the manuscripts consider as part of the same poem?[7] In my view, they are essential to the poem. The key word is *otium*, implying, in this case, a sensuous sort of daydreaming. Taken in this sense, the entire description of Lesbia and of Catullus' own reactions are a sensuous daydream; the very adaptation of Sappho's elaborate description of passion underlines the fact that the situation is unreal, it is merely in Catullus' fervent imagination. In this way Catullus justifies himself, as it were, for borrowing the description from a Greek poem; a literary borrowing would precisely fit an unreal daydream.

A further extension of Setting is the notion of Landscape, which we shall treat in detail farther on. It becomes useful in criticism when there is a constantly recurring setting, especially of a broad geographic sort, which functions as the backdrop for the poet's imaginative stage. Some literary genres, for example pastoral, have usually been associated with definite sorts of landscape. But we shall reserve the treatment of this for the next chapter.

3. SENSE

By the sense of a poem we mean the poet's total message. It is delivered, as we have suggested, in a particular setting and in a special tone of voice. Or, again, the poem may be thought of as a kind of drama being enacted, symbolically, on an imaginative stage. Different poems will lend themselves now to one, now to the other sort of analysis. To get at the sense, one of the best means has been the method of translation or paraphrase. Of course, the total sense of the poem cannot be separated from all the other elements—many of which cannot be expressed in another medium—but by translation or outline we can help ourselves to penetrate the concrete experience of the poet and appreciate it. All such devices and, indeed, all analyses, are merely means to an end. They are never substitutes for the poet's actual creation.

By way of summary, therefore, we may ask ourselves: what is the theme of the poem? In ancient poetry this is not always easy to answer; in the longer pieces, such as the epics, and in the plays, theme is much more elusive than it is in shorter lyrics. Indeed, in our search for theme we may often find that ancient poetry lacks the sort of imaginative, structural unity that we are used to from modern literature. To speak of theme in the *Iliad*, for example, should not lead us to expect a tighter unity than the one we actually find. Stated simply, the theme of the *Iliad* is the mental and spiritual growth of a young hero doomed to an early death: it is the story of Achilles' growing awareness of the meaning of war, suffering and pain. But to put it this way does an injustice to the richness and variety of the epic canvas which are part of its charm. The structure is even looser in the *Odyssey*. There the homeward voyage and the single hero form a flimsy pretext for a delightful succession of adventures. There is no theme in the strict sense; we find the wanderings of Odysseus much more fascinating than his homecoming. Strict unity is not to be demanded of the primitive epic. It is indeed remarkable that Lucretius in his *On the Nature of the Universe*, is so successful in maintaining a single theme and a unified tone in such disparate material. For not only has he transformed philosophical lectures into poetry, but he delivers them with the fervor of an evangelist. Vergil, too, reveals his superior craft when he is studied from the viewpoint of theme and artistic unity. It is almost as if he has taken the emotional unity of the *Iliad* and the imaginative variety of the *Odyssey* and fused them into a poetic whole. The *Aeneid's* singleness of purpose cannot be mistaken.

As a clue to the meaning or general theme of a piece of literature, we sometimes find a central or focal passage or, in a shorter work, a central, dominant image. Such a focal passage occurs in twenty-fourth book of the *Iliad* (468-644), in the pathetic interview between Achilles and Priam: it reflects, as no other part of the poem, the meaning of the epic insofar as Homer himself understood it. The *Odyssey* has no focal scene in this sense, even though the poetic centre of gravity hovers about Odysseus' sojourn at the court of Alcinous and Arete in Phaeacia. In the *Aeneid*, however, we have such a focal scene in the Descent into Hell of the sixth book, and especially in the speech of Father Anchises explaining the meaning of Rome's providential destiny.[8]

In shorter poems we will often find a clue to the meaning hidden within a central image. Images of this sort can be seen, for example, in the vision of the Elysian fields in Tibullus 1. 3, in the food-images of Horace, *Satires* 1. 1 (which embody the philosophic concept of moderation), in the Hades of the lyric poets of Horace, *Odes* 3.13. We shall discuss the function of such images farther on; suffice it for the present to indicate the importance of the image as a source of symbolic unity.

4. FEELING AND TONE

By "feeling" in poetry is meant the emotions or sentiments suggested or portrayed within the dramatic action of the poem. A person may be pictured as experiencing an emotion, as Attis in Catullus 63, Pyrrha and her young lover in Horace, *Odes* 1. 5. Objects and scenery can sometimes convey overtones of feeling and sentiment, like the pastoral landscape in the *Lament for Bion*, where all the pastures and woodland mourn the poet's passing. Flowers and dew, fruit, trees and young saplings, the light of the moon—all these have special overtones in the poetry of Sappho; the phenomena of spring have a special feeling for Horace; there is a special emotional atmosphere which Vergil creates about such characters as Dido, Camilla, Ascanius. The exact emotion and feeling in ancient poetry is sometimes difficult for us to capture precisely, but the general area and direction can usually be defined.

We must, however, carefully distinguish "feeling" from "tone." By "tone" is meant the poet's attitude, emotional or otherwise, towards his audience. Here, in ancient as in modern poetry, it is not always easy to discover. In the *Aeneid*, for example, how are we to understand the poet's attitude in the scene in the fourth book where Aeneas abandons Dido? What is the precise tone of the final scene of the last book where Aeneas kills Turnus? What does the poet mean to convey by the end of the sixth book where Aeneas comes up from Hades through the Gate of Ivory? In some ancient poets, like Homer, Theognis, Sappho, Catullus, Tibullus, tone is easily recaptured; in others, like Pindar, Horace, Propertius, it can be extremely subtle and frustrating. For example, the tone and meaning of Propertius 4. 7, *Sunt aliquid manes*, would be clearer if we could be certain that Cynthia were really dead; as the poem stands, it could be interpreted as an elaborate and somewhat morbid jest signalizing the termination of Cynthia's love.[9] Another piece of Propertius' that has aroused wide controversy is 1.21, *Tu qui consortem properas*, which seems to be put into the mouth of a dead soldier lying on the desolate battlefield of Perugia. The questions of voice, setting and tone are here most crucial.

The problem of feeling and tone is notoriously acute in the *Eclogues* of Vergil. The intentions of Theocritus and his circle, despite the conventions of their pastoral poetry and its occasional artificiality, are straightforward enough. But with Vergil the tone has changed. The *Eclogues*, however elusively beautiful, are not at home in the Italic countryside, and the frequent allusions to contemporary political affairs cause us to doubt that we have completely understood what Vergil is trying to do. At times the shepherds' names seem mere masks to hide historical personages. There is, for many a modern reader, a complete breakdown of communication. We have not fully recaptured the tone; as a result, the total meaning of the *Eclogues* escapes us.[10]

Tone in Horace is often ambiguous, or, at best, ironical and whimsical. This is largely the source of the difficulty in interpreting his *Odes* 1.2, *Iam satis terris*, especially the report of the various phenomena in the first five stanzas; the so-called conversion ode, 1.32, *Parcus deorum cultor*; the ode to the fallen tree, 2.13, *Ille et nefasto*; the peculiarly ambiguous *Epode* 2, on wealth, *Beatus ille*, with its surprising, cynical close. There are many more, and some I propose to treat farther on in my discussion of Horatian imagery. The manner in which Horace may have declaimed such poems, or the circumstances in which they were written, may perhaps have helped to clarify their tone and meaning. But as they stand, on the printed page, read by an audience so far removed culturally and chronologically, they remain tantalizingly ambiguous.

5. SYMBOLS AND IMAGERY

The fifth element in our analysis is perhaps the one that has been most seriously neglected in our study of ancient literature. And yet it is only by penetrating into the imaginative process of the ancient poet, into the religious and cultural imagery on which he drew, that we can truly be said to appreciate his work. The images of the ancient poet are too numerous to allow classification: they are drawn from city and countryside, from the habits and pursuits of men and women, from the process of life and death, mar-

riage, procreation, war and peace, religious ritual and superstition. Here is the particular area wherein the scholar of
ancient civilization can help the literary critic. The ancient
fear of *fascinatio*—like the later fear of the evil eye—lies behind the imagery of Catullus' kissing poems, *Carm.* 5 and
7, and modern scholars have detected imagery taken from
the use of the abacus or from finger counting. The great
emasculation of Catullus' galliambic hymn, *Carm.* 63, though
taken from Greek and Oriental mythology, reflects a severe
emotional upheaval in the soul of Catullus himself; emasculation, whether actual or metaphorical, was undoubtedly
not far from his thoughts, particularly during his stormy
relationship with Lesbia. To seek union with her, his *era*
or mistress—much as Cybele was to Attis—was doomed to
frustration.

Oftentimes, we find an image which has a symbolic dimension. To give an example, I may refer to the imagery of
the lover's apple in Catullus (*Carm.* 65. 19-24). Catullus uses
it to express the shame he feels at remembering his obligations to the orator Hortensius; on another level the apple,
as a love-gift, *furtivum munus*, sent to a young maiden, *casta
virgo*, might imply a certain sexual symbolism, but this perhaps is not uppermost in the actual poem. On the other
hand, Lesbia's *passer*, the blue thrush she kept as a pet, becomes by a kind of suggestion, a symbol of Catullus himself
(*Carm.* 2). Both Lesbia and Catullus suffer from the *ardor*,
the *dolor* and *curae* of love; the love of the bird binds them
together. Yet one cannot help feeling that Catullus envies
the little thrush in its intimacy with its lovely mistress. Again,
in the lovely poem to Sirmio (*Carm.* 31), the little villa on
the lakeside becomes more than a mere home welcoming
its master after a long trip; it is symbolic of the ultimate
and ideal Haven, offering peace and security from the *tanti
labores* of life's great journey. A real place and an actual

return become transformed, in Catullus' poetry, into something ideal and multidimensional.

6. MYTHOLOGY

By a poet's mythology I mean the intellectual and religious frame of reference within which he creates his poetry. This may, of course, involve his actual belief in ancient 'mythology' in the strict sense, but the term in our sense is a wider one. It embraces the poet's complexus of ideas and beliefs as they are regularly reflected in this work. But to use this accurately in our analysis we must be careful not to assume, without reasonable proof, that our poet accepted all the ideas and conventional beliefs of his time. It can be seriously misleading to offer heavy documentation about the customs of ancient Greece and Rome whenever an author gives us the slightest pretext. Historical footnotes to poetry must always be severely restricted by their criterion of relevance. And relevance in the case of a particular poem demands that we show the influence of certain contemporary ideas upon the poet's creative imagination.

Thus, the poetic mythology of Pindar, in this sense, is quite different from that of Sappho, Archilochus, and Theognis. Even two people so close as Horace and Vergil appear to have a totally different approach to the problem of belief in the gods; and this would seem to correspond with their quite different views on the ultimate meaning of life. The same may be said of most of the poets of antiquity: their mythology will ultimately be a function of their entire philosophy of life, at least so far as they present it in their artistic creation.

By considering, therefore, the setting, tone, imagery and mythology of a poem we are striving to enter into the poet's imaginative world. Great poets in the history of literature have always created a world-vision of their own, and our primary task as critics is not to pass a moral judgment, but rather to explore these various poetic worlds, to reveal their hidden beauty and consistency. We may, of course, contrast the narrow, almost adolescent world of Catullus with the mature, transcendental universe of Vergil; the cluttered, obscure, and pedantic world of Pindar with the languorous, sensuous atmosphere of Sappho; the theological seriousness of Sophocles with the ambiguous, provocative world-view of Euripides. But such comparisons reflect not so much definitive value judgments as attempts to enter critically into the creative process of the ancient poet. Here as elsewhere the ultimate task of the scholar and critic is to allow the poet to communicate to us without any semantic or psychological obstacle, so far as this is possible.

* * * * *

There are many other elements which make up the poetic construct: for example, the historical background, the poet's diction, dialect, and prosodic form. But on these, too, much emphasis has perhaps been laid in the past to the neglect of others that more nearly touch the artist's imaginative genius. Again, it is not our purpose to speak slightingly of earlier methods of analysis which tended to stress even in poetry the rhetorical figures of diction and thought.[11] Modern criticism is the result of centuries of trial and error. At the same time it will be useful to clarify the differences between the ancient and modern approach and to point out the areas in which all poetic criticism is in agreement.

Most ancient literary critics were not poets themselves. Horace is the obvious exception; the epigrams attributed to Plato in the *Garland of Meleager*, and Aristotle's ponderous

Hymn to Virtue are not significant enough to disprove the general rule. It is to Aristotle's credit that he realized that the heart of poetry was metaphor; and, for the most part, he did not analyze poetry as though it were rhetoric—a defect common to Dionysius of Halicarnassus, pseudo-Longinus, and Alcuin in his *Dialectic*. Again, no ancient critic has left us an extended treatment of poetry as such, in our modern sense. For Aristotle, of course, ποίησις includes artistic prose as, for example, the dialogues of Plato. And in both Aristotle's *Poetics* and Horace's *Art of Poetry* the long discussions of dramatic or theatrical technique, however important in themselves, involve problems that are strictly irrelevant to the nature of poetry itself. Demetrius, Dionysius, and pseudo-Longinus all treat poetry and rhetorical prose very much as though there were a common yardstick by which both could be measured—or as if there were a specific effect (for example, pseudo-Longinus' ἔκστασις, "rapture") which all great literature, whether poetry or rhetoric, had somehow to produce. It seems clear, however, that even if Aristotle's theory of the metaphor is criticized as being too intellectual, his general approach to the problem of imitation has indeed set the stage for all later poetic theory.[12] To pseudo-Longinus, on the other hand, we owe a more developed discussion of the place of the emotions in literature, of the 'manic,' the irrational; and the stress he lays upon organic structure (σύστασις) is perhaps derivatively Aristotelian.

Two very important ancient texts attempt to treat of the difference between poetry and prose, Gorgias' *Eulogy of Helen* and Horace, *Sat.* I. 4. 39-48, and these we shall proceed to discuss.

If we may trust our sources on Gorgias' life and work, one of the obsessing problems of his career was to endow the spoken word with the power to move men's hearts that poetry had. Of all the various things Greek poetry traditionally did—to tell a story, mythologize, sing of the gods, mourn a death, or celebrate a festive occasion—Gorgias, as a rhetorician, envied the grasp it seemed to have on men's minds and hearts. Although the point seems somewhat irrelevant in the *Eulogy of Helen*, Gorgias still feels constrained to discuss it; when men listened to poetry, he tells us,

> there entered into them a terrifying shudder, a pity full of tears, a longing full of grief; and the soul by listening to the words experienced its own peculiar sorrow [πάθημα] at the misfortunes and catastrophes of other men in other circumstances.[13]

Here was the basic insight—erroneous, though it may seem—that influenced the creation of Greek rhetoric. The tools of power that men wished to yield by the spoken word are found to exist within the framework of poetry; and, by a curious reversal, later critics will take the artificial norms of the developed manual-rhetoric to criticize poetry. In any case, what is important in our present text is fact that Gorgias' view seems to reflect a commonly accepted Greek view of the function of literature even at this early pre-philosophical period. Ποίησις, as Gorgias conceives it, was from the beginning committed: it spoke to the soul, within the framework of the primitive community. It told of the deeds and the feelings of men, but in such wise as to involve the soul in its own private "suffering," πάθημα. There was thus, in his view, both identification and empathy, and the moral goals later specified by Plato and Aristotle were not yet envisaged.

But how did the ancient poet attempt to involve the soul? In answer to this question perhaps some of the most important passages are to be found in Horace, although, oddly enough, not in his *Art of Poetry*. For it is precisely when the ancients spoke of poetry as an art, a τεχνή, that they would often confound poetry with rhetoric, art with what

27

they believed to be science. Hence, the most illuminating discussions of our problem among the ancients (and this is partly true, also, of medieval literature) are not to be found in the technical treatises. Horace, for example, in *Satires* I. 4, attempts a kind of public self-analysis by way of offering an apologia for writing satire. In a peculiarly self-depreciating passage, he suggests that his satires are not, after all, poetry (*Sat.* I. 4. 39-48):

> First of all I shouldn't include myself
> In the list of those whom I consider poets.
> It is not enough, you would admit, to set
> A line in metre; and surely you wouldn't consider
> As poetry the sort of conversational stuff
> That I write. Reserve the honor for the man
> Of special talent, who speaks a kind of prophecy,
> With a mouth producing great sounds. Hence it is
> That some dispute whether even comedy is poetry.
> It has none of that passionate inspiration and power,
> Either in content or in style. If it weren't for the metre
> It would be nothing but conversation.

It is here (and in *Epist.* 1.2) that Horace comes closest to an intrinsic description of poetry—as opposed to the more external elements of the craft, which preoccupy him in the *Art of Poetry*. First of all, in our present passage the distinction between the poet and his poem reminds us of the divisions of the *Art of Poetry*. Again, the poet must possess a special *ingenium*, talent—and this surely is the meaning of the "wisdom," *sapere* of the *Art* (309). But the "mouth that can produce great sounds," *os magna sonaturum*—if the translation produces the tone of the original—sounds almost comic and mocking; it is the prophetic voice of poetry, the *mens divinior*, that Horace is here referring to. But as in other places, he cannot resist being whimsical when speaking of epic or "serious" poetry; it is always the way he was to handle a genre in which he was never able to be successful.

The internal qualities of great poetry correspond to the poet's peculiar gift. First of all, metre is essential, but it is not in itself sufficient. There must be both in diction and in material content—and this is most important—an *acer spiritus ac vis*, a passionate inspiration and a peculiar force and impressiveness. There must be a deepening in thought-content as well as atmosphere. We cannot take, as was sometimes done in comedy, the mere actions and words of ordinary life; there must be some transformation, and the diction should reflect and embody what the poet has imaginatively created.

If the prophetic dimension of this passage were to be taken seriously, it would of necessity exclude a good deal of Greek and Roman poetry as it was actually written. Horace is again mixing humor with sober doctrine, his own views with commonplace Hellenistic poetic, just as his exclusion of himself from the rank of real poets would seem to be conventional mock-modesty. Horace's true opinion of his own accomplishments is clear enough from the *Odes*, especially 3.30, *Exegi monumentum*, the "seal" which he composed to close the book, even though elsewhere his remarks about himself are always whimsical and deprecatory. But even in the last book of *Odes*, 4.2 *Pindarum quisquis*, where he compares himself unfavorably with Pindar, his evaluation of his own work is clear; he may not speak with Pindar's "profound voice," *ore profundo*, or use Pindar's liberties with metre, but the lines *per laborem... carmina fingo*, "I fashion my songs by toil" (29, 32) is as much a challenge as an honest pride in craftsmanship. Horace has for poetry the feeling of an artisan, and he makes this admission with a sense of accomplishment.

To return then to our passage in the fourth Satire, we see that Horace offers us a sound view of the nature of poetry, although he cannot elaborate every detail: by metre and

rhythm the gifted poet conveys a message of profound meaning, his own intense awareness of things through the *mens
divinior*, transformed mysteriously by means of a certain power
(*vis*) and inspiration (*spiritus*).

Horace reveals a later, more philosophical view of the
function of poetry in *Epistles* 1.1.33ff. Here he develops the
view that poetry and literature have a primarily therapeutic
or ethico-religious value; for this surely is what is meant by
the book and lamp we are to ask for before daybreak, under
pain of tossing sleeplessly with love or jealousy. The
word here functions as a magical incantation, *piacula* (36), to
dispel the diseases of the soul. This concept of literature is
very close to Gorgias', and must ultimately have been connected with the Pythagorean theory of music as a cure for
madness.[14] St. Augustine quotes with approval this very passage of Horace, and adds that we may thus "by the medicine
of the word, heal, as it were by incantation, the serpent's
bite."[15] And it would appear that the psychotherapeutic theory of literature, on the view that the passions were diseases,
became very prevalent in the ancient world.[16]

Horace tells us more clearly how this effect is achieved
in the first part of the Epistle to Lollius Maximus (*Epist.*
1.2.1-31). It is clear, he tells the young man, that the *Iliad*
and the *Odyssey* are better guides to moral philosophy than
the manuals of Chrysippus and Crantor, the representatives
of the Stoic and Academic traditions. The *Iliad* portrays the
stupidity of men's passions, and shows how the many may be
punished for the sins of the few. The *Odyssey* is the other
half of the diptych: it teaches us the power of wisdom and
virtue in the example of Ulysses, in his perseverance and
self-control. Further, according to Horace, there is a process
of projection or identification; we are the wastrel suitors of
Penelope, we are the noble subjects of Alcinous who passed
their lives in comfort (ibid. 27-29):[17]

> We are but ciphers, born to eat earth's food,
> The worthless suitors of Penelope;
> The men of King Alcinous, whose only thought
> Was the care of their own bodies.

It is a striking text, and reflects the earliest attempts to interpret Homer allegorically. For even more than the *Art of Poetry*, the Epistle to Lollius attempts more subtly to probe into the nature of poetry and to make sense of the Aristotelian dictum that "poetry is more philosophical than history."[18] Here the philosophical value, the universal significance which Aristotle speaks of, Horace would seem to derive from the symbolic dimension of poetry. It is through this symbolism that we can identify ourselves or our passions in the poetry before us; and it is in this way that the music of the word can charm away the ills of the soul just as medicines work upon the body.

How far the ancient poet *intended* his work to be taken symbolically will perhaps always remain a matter for dispute. It surely was not the self-conscious symbolism of Blake and Poe, Baudelaire and Mallarmé. Yet the doctrine of Gorgias and the philosophical analysis of Horace suggest new dimensions in ancient poetry hitherto unsuspected. In any case, the symbolic approach would seem to be an authentic modern path into the labyrinth of the ancient imagination.[19]

Of all the ancient critics it is Horace who gives us the most subtle, albeit whimsical, characterization of the art of poetry. In *Epistles* 2.2 to his friend Julius Florus, Horace tells the story of the old man of Argos (128-40). The perfect husband and master, he had but one flaw: he was slightly mad, and his madness consisted in his going to an empty theatre and enjoying the hallucination of a dramatic performance. His relatives were deeply disturbed by the old man's eccentricity, and had him cured with a good dose of hellebore. But as reason begins to dawn—and we are reminded of Cervantes' picture of the dying Quixote—he curses his misguided kin for destroying his life (*Ep.* II. 2.138-40):

> Alas, my friends! You've killed me. You've robbed
> Me of my only pleasure, for you've destroyed
> This most charming aberration of the mind.

"This most charming aberration of the mind," *mentis gratissimus error*, is Horace's final symbol for the art he so loved. It is the poet's loveable madness, his *amabilis insania*—his right to live in the land of illusion—that has brought so much good to men.

It may be, of course, that the final nonsense symbols of the *Art of Poetry* are put forward by Horace to prevent his message to the Pisones from being taken too seriously. For there is, at the end of the poem, still more vivid imagery to come. In a final burst, the mad poet Empedocles becomes an enraged bear bursting his bars (473), and then at last an ignoble leech gorging itself on the blood of its victims—in this case, the audience that must listen to his poetry (476). For the leech is Horace's final symbol of his own poetic achievement—this insignificant creature living on borrowed blood.

POETIC LANDSCAPE AND THE GREEN WORLD

VERY IMPORTANT FOR THE APPRECIATION OF ANCIENT poetry is the concept of landscape. By landscape, I mean the imaginative poetic world which some writers invariably use as the backdrop for the action or drama of the poem. At its best, it is a self-dependent, self-consistent world which is coordinate with the author's tone and the habitual treatment which he tends to give to the characters of his imagination. Once established, it builds in the reader's mind an imaginative pattern which makes the poetic message more intelligible. It is, in fact, merely an extension of the *Scaena*, or setting, which we spoke of in the previous chapter. Some types of literature, comedy, for example, pastoral, and elegy, require a more restricted form of landscape than others. It may in in general be said, however, that great writers usually succeed in constructing an imaginative landscape which is uniquely their own.

In Homer the geographic setting lends a peculiar charm. In the *Iliad* the constant vision of the Trojan plain gives the poem a stability and power which is easily overlooked. As we read on, we become more and more involved in this miniature world which stretches from the Hellespont to the towers of Ilium, crossed by the intersecting streams, the Scamander and the Simois. Here and there are famous monuments, well-known trees, a wall, a rise, marshland and ford. And somewhere in the distance is snow-capped Olympus rising high into the *aether* and commanding a view of this narrow world wherein men enact their sorrows, hates and loves. And it is only rarely that we get fleeting glimpses into another, more peaceful landscape: the poet opens, as it were, an imaginative window in his similes and, especially, in the scenes painted on Achilles' shield, on a world of normalcy and nostalgic calm. This tension between the heroic landscape and the window-world of the real, as seen through the similes, is intimately connected with the theme of the entire poem.

The result is a very tight structure, much tighter than, for example, the *Odyssey*. There is a relentless quality about the constant, unchanging face of the sunlit plain, which fits into the poet's scheme of the length of the war. There is a weariness and a bitterness, which is sharpened by the dreary, unchanging scenery. That Achilles should sulk on the fringe of this battlefield fits precisely into the poem's general message and theme: it is a probing of the mystery of human life and death, and hence it is only proper that there should be no distraction. The grim setting is fixed—much as the fates of the men who came to Troy. Even Zeus cannot change the tragic stage on which the actors are doomed to play their roles to the end. Their choices, such as they are, are extremely limited, their joys few. It remains for them to ponder, while they act, the ultimate meaning and direction of their lives.

The theme of the *Odyssey*, however, if we can even speak of a theme, is, like its geographic setting, totally different. In the *Odyssey*, the scene is the fantastic coastline of the Mediterranean, stretching from the Troad to the Pillars of Heracles. The ancient οἰκουμένη, or the "inhabited world" now becomes a vast, god-made fairyland, a trick stage, set with moving rocks, weird and exotic anchorages, and volcanic isles of mystery. It is a suitable canvas on which to project the fabulous adventures of the all-resourceful Odysseus. The scenes move swiftly like a great kaleidoscope, charming ear and eye. We never want Odysseus to rest, because then the scene will stop moving; there is everywhere an atmosphere of enchantment, and it appeals to the childlike sense of wonder in all of us.

In each case, of course, both in the *Iliad* and the *Odyssey*, we must not imagine any detailed geographic research: the landscape painting is primitive, the results of many decades of bardic creation. But how well the unchanging scene of the *Iliad* suits the relentless unfolding of its tragic theme; whereas in the charmed landscape of the *Odyssey* it seems preposterous to ask the poet for a clear statement of theme or a more organic unity. Indeed, when the *Odyssey*, in books 13 and following, settles into its final phase and the wandering hero is perforce brought home, we experience a twinge of disappointment. The lark is over, and yet we would prefer to stay with the Lotus-eaters and Circe rather than consort with the more mundane, scheming suitors who storm the palace of Penelope. True, Odysseus' Journey is meaningless unless it is a Return, a Νόστος. But the poet's artistic scope —and here, I feel, is evidence that the same poet did not write both epics—lay rather in exotic travel than in humdrum domesticity. The tension between these two levels in the *Odyssey* reveals at once its strength and its weakness.

Vergil, however, adapts the landscape of the *Odyssey* ni

a most striking way. For him the episodes are not pure adventure: they are organically integrated into the entire texture of the *Aeneid*: they are the *tanti labores*, the sweat and blood that went into the building of Rome. Even the Descent into Hell, in Homer a mere interlude, sheds new light on Aeneas' destiny; and in Anchises' prophecy (Vergil is here imitating Odysseus' meeting with Teiresias) the whole meaning of the *Aeneid* and, indeed, of the Roman empire is laid bare. Vergil's adaptation cannot but reflect his own profound vision of life. Hence his landscape, though in part derived from the *Odyssey*, includes a further, prophetic dimension, in which past, present, and future are one. But just as the *Odyssey* loses much of its interest when Odysseus' adventures are over and his final work at home is to be done, so too the *Aeneid*, when the landscape changes from the sea voyage to the countryside of Latium, suffers through lack of incident. The last six books of the Aeneid are more tightly unified as Aeneas' goal nears realization. But the scale is too vast—six books are too long—in comparison with the meagreness of detail; and the landscape is correspondingly dull, colorless, and uneventful. It is lack of proportion which chiefly reveals the artistic defect; but it is reflected as well in the landscape.

In pastoral poetry especially the successful handling of plot and character, can only be achieved against the proper bucolic background.[1] Here is precisely where many of the later poets, writing in English or French, have failed: their settings were totally artificial, and they were often little more than clever imitations. Seventeenth and eighteenth-century bucolics can be boring. Not among their least defects was the inauthenticity of the setting.

Theocritus, as the first extant pastoral poet, scores very heavily here. His is a Sicilian Arcadia, based upon the scenes of his boyhood. The bounds of this world are severely limited, and there is no real sense of tragedy or of sin. Life is lived in a magic woodland inhabited by rustic gods and spring-nymphs. Daphnis is its archetypal hero, whose death both gods and jackals mourn, and kids and calves come to rest at his feet. It is a perpetual, green pastureland where sheep may safely graze and man's livelihood is not hard to come by. Whatever Theocritus had seen of the hard life of the Sicilian or Coan goatherd and shepherd is in his poetry totally transformed. And yet he is of all pastoral poets the most authentic and the closest to the soil. There is still on his pages the smell of the goat. But yet it is wrong to suppose that he portrays the actual lives of pastoral folk; his landscape is a bucolic wonderland where life's only sorrow is unrequited love, and, of course, the awareness that death brings an end to all pastoral song.

It is thus difficult for us to recapture Theocritus' poetic tone, this mingled convention and truth, rustic spontaneity and arch naiveté. His is a vision of a Golden Age, of a simple, unspoiled humanity imposed upon the Greco-Italian countryside, and toward this his meagre range of characters and plots are totally directed. The plots, of course, consist merely in the calming of frustrated love, the winning of a singing contest, the wooing of a coy maid or winsome boy. There is little below the surface, and yet all is as it should be. For, in the stylized gestures and courteous manners of these goatherds and girls, who seem to act out their roles on a stagelike Arcadia, there is the poignancy of a dream unfulfilled. It is therefore not completely wrong to suggest that the bucolic for Theocritus and his audience was a vehicle of escape: escape from the brutal world of the Hellenistic kings, from the grinding poverty and taxation of country and city alike. But it was still more. In an age of economic and moral stress, Theocritus sang of the godlike existence of naive countrymen projected against an ideal landscape. His pipe and his song are rustic Sicilian, but his message is of a peculiar subtlety and elusive charm: it is a nostalgic recall to hope and wonder, to the simple pleasures of life and love.

Neither Theocritus' finished craft nor his message survived in the minor pastoral poets who succeeded him. There are rare flashes of inspiration in Bion's *Lament for Adonis*, and few or perhaps none in the anonymous *Lament for Bion* —poems that enjoyed such favor among poets like Milton, Shelley and Arnold. Bion's *Lament* is constructed on the model of the ritual Adonis-song of the Hellenistic Adonis festival; the song would usually explain Adonis' untimely death and Aphrodite's love, together with some reference to the ritual pageant or statuary group representing Adonis and Aphrodite in a final embrace; it was a sentimental song, intended largely for female votaries. There is no intrinsic connection between the Adonis-song type and pastoral poetry as such; it was simply that Bion was a pastoral poet and adopted the pastoral technique for this *Lament*. Just as in Theocritus' *Idyl* 1, on the death of Daphnis, all nature shares in lamentation for Adonis' tragic passing; and as Adonis' blood brings forth roses, the goddess's tears produce anemones. The same technique is used in the verbose, rhetorical *Lament* written by an anonymous disciple at the death of Bion, a piece once wrongly attributed to Moschus. The poet here calls on all nature and all the woodland spirits to join in lamentation. For now all beauty is dead:

> Echo mourns amid the rocks, now silent,
> And no longer follows the sound of your lips.
> The trees have lost their fruit, and withered
> Are the flowers at your passing. No longer
> Does sweet milk flow from the ewes: no longer
> Honey from the hives. For it has died of grief
> In the comb. What need is there to gather it,
> When the honey of your song is dead? (30-35)

But this is no longer bucolic poetry in the strict, Theocritean sense, and the gay landscape has been turned into a vehicle of the pathetic fallacy in a most undisciplined, sentimental way. Indeed, the honey has spoiled in the comb: the pastoral dream has vanished.

That Vergil should achieve some success in his *Bucolics* is proof of his early power and craftsmanhip. Here his master is Theocritus. But the disarming simplicity of the *Eclogues*— and, it should be recalled, the Messianic Fourth is not strictly a pastoral—makes the mystery of their meaning all the more baffling. Once again the scene opens to discover shepherds and their maids. Tityrus, Amaryllis and all the rest—just as in Theocritus. They speak and move within the framework of the expected pastoral plot, somewhat more scrubbed and cleaned to suit the sensibilities of the Roman aristocracy. Vergil's Arcadia is, again, an adaptation from Theocritus; but it is the Italian countryside, the goat-paths and woodlands he knew as a boy in Cremona.[2] But now all the landscape and its puppet-like figures are bathed in an atmosphere of allegory, a mood quite foreign to the pastoral of Philetas and Theocritus. For the clear references to Caesar and Octavian, to the land evictions and veteran settlements suggest that there are many more contemporary references if we would but find the key. But we are more interested here in discovering Vergil's tone: it reveals itself as more meditative, more aloof, more removed from the soil than was Theocritus'. Theocritus' shepherds were naughty and gay, and he does not hesitate to make them into malicious caricatures of city-folk. Vergil's compositions are more subjective; they unfold slowly in a quiet, serious atmosphere. His characters never come alive, and their movements resemble some sombre spring ritual. And yet Vergil reveals his charm precisely where he does not imitate his master, when we catch in his verse a glimpse of the sad Italic countryside—sad because it reflects the poet's own mood—and of the animals and rustic people whom he knew and loved.

To understand Vergil, therefore, one must appreciate this tension which results from his relationship to his predecessor as opposed to his own personal message and achievement. And we must not lose sight of the fact that what was often an effortless element in the creativity of Homer and Theocritus, must have involved, for Vergil, enormous archaeological research. It is this aspect of Vergil's genius that becomes clear when we examine his adaptation of the Greek epic and pastoral landscape.

There is one further application of our theme. Ancient as well as modern comedy may be considered as a fusion of two artistic elements: (1) the manipulation of the laughable, the comic, in verbal and visual humor; and (2) the dramatic rhythm of plot and characters set against a peculiar background or atmosphere. Now it is the second element that more nearly concerns us here, insofar as it touches the general problem of poetic landscape. The conventions of a comic plot are drawn somewhat more tightly than they are in tragedy. The tragic plot always hovers on the brink of disaster precisely because the possibilities are limitless— almost as they are in real life. If nothing else, there is always the possibility of error. But in comedy choices are limited; tragic avenues are definitely closed, and, if they seem to be open, this is only to enhance the amusement. The audience well realizes that ultimately no tragic catastrophe will spoil the fun. The usual setting for a comedy, therefore, and we are thinking primarily of ancient comedy, is a world far removed from the humdrum responsibilities of daily life. It is a mirror-world, one that exists in another dimension, the realm of the playwright's fancy. Here rogues and courtesans are lovable, fathers are old fools, and magistrates are figures of fun. Thus, in this world of distorted mirrors, the serious vocations of life are viewed in exaggerated proportions. One may not of course generalize, for there is so vast a difference in plot and characterization between Old and New Comedy, between Aristophanes and the Romans. But their rose-colored mirror-world is much the same, and to enhance this world many comedians have relied on a peculiar, fairyland setting in which the suspension of pain and tragedy might be more convincing. Here Aristophanes was a master: in Cloudcuckoo-land and in the Hades of *The Frogs*, in the women's world of the *Lysistrata* and the *Ecclesiazusae*, anything can happen; fun is the order of the day. This, too, is Shakespeare's charm in the fairyland he creates in *The Tempest*, *As You Like It* and *Midsummer Night's Dream*.

This comic greenland is analogous to the countryside of pastoral poetry and its function is not dissimilar. It is a vehicle of escape, of projected wish-fulfilment. It is an embodiment of the release that Comedy achieves, and it is symbolic of its optimism towards life in general. To the lover, to the courageous, all things are possible; man lives in the present by his wits and his animal spirits. The only sins are stubborn pomposity, inhibited aloofness, and resistance to good fun. Sorrow, sickness, and death are barely given a thought. As in the world of Don Quixote, the mad eye of the poet has created for us a new Golden Age full of childlike happiness and excitement.

Now the effect of this landscape is achieved in the Roman comedians, and more successfully perhaps in Terence, by the very fact that they borrow their setting from Greek New Comedy. They thus achieve a charming aesthetic distance by the very tension which exists between their characters who are very often Romans in Greek dress, and their Greek, and usually Athenian, environment. For the Italian audiences, the scene, whether set in Aetolia or Thebes, Ephesus or a seacoast near Cyrene,[3] would imaginatively be Italy at one remove—it is the Never-never Land of Comedy.

In this way, W. Beare's view,[4] that Terence's adaptation of Greek plays should not strictly be called *contaminatio*, and that he reveals more originality than had hitherto been allowed, may find further confirmation from the study of his use of comic setting. The fields of Attica, the streets of Athens with its homes and dingy shops, achieve for Terence precisely the effect of the fairyland, the greenland, in which he can more easily deploy his characters with creative abandon. Terence's Athens, its laws and magistrates, its conventions and social classes, are simply a comic mirror of Rome; his array of rich, ripe characters are Italians dressed in the pallium, the product of Italic dramatic traditions as much as they are of Greek.[5] Indeed, Terence is beginning to develop a kind of choral character, a Leader of the Revels, very much like those we find especially in Molière and Shakespeare, who seem almost free at times to step in and out of the mirror. Such are, for example, Bacchis in the *Hecyra*, Phormio in *Phormio*, and Micio in the *Adelphoe*. They seem at times less bound to the comic conventions and limitations than are the other characters; psychologically they seem to move back and forth between Athens and Rome, creating a special bond with the audience and heightening the tension created by the bounds of the comic world. The master of this technique was Molière, but it is surely foreshadowed in Terence. For the adaptation of the Greek setting was far more subtle than has perhaps been supposed, much more than a common trick of the playwright's stock-in-trade. It was, at least by the time of Terence, an artistic device that was retained for its symbolic function in the achievement of the total effect.

The subtle tone of ancient New Comedy and its transformation of the poetic landscape is beautifully illustrated in the latest of the discovered comic fragments of Menander, *The Dyskolos*, or *The Curmudgeon*. It is a quiet play, from the earliest transitional days of Middle Comedy, but the original spirit of the *kômos*, the Dionysiac revel, is still vigorously present. The setting of the play is before the grove of Pan and the Nymphs, perhaps flanked on either side by the homes of Knemon, the Curmudgeon, and of his estranged wife and son. For these are the two homes that Pan will bring together at the end of the play. The day is Pan's feast, and the Chorus are the Pan-revellers with all their paraphernalia. Fittingly does Pan have the prologue: for he, the ithyphallic goat-man, symbol of life and love, fertility and benevolence, will bring the lovers together and transform the Curmudgeon. For there is a fine tension in the atmosphere: the revelling of the god's devotees contrasted with the ill-temper of Knemon, the misanthrope. And in the midst are Knemon's charming daughter (whose name is perhaps Myrrhine) and the generous young man Sostratus.

The theme of the play, then, is nothing less than the destruction of Knemon, the Ogre, by the spirit of Comedy, by the spirit of the Revel. Almost as in an ancient fable, the Ogre guards the innocent maiden—and Myrrhine has indeed been protected from all contact with the evil world by her father—and the hero must perform certain labors in order to gain her. She is the ideal Maiden, and she is won by the forces of Comedy. Sostratus' labors—with mattock and hoe—are an imitation of Hercules' whose name is frequently invoked (at least in oaths) throughout the play. The labors are again the work of Pan, the field-god, as becomes clear from the symbolic dream related by Geta, the slave associated with the Pan-revellers (410 ff.). It is in the spirit of comedy that the hero's labors should be trivial—Pan's labors are always pastoral and pitched, as it were, in a minor key—and thus, too, the taming of the Curmudgeon is achieved

43

by the ridiculous incident of the pot and the mattock falling into the well. The Ogre, now a kind of scapegoat symbol, upon whom all sorts of comic abuse can be heaped, is raised from the well by his disowned son Gorgias. It is a kind of comic resurrection; and by it the pessimism of Knemon is healed and transformed by the boy who had nothing to gain from saving him. The resurrection from the well effects a complete change in Knemon's outlook on the world. He thought, he said (714 ff.), that he had no need of men, that he could be completely independent and self-sufficient. Now he sees the value of love, the benevolence that, as we have seen from the beginning of the play, has Pan as its symbolic source. If all men were benevolent, he now sees (743 ff.), there would be no need of prisons, law-courts, or wars. The transformation is, it would seem, almost too sudden and miraculous. The message of benevolence is again stressed in the character of the young hero Sostratus. Man's only true wealth is goodness (809 ff.); money, if one has it, should only be used to make others happy. The inner spirit of the play, which corresponds to the outer revelry in Pan's honor, is the spirit of trust and benevolence—a spirit which, as Knemon himself admits, would mean the destruction of all civil strife. This is exactly the spirit which inspires Knemon, the disenchanted Curmudgeon, to restore his estranged wife and son, and to give his daughter to Sostratus after he had kept her in calculated ignorance of the world he loathed and distrusted.

Thus in the final scenes of the play the two strands of the action are united by Pan. The bustling of the revellers, which had constantly irritated Knemon, culminates in a rousing feast, and the captive maiden is finally released from bondage by the destruction, that is, the disenchantment of the guardian Ogre by the spirit of benevolence. Indeed, the festival of Pan and the Nymphs is the fitting occasion for the transformation. The raising from the well of despair is climaxed by the comic scene in which Sikon and Geta force the sickly Knemon to rise from his couch and join in the dancing. It is, as it were, another resurrection scene, and the punishment of the Curmudgeon is complete when he is forced comically to join in the fun. The scene around his cot is a kind of incantation, a final exorcism of the demon of malignity and distemper.

With all its spirit of revel, the serious theme of the play is projected in a most subtle, delicate way. It dramatizes the inner tension of every man who is torn between the conflicting drives of love and distrust of fellow men. But, as Sostratus says (860 ff.), all things are possible for human energy and toil. It is the voice of optimism and youth—indeed, the voice of Comedy. In the play the inner polarity of egotism versus altruism is resolved. For Knemon soon discovers that, despite the inherent weaknesses of human nature, a man cannot live without his fellow man. Thus in the end, the spirit of Pan, the spirit of life and love, conquers and destroys the Ogre. But the solution is not merely on the surface. The play breathes an inner beauty which reminds one of Socrates' great prayer to the god in the *Phaedrus* (279B): "O dear Pan, grant that I may become beautiful within." It is this inner beauty that the play celebrates. There is no more profound expression of the spirit of ancient Comedy at its very best.

In conclusion, then, in ancient as in modern criticism it is important to analyze the function of the poetic landscape as an integral part of the poetic tone. Very often, as perhaps in Vergil's *Eclogues*, landscape has but a limited scope; it is a fusion of Arcady and northern Italy. But Vergil has gone further: his shepherds are meant to suggest the intimate poetic circle of Vergil and his friends, and his Arcady becomes the very realm of poetry, where to tend sheep and cows, to weave baskets, and pipe duets are associated together with the writing of poetry in the new Rome. But, as we have suggested, Vergil's *Eclogues* are a unique kind of poetry. The deeper pastoral intention becomes clearer in the *Georgics*. For here the farmer's life is a nostalgic recall to a Golden Age, in which the god is in all things and all men are brothers. Only by clinging to the soil and following the seasons can men ultimately restore the innocent age of Saturn, before the entry of passions and wars. Indeed, in the final book on bees, Vergil's pastoral landscape becomes a miniature Platonic State; it is the poetic blueprint for happiness, symbolized in the harmonious life of the bees.

These are only brief indications of how the ancient technique, the portrayal of poetic landscape, developed from the earliest Greek poets down to the Roman period. If the Greek use of landscape is perhaps more vivildy poetic, it must be admitted that the Roman has a more profound, even more religious, dimension. For the Roman, Mother Earth, *Tellus mater*, was a source of almost mystical yearnings, even while he served her by toil and sweat. She was also the ultimate teacher of wisdom: we are her children, we did not make her laws, and to be happy we must somehow adjust to her bidding. Despite its Epicurean overtones, Horace's image of Mother Earth is fully within the ancient pastoral tradition.

THE GREEK POETIC IMAGINATION

As POETRY WE HAVE ALWAYS KNOWN THAT THE *Iliad* IS NOT merely a bardic reconstruction of a proto-historical Achaean civilization. Generations of men have read it and loved it because—as Gorgias hinted—they felt themselves personally involved in the story of Achilles. The poet of the *Iliad* speaks from an omniscient height—the *mens divinior* of Horace —from which he can see deeply into the minds and hearts of gods and men. His point of view is far from frivolous: it is deeply committed to a serious probing of the meaning of life and death. Though so far removed from us in time and cultural background, his canvas is a symbolic projection of the fortunes of men and women with whom we can somehow identify ourselves as Gorgias or Horace did. For Achilles and Hector, each in a different way, are caught like us, in the mesh of human history, in the web of a senseless human destruction for which

we are not responsible,
But the great god and almighty Moira (*Il.* 19.409-410).

For this is the artistry of the *Iliad*, that almost any one of the major characters of the epic could have been its central focus. As it is, we see the tragedy of the Trojan War chiefly from the emotional standpont of Achilles.

As the story develops, however, we become aware that Achilles' most tragic struggle is within his own divided soul. The conflict between his debt of honor to the Greek army and his private war with Agamemnon is paralleled by the symbolism of the great Choice which Achilles has made before the beginning of the Wrath. The choice of the two Κῆρες is referred to several times throughout the *Iliad*, always as though by way of reference to a tale well-known, to a pre-Homeric bardic poetry now no longer extant. In *Iliad* I. 352-354, Achilles complains to his mother Thetis:

> Ah mother! I was born, indeed to die
> Young—but in this I was to be honored
> By Zeus who thunders from on high.

In the ninth book (410-411) Achilles refers back again to this meeting, but his account of it is not consistent. He explains:

> My mother Thetis of the silver sandals
> Has told me that I have two Kêres
> Each bearing me to the end of death.

If he remains at Troy, his Κῆρ will bring him an early but glorious death. If he returns to his homeland, he will live to an old age without honor. Never does he explain the background of the Choice nor when it was offered him, nor yet the relationship between it and the Κηροστασία, or the solemn Weighing of the Κῆρες by Zeus (22. 210 ff.). It is clear, however, which Κῆρ he has made his own.

Similar imagery occurs in the twenty-fourth book (527 ff.) where we are told of the two great vases set before the throne of Zeus, from which the Cloud-Gatherer measures out happiness or misery to his mortal subjects. It seems a brutal and irrational solution to the problem of pain; it is a bitter lesson for the young warrior to learn as he broods over his frustrated passion.

Parallel with the symbol of the Choice and the Vases of Zeus is the paradox of the Shield of Achilles (18. 478-617). The beauty of the calm and pastoral scenes is like a miniature inset, a tiny mirror-glimpse of reality set within the heroic dimensions of the Wrath. It is a charming window which looks out onto another world, so different from the grim, unchanging landscape of the bloody, windswept plain. Under this aspect the pictures on the Shield bring to a climax all the little window-views that Homer has given us in the similes; and this dual level of the poem creates a tension which is closely bound up with the poem's ultimate meaning.

Studies in Homeric archaeology have made us more aware of the exact structure of the shields that Homer speaks of. From his description, on the outside of the shield there are apparently five circular rings of metal, each diminishing in size until we come to the fifth, which is a small circlet in the center. It is on these five plates that the scenes are wrought, and Homer's description probably proceeds from the central ring to the outermost, although we cannot identify the location of each scene in detail. In the first ring we see the earth and the stars—the setting, as it were, for all man's joy and sorrow, the stage for Homer's drama of war and peace. In the next ring we see the two cities, one at peace and the other besieged by armies; in the third, fourth and fifth rings (it is more difficult to separate them) we have fine portraits of the passing of the seasons, the joys of planting, reaping and harvest, of sheep-tending and hunting; and the last scene is one of a sprightly song-dance festival of men and maidens. That this is the shield that Achilles should carry into the final battle makes the irony all the more intense. It is Homer's presentation, primitive though it may be, of the division within the nature of man.

The author of the *Odyssey*, on the other hand, lacks this serious involvement with the ultimate issues of life. Indeed, his approach to the problem of the gods and the world of human morality is, in many respects, different from that of the *Iliad*. A theme only briefly suggested and, unfortunately left undeveloped is the operation of the divine sanctions for man's misdeeds (*Od.* 1. 34):

> By their own wickedness they suffer
> Misery beyond what is fated.[1]

And if many, since the days of Horace, have seen in Odysseus the *utile exemplar*, the archetype of man's eternal quest for the ultimate Haven,[2] the symbolism should not be over-stressed. For the poetry of the *Odyssey*, for all its charm, is composed in a less dominant, less urgent key. It is primarily folk-entertainment, a morsel from the endless store of pre-literary, Greek bardic narrative. It is adventure of a very high order.

But the poet of the *Iliad* has come closer to Western man's deepest insight in the early evolution of his self-awareness: that consciousness of the frustrating limitations of the world and of the division within his own nature. The poet has touched the heart of the human problem, and thus he is forced to reveal, with almost a cry of pain (*Il.* 17. 446-447)

> There is nothing more miserable than man
> Of all things that breathe and crawl
> Upon the earth.

The *Iliad* is not, indeed, to be allegorized, but it remains, nonetheless, a profound poetic expression of the nature of the human predicament. Achilles has chosen the $K\acute{\eta}\varrho$ of death and glory; but his glory is not as he imagined it. What he had so longed for becomes ashes, and his true greatness is revealed rather in his expression of pity, compassion and human compromise.

One of the most striking images of this early period occurs in Hesiod's *Works and Days*. The wonder is that Hesiod has succeeded in making of the poem something more than a dull Farmer's Almanac. It is prosaic work at best, but certain symbols stand out like nuggets in the rough. Whereas in the *Iliad* we had the image of the *Kêres*, in Hesiod the dilemma of man's personal moral choice is compared with the choosing of a respectable housewife instead of a sensuous slattern (*Works and Days* 287-292):

> The lady Wickedness (Κακία) is easy to find...
> For smooth is the road to her—she lives
> At no great distance. But the immortal gods
> Have placed between ourselves and Virtue,
> Toil and sweat. Long and steep is the path
> That leads to her; stony the ground at the outset.
> But once one gets on top the road is easy,
> That which at first was hard.

True, the moral life which Hesiod offers us is, when all is said, humdrum, unimaginative, nourished from the soil of Boeotia. But the symbol of the great Choice is a charming one, destined to become a commonplace in later pagan and Christian literature.[3] And the archetypal image of Virtue as a Woman has been given a great deal of consideration by the school of Carl Jung.[4]

Greek lyric poetry first emerges from the dark obscurity of its preliterary existence in the person of Archilochus. Of all the many lyric poets whose works are no longer extant, the loss of so much of Archilochus is perhaps the most regrettable, and the recovery of fragments from the papyri has so far hardly been encouraging.[5] But from what we have, we can catch glimpses of his bitter and rapacious view of life, and the primitive sharpness of his vision of death, war, human cruelty, and frustrated love. One of his most powerful poetic techniques is apparently borrowed from the animal fable; in Archilochus' thinking men are like so many shabby, vicious, or lustful animals. The movements or habits of goats and foxes, apes and hedgehogs constantly suggest the uncanny wiles and resourcefulness of men. For Archilochus cannot escape the parallel: Father Zeus is concerned with the good and bad deeds of men as well as the Justice and Hybris of beasts (fr. 94 Diehl). The symbolism has a moral foundation. When he sings of a young girl (fr. 25 Diehl),

> Joyous she was with a sprig of myrtle
> And a rose's tender blossom;
> And her hair fell like a shadow
> Over her neck and shoulders,

it is almost as if the girl herself is the flower, the myrtle sprig. And his stark nature symbolism can be seen when he describes a hillock of his homeland (fr. 18 Diehl):

> Like an ass's back it stood,
> Topped with a savage wood,

or when he paints the approaching sudden terror of the steep storm-cloud over the heights of Gyra as the sea rises (fr. 56 Diehl). But nature imagery and personal expression come together in a fragment of great power and originality (f. 92a Diehl):

> Do you see the steep crag yonder,
> Savage and malicious?
> There I sit, with contempt for your battles.

The setting of the piece is unclear; an eagle perhaps, or bird of prey, broods over a battlefield from a peak set high against the sky. But it is a compelling portrayal of his own magnificently arrogant and aggressive attitude towards the animal-like men whom he despises, toward the wealthy Gyges of this world (cf. fr. 22 Diehl). Whether in love or in war, Archilochus imposes himself upon his environment lest it should somehow deprive him of his independence.[6] The sharp, rich, symbolic thinking that we find in his fragments is unique at this early period and it is all the more to be regretted that we have so little.

The animal-symbol technique is seen at its best in the famous fragment from the *Invective Against Women* of Semonides of Amorgos. In casting about for a reason to explain why women are so different from men, the poet suggests that the god at their creation somehow confounded their substance with that of the pig, the vixen, the ass, the cat, the dog, the mare, the ape, and the bee; stupid women are mixed with earth, and the moody, changeable woman has a kinship with the sea (frag. 7. 1-95 Diehl). It is at once a magnificent and amusing conception, and was to serve as an armory for the ancient poets for many centuries. I need not stress the fact that Greco-Roman literature is, with few exceptions, a literature of men for men. The Sapphos, Corinnas, Praxillas and Sulpicias are quite rare, and it is interesting to speculate what our picture of the ancient world would be like if we were more solidly informed on the woman's point of view. But as it is, in a man's world, the sea with its deceptive calm and sudden squalls remains the dominant symbol for woman from Semonides to Horace; an even worse fate remained in the vitriolic portrait of Juvenal's *Sixth Satire*.

From the viewpoint of imagery and symbolism the fragments of Alcaeus are disappointing.[7] There is the famous political symbol of the storm-tossed ship which Horace borrowed in *Carm.* 1. 14, *O navis*.[8] It is a frequent image in Sophocles' *Antigone* and *Oedipus*, and even in Alcaeus it seems a tired metaphor. It should be recalled, however, that for Alcaeus the ship refers rather to his foundering political fac-

tion, and not to the State as a whole, as Horace later understood it. For like many a poet of modern times, Alcaeus
was rarely on the right side. The image becomes further
involved in another fragment—if the ancient commentator
is right—where Alcaeus describes his symbolic ship as an
old, jaded courtesan. But apart from a few more images
of wine and warmth (which Horace developed in *Odes* 1. 9),
love and war, Alcaeus' contribution along these lines is un-
remarkable. We can only judge from what we have; but
the fragments we have recovered suggest a craftmanship and
versatility without intense feeling or inspiration. This was
perhaps the reason why he is never mentioned by the author
of *On the Sublime*.

With Sappho, however, we come upon what is perhaps
the most original use of symbolism in all Greek lyric poetry
and Viktor Pöschl in his study of Vergil has seriously underestimated her importance.[9] Sappho's poetic world is a striking and sensuous creation: it is a dream-meadow of constantly
blossoming flowers, wherein the time is always spring, and
all the seduction of sight and sound, smell and touch suggests
the fresh atmosphere of young love and young beauty. A
young maiden is like a blushing apple, intact on the bough
despite pursuers (LP 105a),[10] or, again, like a hyacinth that
loses its bloom (LP 105c); a young man is like a slender sapling (LP 115). But in reading Sappho we must not limit
ourselves to explicit comparisons; references to flowers and
fruit almost always carry overtones of youth and young love.
Flowers like the rose, the dewy lotus, the tender chervil,
and the flowery melilot, are associated with the presence of
young girls (LP 96. 12 ff.);[11] it is fitting that garlands of
flowers are made for their hair (LP 94. 12 ff.; 98. 7 ff.; 81b);
and even the simple picture of a tender maid gathering blos-
soms (LP 122) carries, one feels, significant symbolic overtones. In Sappho there is a mysterious association between

young girls and the moon—"the rosy-fingered" moon, if the text is right (LP 96. 8) — outshining the stars with its shimmering light (LP 34). In this all-pervasive setting, even the love for her daughter Kleis, "lovely as the golden flowers, dearer than all Lydia," becomes peculiarly passionate and poignant.[12]

But Sappho's fierce love extended far beyond her dear Kleis. There is the suggestion that Sappho's world is a great battlefield of love, with armies in array (LP 1. 21-8; 16. 1-4) — the symbol of war is, I think, at once a masculine and a sexual image—and a struggle rages between Sappho and her arch-enemies, the ladies Gorgo and Andromeda, for the affection of the maidens Atthis, Dica, Nica, Anactoria and many more (cf. LP 131).[13] In this battle it is only fitting that Aphrodite should be invoked as Sappho's ally (LP 1. 28). By day or night, this demonic female figure hovers through Sappho's world, and we are probably right in thinking that Sappho and her circle paid special homage to the goddess of love and fertility. One of the fragments (LP 2) contains the finest poetic evocation of an ancient shrine that we possess: the sensuous odors of incense and spring flowers, the languid murmuring of water through the leaves, create a fitting symbolic atmosphere to surround the divine presence. But most mysterious of all are Sappho's references to Aphrodite's theophanies. The goddess is portrayed as visiting Sappho in her waking hours (LP 1. 13) as well as in her sleep (LP 134), or the presence of Aphrodite is somehow mysteriously felt during her rustic festival (LP 2; 96. 25-27).[14]

Here a serious psychological problem arises. Are we to take these apparitions as merely literary and poetic—like the visions of the superhuman Lady in the *Shepherd* of the early Christian Hermas? Or do they reflect Sappho's actual experiences in her waking or sleeping moments? That the ancients could dream of gods and goddesses speaking to them

in sleep is not to be denied. It was a problem which contributed to the Epicurean doctrine on the gods; and it seems
to be confirmed by the accounts of actual dreams, such as
we find in the papyri and in the *Dream Book* of Artemidorus
of Daldis. But if we are to understand that these theophanies
occurred while she was awake, then it may be that Sappho was an
emotionally disturbed hysteric, an *hallucinée*. It is not hard to
imagine Sappho with some of the temperament of a Swedenborg
or a Blake; some of her poetry, especially the expressions of intense physical feeling towards the young girls in her entourage,
might tend to support this view. But in default of further evidence we need not postulate anything more than a poetic
embellishment of certain dream phenomena, significant as they
may be. For we may here perhaps be helped by the Jungian
school of depth psychology with its suggestion that a certain
symbolic figure may occur in man's sleeping or waking imagination, which projects his ideal self, his conscience or his
moral goal. In men, according to the theory, the figure is
usually female, the *anima*, and in women it is regularly male,
the *animus*. That Sappho's dream-world should be haunted
by a *female* figure may suggest a psychological aberration
which we cannot now reconstruct in precise detail, but in
any case it would seem to give some slight support to the
view that she was emotionally disturbed.

Here, however, we have ventured beyond the limits of
poetic analysis. From the symbolic point of view we may
only say that the frustrations and longings, the sensuous experiences of Sappho's world enter deeply into the texture
of her poetry. What emerges is a kind of Venus-mystique,
which is to be given fuller, if not more poetically intense
expression in the Hellenistic and Roman elegiac poets. The
poles of Sappho's poetic world are, in a sense, Aphrodite
written in large and in small letters. Whether we accept
the theories of Jung matters little; Sappho's subconscious

life was uniquely projected into her extraordinary music.

The symbolism of Pindar has been subjected to a searching study by Gilbert Norwood.[15] Since the time of Wilamowitz's *Pindaros* (1922) Pindar's poetic reputation had been the object of a good deal of controversy, and now with Norwood's analyses many older views will perhaps have to be discarded. Some of the most important images which he has pointed out are the Bee (*Pyth.* 11), the Captive Bird (*Pyth.* 8), the Eye (*Isth.* 5), the Pebble (*Ol.* 10), the Rose (*Ol.* 7), the Sapling (*Nem.* 8), the Silver Coin (*Isth.* 2), the Triple Diadem (*Nem.* 7), the Triple Draught (*Nem.* 3), the Two Anchors (*Ol.* 6), the War Horse (*Isth.* 7). Others, like the Goblet (*Ol.* 7), Apollo's Lyre (*Pyth.* 1), and the Ship of man's destiny (*Ol.* 12), had been perhaps long obvious. If his view of the fanciful conceit in *Ol.* 2 is correct—that the symbol of the Wheel of Fortune is also expressed by the round Theta, the first letter of Theron's name—it would give us a completely new insight into the subtle complexity of ancient choral composition. Beyond all doubt, Norwood has shown us that Pindar was ingenious, but not, I think, that he was a great poet. His Epinicians offer us incomparable evidence for a study of archaic Greek religious beliefs, and of the ethico-cultural concept of Ἀρετή, the virtue of upper-class breeding. Pindar's work shows a vast range of interests and an amazing energy, but his productivity far exceeded his poetic talent, and much of his work strikes us as cold, commercial, made-to-order. Perhaps Norwood, if anyone, has come close to finding the key to the mystery. And though the symbols he has uncovered cause us to admire the poet's ingenuity, much as we would admire Gongorism or the English Metaphysicals, they bring us no closer to an evaluation of his artistic achievement. It is clear that the ancients were impressed. Horace, who did not perhaps understand Pindar's metrical structure, admits his own feeling of insignificance before the Theban eagle (*Odes* 4.2): Whoever strives to emulate Pindar is like Daedalus and Icarus flying with wax-dipped wings too close to the sun; for Pindar rushes on like a river swollen over its banks "in rhythms free of law." But for many a modern reader there still remains a lack of complete communication; it is, once again a problem of tone.

Before entirely leaving the Greek lyric poets, we may consider the imagery of some of Simonides' fragments. One short piece on Virtue recalls the imagery of Hesiod, which we have mentioned earlier:[16]

> They say that Virtue dwells
> Amid inaccessible rocks;
> And a blessed band of nymphs attend her.
> No mortal eye can ever behold her—
> Unless a man can scale the heights
> Of courage by heart-searing toil.

Aristotle, in a rare poetic mood, uses the same sort of imagery in his hymn to Virtue, written after the tragic death of his friend Hermias; but by now the symbolism seems stereotyped and dull. Simonides' *Dirge* in honor of the soldiers who died at Thermopylae has for its central image the warriors' tomb conceived as a sacred altar and a shrine:[17]

> Glorious is the fortune and fair the fate
> Of those who perished at Thermopylae.
> Their tomb is a sacred altar, washed
> With the libations of memory and the wine of fame.
> Such a shroud neither decay nor conquering time
> Can dim. It is a shrine whose keeper is the glory
> Of all Hellas—witness Leonidas, king of Sparta,
> Who has left an ornament of valor, and an undying name.

The dirge is a quiet one, but the imagery is brilliant. The altar, like an ancient marble temple of the gods, will shine afar, and time will not throw a shadow on it.[18] The libations poured on the altar are remembrance and eulogy—the eulogy indeed of Simonides' own hymn—and the custodian will be Greece's eternal glory.

The most moving poem of Simonides is the Danae-fragment, and its symbolism is quite remarkable. In F.L. Lucas' version it runs:[20]

> When she was set in her carven chest,
> Whirled by the wind from crest to crest
> Of heaving sea,
> On Danae's heart fell horror—her tears began to run
> And babe to breast the mother pressed, crying, "O little son,
> For me is misery,
> But thou, my innocent one—
> Calmly thou sleepest; and nought to thee
> This brass-nailed chest of woe;
> Nought is the starless midnight, nought is the dark-blue gloom
> Of the wave that welters by us and flings its driving spume
> Upon thy curls below;
> Nought is the sea-wind's wailing—so oft thy face is laid
> On mine, within the purple of my mantle fast asleep.
> Nay, terror has no terror, for *thee*—else how dismayed
> Thy little ears would listen, to hear thy mother weep!
> Sleep on, my babe; sleep, restless sea; sleep, boundless ill
> That breaks my heart! O Father, O Zeus, be it thy will
> To save us and to spare.
> Yet, if too bold my prayer,
> If I transgress Thy justice, forgive, forgive me still!

In the young mother Danae and her baby Perseus alone on the sea, we seem to catch a glimpse of the entire human tragedy—of man adrift on the sea of the world, subject to its cruel laws, helplessly naked before the eye of God. The "brass-nailed chest of woe" is like some floating coffin on the sea of providence. And the baby Perseus seems to embody that blissful ignorance of anxiety which all men long for, yet so tragic because the babe must grow to be a man. In Danae's prayer is man's eternal cry to God for salvation, in the midst of a life made painful by human malice as much as by the blind destructiveness of the elements. Danae's feeling towards Zeus is ambivalent; hers is a cry of hope as well as a plea for forgiveness: "Forgive, forgive me still!" And it is all the more profound because the poet has left it without comment.

One further piece should be quoted here, the so-called *Nightsong* attributed to Alcman.[21] Its tone is quite unique in all of Classical literature:

> Mountain tops and gullies sleep,
> Torrents and promontories,
> And all the tribes of beasts that the black earth nurses,
> Beasts in the mountain forest, and swarms of bees,
> And monsters in the depths of the heaving sea,
> And wide-winged birds—all sleep.

The fragment, despite its Homeric echoes, exhibits a striking unity of tone and mood: all nature sleeps, all creatures are one because they come from one mother, Earth, and together take their rest. Most commentators cannot believe that this picture of Night was intended for its own sake and one common view[22] is to suppose that the poet went on to say that, though all nature sleeps at nightfall, he must lie awake for love.[23] This may be true, but as the fragment stands the poet surely stresses the organic unity of all Earth's creatures, repeating the idea of sleep in the first and last lines. As all things are one in origin they are one in rest. It is, in short, a summary of the life cycle, especially if we may take sleep here as a foreshadowing of death. Man alone is missing—and thus the poem remains incomplete, a mystery. Yet its tone, brooding and mystical, seems certainly later than the period of early Greek lyric. Indeed, if man's affinity with the lower orders of creation were mentioned, the poem might even be Epicurean, dating from the Alexandrian period or later.

TRAGIC WISDOM: AESCHYLUS, SOPHOCLES

GREEK TRAGEDY OFFERS A WIDE TERRAIN FOR THE EX-
ploration of the poetic symbol; yet it is in precisely this area
that scholarship has perhaps been the most deficient. In general it may be said that there are five important qualities
which may be found in varying degrees in ancient as well
as modern poetic drama. They are (1) the dramatic rhythm
or "ritual," with which Aristotle is chiefly concerned in his
Poetics; (2) the prosodic element: metre, rhyme, and so on;
(3) that peculiar compression and intensity in the expression
of ideas which Aristotle called διάνοια although it is quite
different from the logic of rhetoric and prose; (4) a special
choice of words; and (5) the use of organic images by a kind
of image-logic based on the laws of analogy and associations.
Now perhaps too much has been said in the past of elements
1-4; indeed, much labor has been expended in the philological and historical aspects of Greek Tragedy, whereas we

have not been completely successful in exploring ancient tragedy as a truly poetic vehicle.[1]

In this chapter I should like to discuss the fifth element
in more detail, particularly insofar as it touches the poetry
of Sophocles. It should be noted, however, that the fallacy
often committed in this matter is that of image counting,
of noting exactly the number of times an image occurs, the
number of lines devoted to it, or, worst of all, the various
categories of ancient life and culture from which the images
have been drawn. Caroline Spurgeon in her pioneering work
Shakespeare's Imagery (1936), tends to fall into this particular
trap in her analysis of Shakespeare. But when all is said,
we are not interested in the question whether Aeschylus liked
to hunt, or whether Sophocles made many sea voyages. The
truth is that the most important quality of an image is its
functional effectiveness. That is, we must explore the relationship between symbol and what is symbolized, the degree of interpenetration between the tenor of an image and
its vehicle, and the organic relevance which the symbol has
for the meaning of the play as a whole. An image-analysis
which uncovers mere irrelevancies—presuming always we are
dealing with great poetry or drama—is fundamentally false,
and serves merely to feed curiosity. It is the artistic function
of the image, in the fullest sense, which is the most important element in this sort of analysis.

It will perhaps be helpful at the outset to situate Sophocles
more clearly, in this matter, with respect to Aeschylus and
Euripides. The religious austerity and epic quality of Aeschylus' plays find an echo in this use of imagery. His richest
plays in this respect are the *Agamemnon* and the *Libation
Bearers*. And as Earp in *The Style of Aeschylus* has shown,
his imagery is predominantly drawn from animals and from
hunting; next in frequency come metaphors from seafaring,
medicine, and athletics. Here is not the place to propose

further lists of these images, which have been adequately drawn up by others. The imagery, whether expressed in metaphor or simile, is for the most part decorative; as in the epic, it serves as a window into a less heroic world, the every-day world of mainland Greece, where the sharply etched countryside looks out upon vast stretches of brooding sea. In his preference for animal-imagery, Aeschylus is perhaps closer to the tradition of Archilochus and Semonides and the ancient folk-fable. It is a more difficult task to demonstrate his use of the organic image or symbol, which is more integrally connected with the plot and dramatic theme.

The uniqueness of *The Persian Women* is that it portrays within a foreign atmosphere a theme dear to the heart of the victors at Salamis and Plataea: the destruction of Persia's pride, her *Hybris*, by Zeus and Atê at the hands of the Greek armies. This is supported by the imagery, especially in the three great scenes of the play: Atossa's symbolic dream, the apparition of Darius, and the return of the defeated Xerxes. In Atossa's dream of Fair Women, she sees her son Xerxes yoking two female figures to a single chariot (190 ff.), obvi-ously Persia and Hellas, and one of them breaks free. The na-ture of Xerxes' *Hybris* is more clearly expressed by the ghost of Darius—himself a wraithlike witness to the fading of Susa's glory. Darius reveals that Xerxes' impetuosity (718) and im-prudence (725) were the cause of Persia's ruin. Xerxes' folly was the building of a bridge across the Hellespont; this was in effect, the yoke that was to bind the two women of Atos-sa's dream to Persia's chariot. The yoke of enslavement (49) that Xerxes in his *Hybris* had tried to thrust upon Greece is aptly symbolized in the yoke (722, 736) by which he tried to bridge the Hellespont, and by the shackles and fetters he tried to put upon the sea. This was Xerxes' final Atê; as Darius explains (749 ff.):

Though but a mortal he thought in his folly

> He could be master of all the gods—even
> Of Poseidon,

the god of the sea. Thus the yoke-enslavement imagery, Atossa's dream imagery, and the fantastic bridge are all thematically united to suggest Persia's pride.

Another cluster of images revolves about Xerxes' ignoble fall from power. Throughout we are told of the pride of the Persian army, the lovely "flower" of the barbarian youth (50, 252, 618, 925). Again the ghost of Darius depicts how, after the land of Plataea was watered with Persian blood,

> Pride blossomed, brought forth a cluster of Atê
> Reaping a harvest of tears (821-2).

Thus, as Atossa had dimly envisioned, the great Persian structure which Darius had raised up was turned upside down and brought down (163-4) by the daemon, by Zeus and Atê with seductive wiles (96-100). The collapse of Persia's manhood is sharply revealed in the Messenger's picture of the soldiers floundering in the sea (558 ff.); this is, indeed the sea of calamity that Atossa had seen bursting upon her people (433-4). The final image of ruin is the appearance of Xerxes himself, symbolizing in his pitiful garb his fall from high estate. His garments have indeed been rent in grief (1030), but they have also been pierced with arrows (1017-33). This is the distance Persia has travelled, and it is strikingly portrayed in the noble wraith of Darius, the king who erected Persia's glory in wisdom and piety, and the ragged runaway, Xerxes, who had presumed in his fantastic schemes to conquer even the gods themselves.

In *The Suppliant Maidens* there are three functional images of some importance which touch the central theme of the play. The first is that of maidenhood as ripe fruit (996-1005). As Danaus instructs the young girls.

> I bid you bring no shame upon my head,
> Now that your loveliness is visible to men.

> Tender fruit is not easy to protect:
> Both beasts and men, of course, despoil it,
> Creatures that fly and those that stalk the earth.

The goddess Cypris causes the ripe fruit to attract the gaze of men, and they shoot the arrow of seduction to gain their prize. The image of flower and fruit is again referred to by the Chorus itself (663-4 and 1015). Connected with this image of fruit threatened with destruction is that of the doves menaced by hawks (223-6); as Danaus bids the maidens,

> Sit on this holy ground like a flock of doves
> Menaced by hawks—birds, too, yet enemies
> Who would defile their own kin, their own blood.
> The bird that feeds on bird cannot be pure.

Again the young girls appeal to the King of Argos (350-352):

> Behold me, a suppliant fugitive, wandering
> Like a heifer pursued by wolves among rocks
> Precipitous . . .

The ripe fruit and tender flower, the pure dove and the pitiful heifer—all underline the motif of the young maidens' refusal to surrender their virginity against their will.

In the *Seven Against Thebes* there is an elaborate blood-imagery. Early in the play we are told of the blood-oath the seven rebel warriors swore (42-48); the Scout reports what he has seen to Eteocles:

> Seven warriors, impetuous captains of their hosts,
> Shed a bull's blood into a black-bound shield,
> And dipping their hands into the beast's gore, swore
> By Ares, Enyo, and bloodthirsty Phobos
> That they would bring ruin on Cadmus' city.

This bloody shield is, it would seem, the dominant image of the play. Clear and persistent images of blood abound throughout the course of the action;[2] the blood that flows has its source in "the bloody stock" that sprang from Oedipus (751-6):

> [Laius] begat his own destruction, Oedipus
> The patricide, who, sowing seed in the holy field
> Of his mother, whence he himself was nurtured,
> Took upon himself a bloody stock....

The image of the shield again returns in the elaborate shield symbolism used in describing the warriors' armor. The rebel Hippomedon's shield represents the giant Typhon breathing forth smoke and flame (489-496); and the intertwined snakes on it suggest all that is evil and malevolent. Against him is ranged Thebes' faithful Hyperbius, whose shield represents Zeus hurling a fiery thunderbolt (512-14), thus foreshadowing Thebes' victory. The rebel Parthenopaeus has the ominous Sphinx on his shield (541). And, finally, Polyneices bears emblazoned on his shield an image of Dikê, the virgin-daughter of Zeus (642-8). She is depicted guiding a warrior with the words, "This man will I return to his home." But the device is merely ironic. As Eteocles says, Justice cannot stand at the rebel's side (669). But Dikê does in the end bring the warrior home, dead, his cause frustrated.

The bloody shield, in which the warriors swore vengeance on Thebes, is then the central image of the play. The blood suggests the "bloody stock" of Oedipus, and also the fact that in this war those of the same blood are fighting against each other. The shield, and especially that of Polyneices with its ironic blazon, suggests the nature of the conflict. Zeus and Dikê are in the end victorious, but not in the way the hapless warriors would have predicted. It seems almost certain that the last scene, from the entrance of the Herald, is interpolated. In any case, the final movement of the play stresses the futility of the war, and the sadness and disgust of those who are left to mourn the misguided warriors. The bloody shield becomes a symbol of frustration and ambiguity.

Of the many images in the *Prometheus Bound* the most prominent and pervasive is that of disease and its cure.[3] But,

because of the nature of the theology we find in the play—
which has, among other things, caused some to doubt its Aeschylean authorship[4]—it is difficult to interpret the meaning
correctly. Among Prometheus' gifts to mortals, perhaps the
most prominent in the play is the art of medicine and the
use of healing drugs (479-483). And yet, Prometheus admits to the Chorus of Oceanids (469-471),

> Despite the devices I have found for men—
> Alas!—I myself have found no way
> To end my present suffering.

And the Chorus replies (472-3):

> Like some poor doctor fallen ill, your despair
> Of finding any cure for your own disease.

But Prometheus' suffering comes from a disease of the soul;
as Oceanus reminds him (379-380),

> Know you not this, Prometheus, that words
> Are the healers of a soul diseased?

On the other hand, Io's disease is god-inflicted, a kind of
mania and fugue (877-886), and her affliction serves as a tragic
counterpoint to the sufferings of Prometheus. But the ultimate meaning of the disease-imagery in terms of the theme
of the play remains unclear. We are situated at the beginning of the third age of the world; the ages of Uranos and
Kronos have passed away, and the day of Zeus has dawned
(96, 200 ff.)—that god who, we are told in the *Agamemnon*
(176-8), leads men to wisdom by suffering. As yet, in the
Prometheus, his reign is fresh; and the compromise effected
by the wisdom of Prometheus had not yet been fully accom-
plished: men were not simply to suffer like animals (441 ff.)
under the yoke of Necessity. If it is true then that Prometheus' bravery achieves this compromise between Zeus and
mankind, as the poet sees it, the suffering of Prometheus
and, indeed, of Io, is merely an illustration of the general

pain of mankind under the conditions imposed by Zeus, by the very nature of man and the universe. But its true significance would perhaps only have been clear from the other play or plays which followed the *Prometheus Bound*. Thus the symbolism, like the theology of the play, remains somewhat of a mystery.

Blood-imagery again recurs in the *Oresteia* trilogy, mingled with symbols of hunting and snaring. The keynote is struck by the Chorus of Elders in the *Agamemnon* (1019-1021):

> The blood of man, once it has first fallen
> To earth, black in death, there is no magic spell
> That can call it back again.

And the same motif is repeated in the *Choephoroi* by the Chorus of women (48):

> What ransom is there for blood once shed on earth?

But farther on in the same entry-song, the black blood spilled on the ground seems to become a symbol of Ἄτη, that daemonic force which the gods send to destroy men (*Choephoroi* 66-70):

> The nourishing earth has drunk her fill of blood,
> And so the avenging gore is clotted
> And will not be absorbed.
> And Atê tears the guilty
> Until he swells with overmastering pain.

It is the blood of kin that has been shed; and this is the trail which must be pursued by the hounds of primeval Justice, the Erinyes; as "the exactors of blood" (*Eumenides* 319) they must pursue Orestes until settlement is made. After a painful journey Orestes makes his plea at Athens (*Eum.* 280-283):

> The blood upon my hand sleeps now and grows faint;
> The matricidal stain has now been purified;
> For while still fresh it was dispelled at the altar
> Of Phoebus by the ritual of slaughtered pigs.

It is blood then that pervades the entire atmosphere of the three plays. To the frenzied Cassandra, Agamemnon's palace is a grave that smells of blood (*Agam*. 1309); and she sees herself as a bloody sacrificial animal butchered by a hot knife (*Agam*. 1277-8). It is this blood-imagery which appears to underlie Clytemnestra's Purple Sea speech in *Agam*. 958 ff.:

> There is a sea—and who can drain it?—that nourishes
> A vast purple stain, silverlike and ever new,
> Containing all we need to dye our garments.
> Of these our house—thanks to the gods—has all
> We need; penury in this it shall never know.

Surely this Sea suggests a sea of blood—sufficient indeed to dye all the garments of the household. Connected perhaps with this, too, may be the great purple tapestries which Clytemnestra lays before the feet of her returning lord; by walking on them Agamemnon somewhat seals his fate.

Side by side with the images of bloodshed are the regular animal symbols we are familiar with in Aeschylus. There is the mysterious portent of the eagles that devour the hare and her unborn brood before the Achaean host (*Agam*. 110-120), suggestive of the pitiless cruelty of human passions, especially as we shall see them exhibited before us in the trilogy. Again, Orestes and Electra are like a brood of eaglets whose parent was killed by a viper (*Choeph*. 247-9); indeed, Clytemnestra is the viper, or even a sea-serpent (*Choeph*. 994-6). The imagery is for the most part purely decorative, but we may detect traces of a recurrent imagery in the symbol of the Lion of the House of Atreus. In the second stasimon of the *Agamemnon* (717-726), the Chorus takes up the fable of the lion's whelp to illustrate the Fate that fell upon Troy:

> A man once reared in his home a lion's whelp;
> Though as yet unweaned it had no mother's milk.
> And while still young it pleasured young and old:

> They took it in their arms like a new born babe;
> Its eyes would glisten at a touch, and it fawned like a cat
> To satisfy its needs.

But soon, we are told, it showed its true colors and retaliated by slaughtering the entire household (727-736). More clearly, however, does Cassandra see the vision of Agamemnon's death as plotted by a craven lion, "luxuriating in its bed" (1224). In her tortured ecstasy she cries (1258 ff.):

> Ah! There is a two-footed lioness who has gone to bed
> With a wolf in the absence of her lord, the noble lion—
> She will slay me . . .

Here we see Aegisthus as the wolf who has slept with the lioness, and Agamemnon as the noble lion. But the tenor of the imagery soon changes. The house becomes a place of sacrifice, a grave filled with the smell of death (1309-11). Agememnon is caught like a fish in a net (1392), trapped in the spider's web (1492, 1516). The images lend the play a brutal, primitive color, but in the *Oresteia*, as in his other plays, Aeschylus' message is on a far deeper, theological level. Quite different from its use in Sophocles, the image in Aeschylus is still in its purely decorative function, and is just barely passing over to the realm of the symbolic.

In Euripides, on the other hand, the symbolic dimension has passed from the realm of actual imagery to that of character and plot. The tone of fantasy is often set by the prologue, as for example in the apparition of the ghost of Polydoros in the *Hecuba*, the address Apollo makes to Admetus' house in the *Alcestis*, the improbable decision of Dionysus at the opening of the *Bacchae*, Helen's delightful speech to explain her presence in Egypt in the *Helen*, and Orestes' feverish delirium in the *Orestes*. Euripides' prologues are crucial insofar as they not only set the play's tone but embody essential clues for the unravelling of the mystery. For the Euripidean plot is not always as straightforward as it may at first appear: Euripides' presentation of the myth is often obscure and ambiguous, and one ventures to suggest that the Greek audience found it so. The symbolic world of Euripidean drama has regularly two dimensions which are always interpenetrating: in the one we have the presentation of the myth, and in the other the uneasy, pervasive suggestion that all is falsehood and deception. The very ambiguity of Euripides' plays is sufficient warrant against any clear-cut, one-sided interpretation. But surely it can be said that Euripides' tragic vision is restricted to the world of the here-and-now, without a theological dimension as such. For it is precisely in the area of theology that Euripides is disturbing and disquieting, and his plays leave us with an abiding awareness of all that is inconclusive and imperfect in life and belief. How much of this was due to a conscious technique and how much, as I suspect, to Euripides' own artistic limitations, will aways be difficult to say. Suffice it here to admit that the method of symbolic analysis tends to be frustrated when applied to his plays.

Between the Aeschylean use of the decorative metaphor and the more abstract presentation of Euripides lies the highly imaginative world of Sophocles. Here the tragic symbol achieves the peak of its dramatic coherence, with a theological depth that will not again be sounded until the great French and English playwrights of the Renascence. For in Sophocles the image is not merely ornamental; rather, it is the vehicle of his profoundest message. It is thus that his position with regard to Euripides and Aeschylus will become clear, and the nature of his supreme dramatic genius made more manifest.

The *Ajax* is a difficult play, and the study of its imagery does not make it easier. The central theme of the play is the devastating, destructive force of Ajax's passion, that disease that springs from his hurt pride, his inability to adjust to the brutality of life and to be content with the meagre favors the gods have given him. This is the force that destroys Ajax himself as well as the happiness of Tecmessa and the child Eurysaces, and the calm and equilibrium of the Achaean camp. The vicious and disgusting slaughter of the innocent cattle, that useless outpouring of blood that Sophocles dwells on so much, is symbolic of the ugly passions that rage within Ajax's soul. It is cattle he takes captive and tortures in his tent (61-65); he flogs and beats them mercilessly (235 ff.), for here, in his madness, Ajax is playing at war, and Sophocles, indirectly, is thus showing us the ugliness and irrationality of war that is the result of men's abandonment to their passions. Ajax is the victim of "a heavenly Ἄτη" (195).[5] His temporary madness is a wound (581-582), a disease and a plague (269, 452), a storm bristling with bolts of lightning (207, 257-278). But even when his sanity returns, his state is not much different than before. "Now, in his right mind," sighs Tecmessa, "he suffers new pain" (259-260), for he has to face life as it really is and take the risk of human responsibility.

Sophocles means to stress the continuity between Ajax's state of madness and his state of sanity. The Chorus agrees with Tecmessa: "Surely now that his seizure is past he has no more joy than when he was sick" (279-280). And the reason is implied: it is because there is a parallelism between Ajax mad and Ajax well, and the ugliness of his frenzied state is meant to mirror the vicious destructiveness of the passions that sweep over him when he is sane. The only bright ray is his love for Tecmessa, and his tenderness for his son Eurysaces, that symbolic shield (574-575), that armor which will stand as a trophy for him after death, for the rest of his armor will be buried in his grave (577). The passage with Eurysaces recalls, thematically, the trivial reasons which roused Ajax to frenzy, the dispute over the armor of Achilles.

Here for a moment Ajax almost glimpses the one resource that can save him. But he lives in the darkness, and the darkness alone is his light (394-395), just as his foul destruction of the cattle was done in the dead of night (285). And yet Ajax is not totally in the dark; he has a vision of the tragedy of life, of the monotony of day-to-day living with evil (473-480):

> When a man is never quit of evil
> It is wrong for him to seek the normal span.
> What joy is there when day follows day
> Now urging us forward, now drawing us back
> From death? To me that man is good for naught
> Who takes his comfort from mere futile hopes.
> The man of worth lives well, else nobly dies—
> That's all there is to it.

Ajax's disease is deep-seated in his nature; no tears can heal it. He cries, unfeeling, to Tecmessa (580-582):

> A woman's a tearful thing. Quick, close the doors!
> A skilful doctor sings no charms
> Over a wound that needs the knife.

Logically Sophocles convinces us that by the reasoning of passion only one solution is possible: the "noble outlet," as the later Stoics called it. And yet we are aware that somehow the solution is all wrong; it is merely the corollary of madness. The long debate over his body, though somewhat alien to our modern tastes, is necessary to establish the equilibrium that has been disturbed by Ajax's violent spirit. It does, indeed, take the place of an epitaph: he was, as Odysseus must admit, "a brave warrior" (1344-1345). He was in short, a man.

In the *Trachiniae* Sophocles explores the destructive effects of another overwhelming human passion, jealous love. In this case, however, the instrument of the divine Ἄτη (1274) is one of the tenderest and most charming women in all Greek tragedy, Deianeira, the wife of Hercules. She is like a pathetic, helpless bird (105), or a tender, sheltered plant (144 ff.) and her innocence makes her slow to suspect the ugliness and malice that is in man. And it is the irony of the play that the invincible Hercules, the son of Zeus, should meet his fate at the hands of a helpless woman.

Indeed, the Chorus set the tone when they describe Hercules' life like a stormy wind-swept sea (114-115); for Iole, his mistress, comes to Deianeira like a baneful ship's cargo, destructive of her peace (537-538). And the tragedy steals upon them relentlessly, like the eternal wheeling of the Bears in the nightly sky, joy succeeding sorrow, and sorrow joy (130). Deianeira cannot brook a rival for her lords' affection, and it is this πόθος, this jealous desire (106) that is the source and spring of the catastrophe.[6] "The Cyprian goddess indeed," as the Chorus sings (860-861), "is clearly the silent cause of this destruction." In her rash simplicity, Deianeira recalls the blood of the centaur Nessus, which she had kept locked in a secret place (579), and the promise that this would be a "charm for the soul of Hercules" (575-576). But it is rash of her to trust the words of this monstrous creature, and Deianeira herself is self-conscious about it (586-587). It was blood bred of lust and envenomed with hatred; it was "a venom begotten of Death" (834). She should have suspected, but her own desires, her eagerness to win a victory over the young and graceful Iole, are too strong to resist. The blood of Nessus is, in a sense, the focal symbol of the entire play: it stands for the forces of hate and jealousy (so mixed up with love) that, when unleashed, can be so destructive of man's happiness. In the hands of the rash but innocent Deianeira it brings low the hero who has conquered all the perils of the world. Thus the vivid and disturbing descriptions of the poison's operation are most important for the central theme of the play (672 ff., 765ff., 1053 ff.); it is, as it were, the operation of the passions within man's own soul. Closely connected with this, too, are the clothing-symbols. Deianeira takes the poison and with it prepares a new tunic for her lord (580); this garment that is to be next to his skin is, for her, a love-token, a sign of her deepest love. The horrifying effects the blood has on pieces of cloth (695 ff.) as well as on the tunic itself aptly expresses the destruction of the love and intimacy which husband and wife enjoyed. It is only fitting that in dying, Deianeira should lay coverlets upon their bridal bed as though for sleeping (915-916), violently rip her own peplos (923-924) and plunge the sword into her heart, the root and source of all her tragedy. But to say that the source is unbridled passion is never, for Sophocles, the sole answer. "In all this is naught but Zeus" (1278), brooding darkly from Mt. Oeta; the mystery of human iniquity is somehow to be sought in him, ruling implacably and impartially like the cold Bears ever circling around the heavenly pole.

In the *Electra* we turn to a new sequence of imagery. For the theme of the play is one of hope. It is that the good of the world—like the "prudent birds of the air" the Chorus bids us observe (1058-1062)—are ultimately protected by Zeus, Themis and enthroned Justice, and sin does not go unpunished (1053-1065). For the providential deliverance of Electra (1509) ultimately emanates from Zeus, "who oversees and governs all" (175). This freedom which Orestes brings to the house of his father is a work of the gods (1270), set in motion by Apollo (32 ff., 1379-1380); he, apparently is the "ever-present daemon" (1306) who assists Orestes and Pylades in their appointed task. And yet, as an act of violence and blood-letting, the murder of Clytemnestra is a sacrifice to Ares (1385, 1420-21); in this sense, Orestes and Pylades are not the bringers of Apolline deliverance, but become the implacable hounds of vengeance (1388), instruments of the god of vindictiveness.

But the main theme of the play, as I have said, is the deliverance of Electra from death by death, and the thematic interchange of life and death is fundamental to the meaning of the play. For Electra's life has been a living death (1152); unmarried and childless (187), she has been kept in cruel captivity as a menial drudge (189-191, 818, 1192). True, death would be for her a happy release, especially if she would be with Orestes, whom she thinks dead (1168-1170, 1320-1321). Indeed, by a kind of symbolic gesture she sinks down to the ground before the house, and vows she will never more enter in to it (817-819). It is a diseased house (1070), infested by two Erinyes (1080-1081), the adulteress and her paramour; it is, as Clytemnestra unwittingly confesses in her hour of death, "a house forsaken by loved ones and full of murderers" (1404-1405).

It is to this house of death that Orestes comes, as a light and a savior (1354), for the "dead are alive" (1477-1478), and "the living have no tomb" (1219). He bears his father's signet ring as a seal (σφραγίς, 1223) of his authenticity. And though his mother is deceived at his coming, she had had a warning vision in a dream. The tale was heard when Clytemnestra declared her dream openly to the Sun (417-425); Agamemnon was with her as of old, she dreamed, and took his sceptre and planted it in the earth of the palace hearth. The sceptre is both a regal and a phallic symbol, and its flowering suggests the rebirth of Agamemnon's only son and his consequent conquest of all Mycenae. In Clytemnestra it is an anxiety dream; but its content enshrines the substance of the play.

Orestes' entrance is heralded mysteriously by the disguised Paedagogos, his long, and perhaps to us wearisome, account of Orestes' death is made vivid enough to be convincing and thus to forestall any possible suspicions when Orestes finally does appear. Psychologically, too, the story of his death embodies for Clytemnestra a kind of wish-fulfilment (766-768); and yet her paradoxical grief poignantly reflects the heart of the woman and the mother, which has now been so over-coated with hypocrisy and lust. But here, in a word, Soph-ocles expresses the emotional paradox of the play (770-771):

> It is a terrible thing to be a mother:
> No matter what her woe, she cannot hate her child.

For the poet's profound insight entails its opposite: a child can never hate its mother. And it is precisely this unnatural feeling that Zeus and Apollo impose upon the obedient hero.

The funeral urn, supposedly filled with Orestes' ashes (1117 ff.), serves as a kind of talisman to unite brother and sister in love and impel them towards their final decision. It is a symbol of their death-in-life, of what Electra was, of what Orestes might have been. For Orestes is "dead by a strate-gem, and by a strategem alive" (1228-1229). For by a feigned death Orestes rescues his father's house from the bondage of sin and brings Apollo's light and redemption.[7]

The *Philoctetes*, on the other hand, explores the problem of spiritual desolation and rejection. It is, in a sense, many plays with as many different conflicts. There is the theme of Neoptolemus' moral dilemma, and the conflict between politics and morality. There is the emotional relationship between the old man and the boy, and the masterly por-trayal of Philoctetes' warped psychology. But all these are composed as counterpoint to the dominant theme; and this, if we may express it simply, is the poet's vision that the prob-lems and sufferings of life are best solved by human faith and love, by the sympathy and understanding of our inter-personal relationships.

But the symbolic dimension in the *Philoctetes* is restricted to the actual setting rather than developed by any use of metaphor. Almost more than any other of Sophocles' plays, the plot is developed by action without the use of description or imagery. The rocky isle of Lemnos, for example, suggests the very barrenness of Philoctetes' life, the desolation in which he has been abandoned because of the unfeelling cruelty of the Achaean army. It becomes in the course of the play almost a part of his whole character, and when he bids it farewell in the closing lines of the play (1452 ff.), we realize that he is breaking away from what had been the dominant atmosphere of his life. As the play unfolds, we realize that two important elements in Philoctetes' character are symbolically juxtaposed: the festering wound, which makes him repulsive to himself and to men, and the magic bow which is the reason for his survival and the source of his power.[8] It is clear that such power must be harnessed to the Greek cause, despite Philoctetes' affliction and warped personality. But how is this to be done? Odysseus stands for the point of view that men must be made to conform, regardless of pain or personal unhappiness. And even in ancient times it must have been felt to be a traditional point of view, which owed its continuance precisely to the ruthless effectiveness of its policy. Individuals must be subordinated to the community, and, from this point of view, all means are good which achieve the desired result. Such a system deliberately overlooks the intrinsic value of the human person, and refuses to recognize the hierarchy of values within the individual. Thus in the exploitation of Neoptolemus, we have not only the portrayal of youth's first experience of moral evil, but we see the brutal manipulation of innocence for the attainment of political ends. From this point of view Sophocles exhibits the maturing and development of Neoptolemus, who learns to see human beings as they really are.

But the core of the play, as I have suggested, concerns the spiritual state of Philoctetes and his emergence from the

78

psychological darkness in which he has lived so long. The desert isle itself is suggestive of the waste-land of his soul, and the cave in which he lives fits in well with his darkened mind as well as his almost animal mode of existence. Alone on Lemnos, he finds his sole source of security in the miraculous bow of Hercules; it becomes almost the center of his entire life. But the chief focus of his attention is the disgusting, ulcerous wound, which has made him warped, morose and self-centered; as the wound has grown and become more noisome, it has, in a sense, fed the vicious hatred Philoctetes has for the Achaean chiefs (792-795). But it is due to Sophocles' art that we can observe the change in Philoctetes' soul against the background of his growing affection for Neoptolemus. He rediscovers himself when he discovers the tenderness of human love. His conflict resolved, Philoctetes is cured, in a sense, by Neoptolemus even before the theophany of Hercules. Before the joy of their friendship and reconciliation, the problem of the bow and the sack of Troy fades into the background.

It is primarily in the two great Theban plays, the *Oedipus* and the *Antigone*, that Sophocles exploits his genius for imagery to the fullest. For the imagery of the *Antigone* there is very little that one could add to Robert F. Goheen's monograph, *The Imagery of Sophocles' Antigone*. I should not here attempt to summarize the entire book, but one of its chief contributions was the discovery of six dominant image-sequences throughout the play. Four recur with marked frequency, according to Goheen: the imagery of money and merchandising, of warfare and military activity, of animals and their control, and images of the sea and sailing. Two sequences are more restricted in diversity and application, namely, images of disease and images of marriage. Goheen's analysis of these image-sequences is indeed a most remarkable achievement, even though, when he wrote, he was perhaps too much impressed with Caroline Spurgeon's work on Shakespeare. At times the grouping of the different images (for example, those dealing with animals) seems highly artificial, and the dominance of animal-imagery does little, when all is said, to explicate the fundamental meaning of the play. And yet, as I have said, our fundamental concern in image-analysis should be the functional bearing of the image or symbol on the central theme, on the dominant dramatic rhythm of the play. But the soundness and caution of Goheen's ultimate conclusions more than make up for any deficiencies one might find in his initial approach.[9]

Of the many possible readings of the Antigone, I still feel that Sir Maurice Bowra's view is the closest to what Sophocles actually intended. For the meaning of the play must surely be in the area of conflict between Creon and Antigone; it is, indeed, a conflict of character and outlook in which the justification of Antigone entails the humiliation of Creon. As the play unfolds we see that not Antigone, but Creon is the victim of folly and infatuation.

Now it is interesting to note that an image-analysis of the play does yield two predominant image clusters, one centering about Antigone and the other about Creon. Those about Antigone mainly symbolize her youthful love; and those about Creon suggest the world of the ruler and the politician. Antigone is "in love with the impossible" (90). She sees her life as a brief journey whose goal is the Otherworld; her love is in Hades (75-67, 524-525) and there her marriage rights will be celebrated. As an innocent young girl, she thinks of her final march to execution as a bridal procession and the rock-bound tomb is her bridal chamber (804,891). Fully does she embody the ideal of human nature expressed in the famous choral ode on the wonder of man (332 ff.), for surely the climax in man's ability to control his environment and himself is the deliberate determination to choose death as the only expression of one's view of life. For Antigone, the only tangible motives she is able to express are her respect for the Unwritten Laws which govern the right of the underworld gods and (if the passage is authentic[10]) her deep-seated natural love for her brother.

Creon, however, inhabits an entirely different world of ideas. He is the sole captain of his ship (162-163, 189-190), its sole pilot (994), who takes counsel, however, from Teiresias. But on his ship there is no democratic rule (736), and all interests must be subordinate to its successful voyage (162-163, 189-190). But, by implication, Creon considers all his subjects as mere slave-rowers, who must submit to the yoke of subordination (291). Creon's view of human motivation is primarily a materialistic one; as Goheen has pointed out, he thinks along lines of strict external subordination in affairs of state, and any deviation he readily attributes to bribery and private gain.[11] Thus at the outset of the play he is completely incapable of understanding the complex motives which impel Antigone to break his command. But as the play draws to its close the veil lifts and we begin to see who the guilty one really is. Creon is guilty of ἀβουλία, and δυσβουλία, lack of foresight (1242-1243) in disregarding the gods' established laws. Indeed, he has committed sacrilege against heaven, and the avenging Furies of the lower world lie in wait for his soul (1068-1076). This is the judgment of Teiresias—and therefore the judgment of the gods themselves. Creon himself confesses at the end that his sin has been one of stubbornness as well as folly (1261-1262)—the two precise faults which he had, at least by implication, attributed to the guiltless Antigone. For she was, he had said, like a wild horse that would not yield to the bit (477-478).

But the two major image-sequences, Creon's imperious ship and Antigone's child-marriage with Hades, are united in two ironic ways. Dramatically the two symbolic worlds are brought together through Haemon. Haemon is the one member of Creon's crew whom he thinks should be most submissive and obsequious; he is his son (639 ff.). Yet it is he who rebels most openly and, as it were, celebrates the symbolic death-marriage in the rocky grave. As the messenger relates,

> There they lay, side by side in death,
> And he, poor boy, had won at last
> His nuptial rites in hell (1240-1241).

Creon's ship-imagery is also, though not so explicitly, organically connected with Antigone's disaster. For in the second stasimon the Chorus describes the Ἄτη, the dark fate that broods over the Theban dynasty, as a violent, stormy sea (583-591). There in the roaring, frightening swells, that dredge up ugly mud from the sea's depths, Sophocles has painted the awe, the brutality and the mystery of the universe. And the raging Thracian sea-winds (589) recall the gusts of passions which the Chorus later notices in Antigone (929 930). For the Sea of Ἄτη is only horrifying to man when human passions cooperate in ruin and destruction.[12] The black silt that the sea casts up (590) suggests the ugly and unexpected which passion causes to emerge in men; it is perhaps, the dark mystery of the subconscious.

Steering by folly, and abandoning the path of justice, it is on this Sea that Creon's ship is sailing. Once again the symbolism is linked together by a remark of Haemon's. In cautioning his father against rigidity and inflexibility in human affairs, he sets forth two parables: the stiff and stubborn trees that do not bend as the torrent rushes past them are uprooted and destroyed (712-714), and the ship that sails before the wind with too taut a sheet is ultimately overturned on the sea (715-717). Hence Haemon pleads for a μετάστασις, "change," "adaptation," that flexibility that is the condition of all life. The image seems to set the vital reaction of young saplings against the stiffness and toughness of the old tree. But the image of the sailing ship directly hits the mark; for we are made to think of Creon's ship, wherein his decisions are absolute; it is a treacherous sea, and imprudence—in this case inflexibility—can be disastrous. Life can be, as the Chorus suggests, like walking amid hot coals (618 ff.), but evil seems to fascinate those "whom the god is leading towards Ἄτη" (622-264).

But the final linkage occurs in Creon's last pathetic lament over the broken body of his son, the "significant memorial" of his crime (1258). After confessing his crime, his folly and stubbornness (1262 ff.), he pictures the god as swooping down and striking his head with great force (1272 ff.), overturning and trampling him. And finally, at the news of his wife's suicide, we hear the anguished cry: "Ah, harbor of Hades hard to appease!" (1284). The play has come to its term: for that same Hades, which was for Antigone a marriage chamber, a θάλαμος, has really become the ugly port towards which Creon's ship has been blown over the Sea of disaster.

It is not the place here to dwell on the stark and primitive religious setting in which Sophocles sets his parable to lend it color as well as aesthetic distance. For the tale is set in a dark prehistoric era, when defilement brought immediate sanctions, when truth was tested by the ordeals of fire and molten metal, and guilty women were immured to avoid contagion among the people. Sophocles' parable of conflict between a man and a woman has perhaps a deeper meaning. For the clash between Creon and Antigone is between two fragmentary views of the moral world. Man's wisdom is his characteristic genius; it has enabled him to rise above the world, but not above the gods or the mystery of deaths Man is not infallible; truth is not in him as it is in Apollo's servant. And Creon? He is to blame, and yet not to blame. In his fate we see the paradox of moral evil in the world. It is only by constant caution and flexibility that we can abide by Zeus' Unwritten Law, avoid the sea of Ἄτη and the pit of hell. But can we? Can one lay down the rules for happiness? Sophocles does not answer because he has no answer. Only by chastening can a man learn. Only in old age can he learn wisdom (1348-1353).[13]

It is perhaps in the *Oedipus* that Sophocles achieves his greatest symbolic masterpiece. In the early part of the play, he proceeds by laying down a series of fundamental images; then the most important of these, the predominant or leading images, are taken up and developed like musical themes and allowed to acquire deeper connotations as the play comes to a close. It is this developmental process in the *Oedipus* which I wish to illustrate here.[14]

Up till the end of the *parodos*, the chief image is that of the great plague, and in Sophocles' hands it is not only a dramatic event but also one of his most effective symbols. It should be recalled that for the Greeks as well as the Romans the word "plague" had no definite pathological denotation: it was simply an outbreak of wide-spread disease.[15] In any case, how far Sophocles incorporated the actual symptoms of the great Athenian plague, or what was the real nature of the plague as described by Thucydides, need not concern us here.[16] But it is important to note that the Theban plague as created by Sophocles consisted of three aspects: it was what we today would call an epidemic, affecting human beings; there was, as well, an epizootic, or epidemic among the animals (*O. T.* 16), and a blight upon plants and vegetative life (25, 254). Further, the symptoms of the Theban epidemic were complicated by the outbreak of what would seem to be puerperal sepsis or fever (26, 173-174), affecting, therefore, merely women in childbirth. Now whether or not we may find historical examples of such a coincidence, the details, which Sophocles has added, of the blight and the puerperal fever are, I think, significant. For it woudl

appear that Sophocles has conceived of the plague as a daemonic force attacking the very source of life. Oedipus' unwit-
ting crime has caused a profound disturbance in those mysterious laws which govern relationships between parents and
offspring. For this he has incurred a ritual μίασμα or defilement, and it was only fitting that the penalty inflicted on
Thebes should somehow symbolize the nature of the crime.
To the Greek mind defilement was incurred as though it
were a disease, without full awareness being necessary. Its
infection can taint a family, an entire city or even, as we
know from the *Antigone* (1080-1083), a surrounding ring of
cities. It can be transmitted by the mystery of Ἄτη to one's
descendants. And, in certain cases at least, it may be cured
by isolating the defiled individual from the community and
forcing him to undergo either death or exile, or else by im-
posing certain ritual purifications suggested by the god offended or his legitimate ministers.[17] To think of defilement as
a disease is, of course, only an analogy, but it was perhaps
some such natural association of ideas that made the Athenian plague, with the various changes which Sophocles adopted, an extremely suggestive symbol for the opening movement of the *Oedipus*.

From the plague-symbolism, we pass on to the symbolism
of the sailing vessel. The origins of the ship-metaphor to
describe the city-state we have discussed in an earlier chapter. For Sophocles it is throughout a kind of sunken metaphor, not always explicit coming to the surface. It first appears in the priest's petition to King Oedipus:

> Our city, as you know, now dangerously tosses;
> It cannot raise its prow from the depths
> Of the empurpled swell (21-23).[18]

In the word "empurpled" (φοίνιος), really "blood-red," we
have the point of fusion between the two sequences, that
of the ship-imagery and that of the plague. Thebes is the

ship now becoming "empty of crew" (55-56): it is "blood that is causing the storm" (101). Oedipus is the captain-pilot who in the past had steered according to a good course (104, 695-696). His crew now become terrified to see him frightened (922-923), for they had so long been accustomed to sleep soundly under his guidance (586, 1221-1222). And the course that Oedipus eventually adopts is, he feels, the only cure for his ailing subjects (60-61, 68).[19]

Intimately connected with the ship-metaphor is the harbor-haven symbolism which first occurs in Teiresias' ominous prediction (421-423):

> What haven (λιμήν) then will not receive your cry
> ...When you realize the marriage to which you've come,
> Like a harborless haven, after a fair voyage!

Actually the image of the 'inhospitable harbor' had first been expressed by the Chorus in their petition of the *parodos* (196-197), where they prayed that the plague-god Ares might be dispatched to the savage region of the Euxine Sea. They are unaware that they are really praying for the exile of their captain Oedipus. Again, in the *stasimon* which follows the great revelation (Aristotle's *peripeteia* and *anagnorisis*), the Chorus pictures the marriage of Oedipus and Jocasta as a harbor-haven (1208-1210).

> The same great harbor (λιμήν) sufficed
> For son and father to come to as a bridegroom.

Here is a passage teeming with ambiguities. The Greek may mean that it sufficed Oedipus as father and as son (as Jebb takes it), or it sufficed Oedipus as son just as it did Laius his father (as I prefer), but I think that both levels of meaning are involved. Further, the Greek word I translate "come to" (πεσεῖν) means, of course, "fall (into)," and this may have various connotations: to fall into someone's arms, to fall as to one's lot or fate, to collapse in ruin, and to fall from the

womb as a new-born baby.[20] "Harbor" is an obvious symbo
for the womb, and, indeed, Empedocles uses the Greek word
λιμήν in this sense.[21] Thus in this one choral passage the
images of ship and harbor and the mystery of fate and human
birth are subtly interwoven. Again, the passage is immediately followed by the symbolism of the plough and the field
(1210-1211), which is familiar enough from other ancient
sources.[22] The ploughed and planted field is another under-
current theme of the play (1257, 1485, 1497-1498); Oedipus
obliquely refers to it even before he is aware of his own birth
and incestuous marriage (260; and 460, with obvious irony).
The blight that affects all living things may be thematically
connected, and I am not sure that Oedipus' curse upon the
murderer's harvest and offspring (270-271) are not part of
the same texture.

It is clear how the imagery has shifted. For now, instead
of being the pilot of the ship of State, Oedipus becomes, as
it were, the ship itself. His life up till now, as slayer of the
Sphinx and the inaugurator of a new era for Thebes,
has been a 'fair voyage.' But the harbor in which he has
at last arrived—his mother's womb—is no harbor at all, or
at least one in which he should never have sought a haven.
The marriage which for Greek men would have been the
climax of their career was, in this case, one disruptive of
the laws of gods and men.

Then, from the ship-metaphor on its second level we can
also see how the poet has passed almost imperceptibly to the
symbol of the plough and the arable land: the obvious analogy between the motion of a ship over the sea and that of
a plough over a field leaving a furrow behind it. Rudolph
Pfeiffer has said that the ship-plough image is not certain
until we find, in a fragment of Callimachus, sailors referred
to as "ploughmen of the sea."[23] But in Sophocles the suggestion is, I feel, at least implicitly present.

The infectious plague, the rocking ship, the womb-haven of Oedipus and the mystery of the ploughshare — this is the image-chain which I find to be predominant throughout the *Oedipus*. There are, however, a number of other images which, though not so extensive, are important for the interpretation of the play.

The first of these is the bipolar image of vision-blindness, which seems also to be connected with the theme of wit-stupidity (especially in the solving of the riddle) and revelation-darkness.[24] The theme is first developed in the priest's praise of Oedipus for his destruction of the Sphinx (37-39). It is obviously the same dangerous talent which he is going to use to solve the murder of Laius (120-121), in scrutinizing every clue (220-221, 291). It is precisely Oedipus' skill, says Teiresias, that will damn him (440-442), even though he is a "know-nothing Oedipus" without the gift of prophecy (397). Here we have the familiar antinomy: in his vision Oedipus is blind (367), whereas Teiresias, though blind, can see. Then, in the enigmatic lines, Oedipus taunts the prophet (374-375):

> Night alone is your nurse; you cannot harm
> Me or anyone who can see the light.

The reference here is difficult. Teiresias cannot harm those who see the light, true; but Oedipus is blind. But what is the meaning of 'night alone' or, more literally 'one night,' μία νύξ? This can mean: (1) Night is Teiresias' *only* parent or nurse; (2) *one perpetual* night is the parent, without change, so that Teiresias never sees the light; (3) one (= *a kind of*) night, a metaphorical night; (4) ironically, *one and the same* night was the parent of both Teiresias and Oedipus. Again the verb "to nurse" (τρέφω) may refer to the custom of keeping a child sheltered in the women's part of the household until he is of age; thus it would be a taunt at Teiresias,' childish senility. Or again it may mean "to carry in the womb," and this is the meaning that I should prefer in the passage.

88

Hence the final meaning is: "You are living in the womb of one perpetual Night," and the taunt is as true of Oedipus as it is of Teiresias.[25] There are many other more obvious references throughout to this vision-blindness motif, but they ultimately refer back to the initial paradox enunciated by Teiresias. For Teiresias, along with the oracular voice of Delphi, is the dramatist's constant symbol of the immutability of Apolline truth, a truth not seen with the eyes of this world. For I think that particularly in the *Oedipus*, and to a lesser extent in the *Antigone* and the *Oedipus Coloneus*, Sophocles is struggling to express the deeper problem of man's vision of the world and its meaning. Zeus and Apollo are all-knowing (cf. 498-499); but their view of truth is inaccessible to men and is like the darkness of night. What counts for blindness and narrowness on earth is perhaps the deeper vision into the forces which rule the world. When Oedipus finally sees the truth he can only scream and tear out his eyes.

There is another image train which is subordinate to the wit-stupidity theme, the hunting or tracking metaphor.[26] The first inkling of this is in Oedipus' reference to the "obscure trace of such an ancient crime" (109; and cf. 220-221), with Creon's sententious reply, that "what is searched for is found" (110-111). Here, of course, on the first level the reference is to the murder of Laius. But the line may also be taken to refer to the ancient crime of Oedipus' exposure on Cithaeron. The hunting theme is taken up by the Chorus in the first *stasimon*, as they picture Apollo and the Κῆρες unerringly dogging the criminal (469 ff.). Here the murderer, in a passage which has not yet found a satisfactory solution (475 ff.), is pictured as a frantic beast, separated from the herd, stumbling bewildered among the steep rocks and wild underbrush in an attempt to escape its pursuers. It is fitting that the trapped beast should be a bull, the king, as it were, of the herd and the object of certain cults.[27] But the track-

ing image is soon dropped, and it is perhaps mere specula-
tion to connect it with the Chorus' words in the final *stasimon* (1213-1214):

> All-seeing Time has found you out
> Despite your struggle, and has long ago
> Condemned this fatal marriage.

Oedipus, too, like Creon in the *Antigone* (*Ant.* 1272-1274),
refers to the god as springing or swooping down on him
(*O. T.* 1311). The image may be from armed combat or
perhaps from the swooping of birds of prey.[28] Associated
with it is the obscure metaphor, perhaps taken from jumping
contests, used by the Chorus as they first see the mutilated
Oedipus groping his way from the palace doors (1299-1302):

> Poor man, what madness has seized you!
> What daemon has leaped upon your unhappy head
> With a surpassing great bound?

There are indeed other symbols connected with ancient ath-
letic contests, such as the "wrestling-lock" that is favorable
for the city, and the hold the Chorus claims to have upon
the champion god (879-881). There is here perhaps a suggestion of the same sort of primitive religious thinking that
we find in the story of Jacob wrestling with Jahweh's
angel in *Genesis* 32. 24-26. "I will not let thee go" says Jacob,
"except thou bless me." There is the further idea in Sophocles that conflict can be a good; the Chorus prays that their
struggle with Apollo, the god of truth, may have a happy
outcome.

There is also the image of Oedipus' superior bowman-
ship of which the Chorus speaks (1197-1198), but it seems
here to be purely decorative and without further significance
for the theme of the play. There is the image of the walled
city (56); Oedipus, in fact, had stood as "a fortified wall
against Death" (1200-1201). And despite the state of the

text, it may be that the familiar image of the climbing and fall of Hybris to deepest ruin (874 ff.) refers to the scaling of a city wall during a siege. One is inevitably reminded of the fall of the Argive warrior Capaneus that forms such a vivid picture in the *parodos* of the *Antigone* (Ant. 131 ff.). But so far as the *Oedipus* is concerned, we cannot be sure; the concrete reference may even be to the climbing and trapping of a beast, such as the bull among the rocks of the first *stasimon*. Whatever the metaphor, it would surely foreshadow the more abstract statement the Chorus makes later on (1189-1196) about the rise and fall of Oedipus with the application of Solon's maxim on avoiding the divine envy.

There are many other images scattered throughout the play, but they clearly are of a minor sort. For example there is the interesting metaphor of the βάσανος or touchstone in the first *stasimon* (494 ff.). This was a slate-like piece of schist or jasper, sometimes called the Lydian stone, on which the ancients would test the purity of gold by noting the color of the streak it left on the stone and comparing it with the streaks left by gold pieces of known content. The Chorus here wishes that it had some such tangible touchstone to determine the truth of Teiresias' accusation against Oedipus. On a deeper level, perhaps, they are asking for an ultimate criterion of truth and falsity, of moral good and evil (cf. 895-896), and Sophocles would appear to be suggesting that human issues are never of the sort that can be solved by such simple empirical means. But it may be that I am pressing the symbolism here too far.

Another minor image which should not escape us is that of the scales which incline towards Oedipus' guilt (847), and with this we ought perhaps to compare the "slight tilt" which puts old men to sleep (961) in speaking of the death of Polybus, and with perhaps ironic overtones of the murder of Laius, who was effectively tilted out of his chariot at the crossroads. The scale-imagery is a familiar one, and we are reminded of the so-called Κηροστασία or the image of Zeus weighing the fate of the warriors in the *Iliad*.[29] But by this time the metaphor may already have become otiose.

But in image-analysis the temptation is usually to ignore or underestimate those ideas which are put forward with little or no demonstrable imagery, and yet it may be that the ancient poet's most important ideas were developed without dependence on such symbolism. In the *Oedipus*, for example, one of the most striking passages, the opening of the second *stasimon*, remains tantalizingly obscure from this point of view. There the Chorus of Theban elders sings of the "high-stepping laws" who are sons of Olympus born in the highest region of the heavens, having within them

> A divine nature which can never be put to sleep
> By Lethe nor can it ever grow old (865-7).

Here the dramatic poet would seem to be creating a new mythology, a new form of divine beings that live in the upper ether, emanating by some mysterious birth from the gods themselves. Nor do they spring from a particular god; rather it is Olympus, the vague heavenly region which was the gods' dwelling, that is called their parent. Here we have a language which is not directly sensuous; it is in fact prephilosophic. And yet it represents one of the most important phases of Sophocles' thought. For here is the suprahuman, even supra-Olympian level of reality which is the source of the world's morality and against which, by an inscrutable law, Oedipus has grievously offended.

Our feeling here is supported by another passage which, on any reading of the play, must be considered important. It is the well-known Solonic section of the last *stasimon* (1189-1196):

> What man, what man is there that ever enjoys
> More than the mere external semblance of happiness,

And after his period of deception fades away?
Taking a lesson from your daemon, Oedipus,
Your fate, how can I ever call any mortal blessed?

Now whether or not we consider this passage in conjunction
with the so-called trochaic ἐπιμύθιον or moral tag at the
end of the play (1524-1530),[30] it is clear that the Solonic
dictum, "Call no man happy until he is dead," is eminently
verified in the person Oedipus.[31] For Solon the good life,
on which alone a beatitude may be pronounced after death,
is the ordinary life of the Greek of moderate circumstances
who has enjoyed good health and family blessings without
attaining wealth or political eminence. Any other life which
rises above the average is fraught with danger because of
the divine envy; for the gods delight in destroying the pros-
perous. The Solonic idea, whether or not the attribution is
authentic, would seem to be essentially a fusion between com-
mon-sense idea of Greek moderation (or at least a commonplace
way of consoling those who had not achieved distinction),
and the age-old folklore superstition with regard to the "envy"
of the evil eye. In any case, I do not think that this doctrine
of the divine envy is explicit in the play of Sophocles; but
if it were, as I have suggested, it is not an idea which could
be adequately treated in a study that would restrict its interpretation merely to what is expressed in sensuous imagery.[32]

One final element of the play remains to be mentioned, the
conflict which the poet sets up between the Apolline oracles
on the one side and the scepticism of Oedipus and Jocasta
on the other. Their attitude is quite human and under-
standable. Their fear and anxiety that the oracles might come
true leads them to interpret them in casuistic or non-literal
ways. This must surely be a reflection of a common practice
among the Greeks of the fifth century, at least those who
would be influential enough to consult the oracles. Jocasta,
for example, suggests that the oracle about Laius' death was

invented by Apollo's priests (711). In the case of Polybus' death, Oedipus interprets the oracle's words (that he would murder his father) as meaning that his father would die "out of longing" for his son (969–970). And the incestuous marriage of Oedipus with his mother is interpreted by Jocasta as referring to a common dream which is not taken seriously by sensible men (981–984). This aspect of the play is handled very skillfully by Sophocles and fits in with the previously mentioned imagery of blindness-vision, and revelation-darkness. The oracles, and Teiresias, represent a grimmer and more tangible aspect of the Laws that "walk on high." This is the plane of truth which, for all its obscurity, makes the world of illusion seem so pathetic and poignant. But very often it would seem that the Athenian playwrights had recourse to the oracles as a convenient device in the machinery of their plot motivation, and hence the importance of the oracles in the play should not be overstressed. It would of course, seem to be reading too much into our text to understand the play as a piece of outright religious propaganda, a religious tract in defence of Delphi.

Of one thing, however, we may be sure. Sophocles will not tolerate any rationalist rejection of the traditional Athenian religious point of view. Thus in Sophocles' portrayal of Oedipus' psychological disintegration, he has him not only reject the oracles but also publicly proclaim himself as a child of Fortune (1080 ff.). In this most obscure passage, Oedipus boasts of his kin, "the months, who have made me great and small." He feels himself a child of the blind physical forces of the universe; like the moon, his fortunes wax and wane without apparent purpose. Tentatively, I should suggest that the passage contains a reference to primitive astrology. For the months that shape Oedipus' destiny would seem to represent the twelve signs of the Zodiac. In any case, the passage reflects Oedipus' complete rejection of orthodox Greek piety and his abandonment to the irrational, symbolized by the constellations and the heavenly bodies. But it is clear, of course, that Sophocles has allowed his hero, in a moment of passionate despair, to go too far.[33]

But the *Oedipus* is a most complex play, and, on the basis of our analysis, it would appear impossible to suggest a single center or focal point from which we could derive a single theme.[34] Rather the play is like some ancient narrative frieze which, for all its charm, need not have a single perspective. Or perhaps we might compare it with a piece of ancient Greek music enriched with many different rhythms and melodic phrases, without necessarily being dominated by a single theme in our modern, western sense of the word. From the point of view of image-analysis, the most important theme is clearly the interlocking symbol-sequence which opens with the plague and unfolds, like the solving of an ancient riddle or the revelation of a mystery ritual, with the gradual discovery of the awful nature of Oedipus' defilement. At the core of the mystery is the harbor-womb and Oedipus' emergence and return to darkness. But even this image-chain cannot be fully understood apart from all the other, sometimes non-symbolic, elements of the play. It may be that modern criticism has overestimated the importance of always finding a unified interpretation in a work of art. For it may be that be that to search for a single theme in the *Oedipus*, whether it be religious or non-religious, is to look for a will-o'-the-wisp. It is a false search, motivated by a false problem. And thus it may be said that the *Oedipus*, in a sense, has no interpretation.

The same need not, however, be said of Sophocles' final play, the *Oedipus Coloneus*, for it breathes the calm of final attainment, a comprehension, almost, of all the problems which Sophocles had himself struggled with in a lifetime of artistic creation. Now he has reached an equilibrium: first, about the meaning of man's life, and secondly, about the character of Oedipus. At last in this play Sophocles allows himself, dramatically, to express the μακαρισμός, the beatitude on Oedipus—and by implication, on all suffering mankind—that the caution of Solon had forbidden him to pronounce before. Nowhere else is there a clearer defence of Oedipus' innocence than the one we find in the *Oedipus Coloneus* (936 ff.); nowhere a clearer vote of confidence in the ultimate beneficence of the gods' inscrutable decrees. If the tradition about the play can be believed, it was also a kind of dramatization of Sophocles' own interment and his epitaph. He brought a blessing to the city that received his bones.

The aspect of Oedipus as he first comes upon the stage, a wandering beggar, like Cain, over the face of the earth (745-746), is in striking contrast with the transformation that is to take place in him. For the entire core of the play is the assumption, the apotheosis of Oedipus, and all the central episodes are more in the nature of a gentle prolongation of the end, like a refusal to part from a dying dear one even though there is nothing more to say. He anticipates his death by a kind of sacramental ritual (465-487), through which he makes his final peace with the Dread Goddesses, and in a wonderfully lucid passage he declares the fundamental innocence of his entire life (963-999). "I shall not be held guilty of sin," he says, "either in my marriage or in the slaying of my father.... Such rather was the evil into which I fell, led by the gods" (988-998). Indeed, the problem of pain in the universe can only be squarely faced when we consider the suffering of the just man, as we see it in Sophocles and in the Book of Job, or the pain of innocent children, as in Dostoevsky's Myth of the Grand Inquisitor in *The Brothers Karamazov*. The innocent and the just—these are the creatures whom Sophocles sees adrift on the winter's waves, lashed by the frightening ᾿Αταί that come from all corners of the heavens (1239-1248). When one considers all the possible disasters of life, it would seem better not to have been born (1225). It recalls the cry of Job: "Why did I not die in the womb?" (*Job* 3. 11). It recalls the cry of the Chorus to Oedipus: "Were you blind," they ask, "from birth?" (*O. C.* 149-150). But the play in general does not long dwell on a mood of despair: it is the story of the "raising up" of Oedipus (395) and his calm confrontation with the final mystery, Death. There are, indeed, extremes of violent passion before the end comes. Oedipus is still human, and after he passes, problems and tensions will continue. But all of this is played against the quiet background of the sacred groves and within an atmosphere of inevitability; the end is always in sight. Even the poignancy of Polyneices' refusal to choose before the dark prophecy of his own doom (1431 ff.) is rather a theme in counterpoint, played in a minor key.

We come at last to the mystery of Oedipus' death. Earlier, in the despairing third *stasimon*, the Chorus has spoken of Death as a savior, an "impartial deliverer" (1220) who comes, without music or the dance, to terminate life's struggle. Then later, just before the fateful thunder-peals are heard, they sing (1450-1455):

> It may be that Moira is finding its mark.
> For I cannot say that any decree of heaven is in vain;
> Time watches, time sees all forever
> Upsetting some, and raising others
> On the morrow to heaven.

Oedipus' final passing has all the dignity of the death of Moses in Deuteronomy. "And Moses the servant of the Lord died there in the land of Moab, by the commandment of the Lord; and He buried him in the valley of the land of Moab over against Phogor; and no man hath known of his sepulchre until this present day" (*Deut.* 13. 5-6). So for Oedipus the netherworld opened and received him without pain (1663-1665):

> His going was not accompanied by anguish.
> By disease or lamentation. It was miraculous,
> Above all mortals.

His daughters may not see his home below the earth (1726); beyond all tears, far off in the Invisible Fields (1681). There is no nobler vision of death in all the ancient world, and as the play closes with mingled peace and mourning, we realize that these tears are not only for Oedipus; they are for Sophocles, and for all mankind.[35]

Sophocles does not allow us easily to summarize his plays, much less his total philosophy of life or his answer to the problem of evil. His plays are, symbolically, explorations of the mystery, with only rarely a glimpse of clear revelation. In the spirit of the Book of Job, he too seems to say to us: "Why queston me? Were you there when the laws of the firmament were laid?" Yet somehow there is redemption in suffering. And there is comfort in sympathy with the suffering of others. Perhaps in the *Coloneus* Sophocles gives us an insight into the meaning of his art (1192-1194):

> Others too are quick to anger
> But they are chastened and charmed from their wrath
> By the songs of those who love them.

It is by Sophocles' charm that the sting of the serpent's tooth is lulled; we are gently chastened into accepting the world with patience and equanimity. Only by chastening can man learn. He cannot trust himself or his inclinations. Only in old age can he learn wisdom.

VI

SYMBOLISM IN THE ROMAN POETS

THE IMAGERY OF ROMAN POETRY IS DERIVED FROM MANY sources. Just as Roman poetry, in the historical period, represented a fusion of the ancient Italic *carmen* with the conventions and metres of Greece, so too the imagery exhibits both an original and a derivative strain. Roman imagery tends to be more abundant and more superficial than the Greek, and very often it does not achieve the same emotional depth. At other times it is more ethical in tone, more philosophical and religious. There is more consciousness, in Roman poetry, of the *utile*; in many of our extant poets there is a moral earnestness that seems almost like an attempt to justify poetry's existence in the eyes of the practical Roman statesman and politician. It recalls the scruple which Sallust mentions in the prologue of his *Catiline* (8.5):

> Rome never enjoyed so great a number of writers [as Greece did], because all her most gifted men were totally

absorbed in activity, and all her greatest men preferred to have others praise their deeds rather than take on the burden of narrating the deeds of others.

The element of religion, too, is sometimes more transparent in Latin poetry, and even in poets like Catullus, Tibullus, and Horace the imagery reflects at times the old pastoral cult origins of Italic song.

One of the most difficult poets to classify, however, is Lucretius, precisely because he was so daring an innovator in the tradition of Latin poetry. Even in Lucretius the abundance of religious and mythological symbolism attests his debt to earlier literature and worship; and yet, the use to which his poetic heritage is put—to achieve the destruction of Italic religion—is responsible for the conflicting, contradictory impression conveyed by the poem as a whole.[1] In the long, encyclopedic exposé of Epicurean doctrine, the movement of the poem comes to rest, as it were, on certain focal passages which convey more clearly the direction and tone of the whole. In Book Two, for example, the brilliant description of the cult of Cybele (600-660) with its swaying, sensuous rhythms embodies Lucretius' ambivalent feelings towards organized religion, his mingled repulsion and fascination with a cult which promised security and ecstatic escape. In this scene, in a sense, is enclosed all the driving frustration that impelled the poet to devote his artistic genius to the creation of this peculiar masterpiece. But central to the entire work is the Third Book devoted to the destruction of the main *idolum fori*, the belief in the immortality of the soul and the fear of death. All the other discussions, and the sometimes undigested chunks of claptrap and pedantry, cluster about the focal passage (especially 3.417-829) like so many planets around the sun: all Lucretius' resources, poetic, rhetorical, sophistical, are poured into the chain of ambiguous sorites and enthymemes in order to destroy the ultimate stronghold of superstition: death. Another theme that moves in an orbit about this central passage is that of the life of the gods and this comes to a focus in 5. 1161-1240. Here we have the *cri du coeur* which embodies the tone of the entire poem (5. 1194-5):

> Unhappy human race, to assign such acts
> To gods as tokens of pursuing wrath!

It was this passage coupled with an earlier one (5. 82),

> For those who have learnt that the gods
> Lead a carefree life—

that appealed so strongly to Horace; they suggest, as we shall see, the tone and ultimate theme of his Fifth Satire, the Journey to Brundisium. Two other passages of thematic importance are the discussion of birth and procreation (4.1030-1287), and the section on plague (6.1090 to the end). In both of these passages there is a kind of fascinated, morbid disgust, and the entire atmosphere suggests that men and women are little more than animals—indeed, little more than peculiarly shaped globs of atomic particles that move and mate, grow sick and die in obedience to mechanical law. The section on procreation is preceded by a discussion of sleep and dreams (4. 907-1029); and here too we have the common Epicurean topic showing the relationship of men and animals (especially 987 ff.) in the activities of dreaming and sleep. It is a motif which we shall find recurring in the dream-poems of Petronius, where the poet stresses the continuity between life and sleeping, between dreaming and the activities which so absorb mankind. But this extension of the symbol is not clearly present in Lucretius. The Fourth Book, however closes with a most striking image. After drawing to a conclusion his discussion of love and seduction, he adds (1286-7):

> Do you not see the water dripping on the rocks?
> Time will slowly pass: the rocks will be cleft . . .

Here, briefly, his theme is summed up: the motion of atoms, the evolution of man, the union of man and woman, the meaninglessness of the Universe.

But Lucretius chose not to end his poem on an abstract philosophical note. The closing horrifying passage on disease and the Athenian Plague (6. 1090 ff.) leaves the reader with a sense of rising nausea and shock. It is like the great canvas of the rat-infested, dying city that the French novelist Albert Camus paints in *La Peste*. For Lucretius, the plague-infested City is man's world, ridden by false belief and superstition, at the mercy of cruel, implacable forces that bring nothing but "noisome wounds" and the "doom of death" (6.1299). The black, disgusting humors that flow from the body, the gangrenous wounds, racking pains and repulsive mutilation— here, says Lucretius, is man. It is an overwhelming picture, but its organic function as a symbol must not be overlooked. Like a primitive Nietzsche, Lucretius merely paints the picture of the dirty, squabbling men (6. 1272 ff.), elliptically, without comment. His message is only suggested in passing (1276-7):

> Now at last gods—worship—counted for naught;
> The immediate grief was too much.

It is perhaps the most depressing poem in all of ancient literature, but it is a sober contribution to the age-long poetic dialogue on the meaning of man.

And yet, in Lucretius, all is not despair. The fundamental ambiguity of his work creates, in the end, truly great literature. For it is not merely the dull bones of Epicurus set to metre; rather, the bleak waste-land of Democritus' improbable universe takes on, in the poem, a new dimension of its own. The entire monstrous, atomic abyss becomes for Lucretius a cosmic symbol which reveals poetically the poet's profound view of man. The creation of *The Nature of the Universe* not only marked the end of long, laborious research; it embodied as well, a bold, personal decision. Paradoxically, it implies a profound intuition of man's superiority over the world of the flesh. And thus it is, in its way, a poem of commitment, preaching a passionate evangelism of its own in protestation against established Italic superstition. Though for us Lucretius' world-view is philosophically incoherent and incomplete, the poem, as an expression of his artistic genius, is a very moving document.

Image-analysis becomes much easier with Catullus.[2] His symbols, when he is not borrowing from earlier poets like Sappho, are meagre but effective. His whole style of composition shows less care and more ease than Horace's. Horace's lyrics show greater reflection, Catullus' more spontaneity and passion. Horace wrote more slowly and, it would seem, with more self-correction; Catullus more quickly, and in the heat of emotion. Catullus' verse strikes us as more youthful and, at times, naive; Horace is always more worldly-wise and urbane. Catullus' poetry is more obviously autobiographical; Horace is more indirect and, when speaking of himself, eccentric and whimsical.

Catullus' poetry is most revealing when it is introspective. Often he tends to address himself, in a way that Horace would never do, chiding himself for his self-scrutiny, as for example in 51. 13 ff., in Copley's translation:[3]

> Catullus, it's bad for you to have nothing to do;
> when you've nothing to do you get all stirred up and excited;
> having nothing to do, in days gone by, has ruined
> kings and rich cities.

His is a sensitive soul—perhaps the *animula miserula* of frag. 4 (Ellis)—whose centre is love, but love in constant torment. His is the heart of a child: at one extreme are the wild joys of the laughing Lago di Garda (31. 14) and the thousand kisses that no evil eye can spoil (5. 7 ff.). But at the other are the deep terrors of the night that knows no waking (5. 6), the "evil shadows of Orcus that devour all that is lovely" (3. 13-14).

Most of Catullus' imagery, unlike Horace's, revolves around love. It is variously described as pain, *dolor*; burning, *ardor*; insanity, *furor*; anguish, *curae*. Much of his love-language is taken from Roman colloquial speech, and we should not always press the metaphor. But in the lovely poem 76, the earliest Latin amatory elegy, we see a subtle self-analysis in which the imagery fully supports the poetic statement.

> O gods, if it is yours to show mercy, if ever
> You have brought relief to those on the brink of death,
> Look down on me in torment; and if my life
> Is pure, remove this plague that is destroying me.
> Subtly to every corner of my body like a coma
> It creeps, expelling every joy from my heart.
> I ask not that she return my love, nor yet
> That she should try the life of chastity—
> This were impossible. My wish is to be well,
> To throw off this foul illness. O gods!
> In return for my pure life, grant me my prayer.

As we can see, after the intellectual analysis of the first part of the poem (1-10), there is a more emotional effort in the second part (11-16) to steel himself against all feelings of remorse and self-recrimination. Then at last, in the passage just quoted, Catullus turns to prayer (17-26). The prayer is deeply Roman in inspiration. As a claim on the gods' favor, the poet recalls his pure life, his *pietas*, as well as the gods' power to heal. His love in torment is described as a plague, *pestis*; a source of destruction, *pernicies*; a noisome disease, *taeter morbus*, seeping through his body like a death-like chill, *torpor*. As the old Romans sang *carmina* to invoke the gods' power against disease, Catullus now calls them in aid against his unmanning passion. The poet was perhaps physically ill as well when he composed these lines; in any case, his analysis of his psychic state is a poetic masterpiece.

But from the psychological point of view, perhaps the deepest revelation of Catullus' subconscious can be seen in the *Attis* (63). Here the almost animal rage (*furens rabies*) by which the goddess Cybele possesses her devotees drives the young man to self-emasculation. The Attis of the poem is not, it should be recalled, the mythological hero who was worshipped as Cybele's lover, but a young Greek boy who is to become an "Attis," one of the leading cult-followers (or even high-priest) of the goddess. The poem is really a Galliambic hymn to Cybele (cf. 63. 9: *tua, mater, initia,* and the close, 91-93), though the great part is devoted to the narrative (1-90). The Greek youth sails to the shores of Troy with a band of companions, and with them he makes his way through the woods to the temple of Cybele on Mt. Ida. After their act of mutilation, they sleep in the temple. The following morning as the young man awakes, he realizes in horror what he has done, and rushes back to the seashore. From the shore he addresses his native country in remorse for his rash act of religious frenzy; now he can never return to the joys of his young manhood. But suddenly Cybele releases one of her sacred lions, charging it to goad the young Attis into frenzy and thus keep him within her domain. The narrative closes with Attis rushing back to the woodland of Mt. Ida to remain the goddess's perpetual servant.

That the young poet should have chosen such a shocking subject is most important for an understanding of the contradictory passions which raged within him. Whether or not Wilamowitz's view is shown to be correct, that Catullus was imitating a lost poem by Callimachus, we may still study it for the light it may throw on Catullus' poetic personality. The final clue to its meaning is perhaps contained in the last three lines (63. 91-93), where the true hymn-like nature of the poem becomes clear:

> Great goddess, goddess Cybele, goddess,
> Mistress of Dindymus, keep all madness

> Far from my home, my Lady. Goad others,
> Drive others to wild frenzy.

It would help solve the ultimate mystery of the poem if we knew the circumstances under which it was composed. As it stands, however, I think that all of Catullus' fears, all his emotional disturbances are reflected in this strange poem.[4] Cybele, whom Catullus calls *mater* and *era*, is perhaps symbolic of both mother and mistress. It is the conflict with Lesbia again revealed under a new aspect. The dual sex of the young Attis represents, in large projection, the great emotional conflict in Catullus' soul, a conflict involving religion, love and piety, but one which we shall never be able adequately to recover. The theme of the poem is the *furens rabies* of which Cybele is the all-powerful mistress, and the lion in her train the clear embodiment. In this *furor* which leaves Attis in the end barely human, screaming wildly through the woods, Catullus has expressed his own torment. The violent solution attemped by Attis becomes an act of frightfulness.

Like Sappho, Catullus uses the imagery of flowers and fruit to symbolize the freshness of young love. The young bride of the epithalamium with "flower-fresh face" is like a white artemisia or flame-colored poppy (61. 186-188); she is like the larkspur in the garden of a rich man (61. 89), or like ivy that grows strong when twined round a tree (61. 33-35), or like a trained vine that brings forth luscious fruit (62. 49-55) and is beloved by all the farmers. Catullus' own love for Lesbia has been cut down like a flower on the meadow's edge after the plough passes by (11. 22-24), and a maiden's virginity is a secret flower growing within garden walls (62. 39-41), ignored by the plough, delicately nurtured by sun, wind, and rain. A lovely girl is to be cherished like ripe, black grapes (17. 16); Postumia, mistress of the revels, is called "drunker than the tipsy grape" (27. 3-4); an apple is "a secret gift" (*furtivum munus*), a symbolic love gift hidden in a maiden's bosom (65. 19-24). In this connection, too, we find clothing-images in Catullus used in a love context: the maiden's soft dress under which she hides the apple (65. 21), the *sinus* (61. 53, 65. 43), or *gremium* (3. 8, 45. 2, cf. 65.20 and 61. 217); the familiar *zona* (2b. 3, 67. 28) or *zonula* (61. 53) of the marriage ritual, the veil (61. 8), the marjoram wreath (61. 6-7) and the slipper (61.10). In writing to Hortensius, the image of the love-apple (65. 19-24) suggests the tenderness of his poetic obligations. And in his poem to Lesbia, the love-imagery in turn gives rise to a fine eschatological symbol: "we must both sleep that one eternal night" (5. 6).

Catullus' emotional life, as we find it reflected in his poetry, oscillates between rapture and despair. The lovely country home at Sirmio, on the *limpidus lacus* (4. 22), becomes transformed into an ultimate haven of security and peace in which his yacht, and Catullus himself (for poetically they are one), can grow old in restful quiet, and on his return from the East the tiny waves of the "Lydian lake" become as so many ripples of laughter to welcome the poet, weary of travel, to his familliar hearth and bed (31. 13-14). In a more playful mood, he all but identifies himself with Lesbia's pet thrush, envying the bird's intimacy with its mistress (2. 1-4); or he plays at keeping accurate abacus accounts of their kisses and then confusing the sums in order to avert the *fascinatio* of the evil eye (5. 7-13).[5]

Yet at the other end of the scale he is plunged into the depths of physical depression and despair. First was the frustration of his love for Lesbia and, probably around the same date, the news of his brother's death. Of Lesbia's renunciation much has already been written and little more need here be said. The bond of their "holy friendship" (109. 6) was broken, the tender flower of their love cruelly cut down by the passing plough (11. 21-24)—an image more poignant when we recall its use in connection with the joyous epithalamia to symbolize the holy surrender of maidenhood. The vile, almost disgusting language Catullus now uses of Lesbia is symptomatic of his deep rage and frustration. Catullus' vocabulary does not show the mature self-control of Vergil or Horace; many of the words recall parallels from the walls of Pompeii, and we are constantly at pains to recall the disarming lines (16. 5-6),

> Chaste should be the poet's life—
> Not necessarily his verse.

Again it is a question of tone; it is difficult to recapture the atmosphere of the short epigram, the *vers d'occasion* of the Republican period.

In 10, the longest of the pieces in which Catullus celebrates Roman low-life, he uses the satirical narrative technique with which we are perhaps more familiar from the *Satires* of Horace. Though in many ways an unsuccessful piece and vastly inferior to Horace's satire on the Bore (*Sat.* 1. 9), it has nonetheless its own charm. The dramatic date is about 56 B. C., shortly after Catullus' return from his profitless trip to Bithynia with the propraetor Memmius. Varus and Catullus are idling in the forum, when Varus suggests they visit a *puella* of his acquaintance, a lady of easy virtue. Once they arrive, however, the conversation develops into a flirtatious battle of wits between Catullus and the girl. The centerpiece of the poem is the mutual bluff: in Catullus' claim that he made enough money in Bithynia to purchase *eight* slaves (not merely the usual four or six) to carry a sedan chair, and in the girl's request that he lend her the men that she might ride in state to perform her devotions at the temple of Serapis. But the poem's conclusion (10. 27-34) seems flat —unless the very ineptness of the lines was intended, in order to suggest Catullus' complete disorder and embarassment. The bluff has been called and turns to bluster.

The plaintive lament (101) at his brother's grave derives much of its charm from the dramatic use of present tenses: "here I am," *advenio* (101-2), "take these gifts," *nunc... accipe..* (101. 7, 9); it is as if the poet is speaking to the "mute ash" right there on the sunlit Trojan plain, weeping as he performs the belated ritual. We but overhear his private prayer; what passes between the two brothers is of an intimate nature; the *haec* are taken for granted, but whatever libations they included, a large part, we may be sure, were Catullus' own tears. In a sense the whole poem is a *triste munus*, a pathetic offering standing as a perpetual, tear-washed monument symbolizing that brief and solitary pilgrimage, hardly long enough for the ritual acclamation, *Ave* and *Vale*, Hail and Farewell.

In discussing the love-symbolism of Catullus it is natural to think of Tibullus and Propertius, with whom he has a good deal in common. What strikes one most forcibly at first, however, is that the atmosphere of the later elegists is so unreal and so much out of contact with the Roman life we are familiar with from Horace and Catullus. For one thing, actual historical references are relatively rare, and Propertius as well as the writers of the Tibullan corpus have already learned the knack of creating an entirely new poetic landscape, a dream country whose boundaries are only vaguely defined. This elegiac tone is surely peculiar to the the Roman poets, no matter what antecedents they may have had in the Hellenistic epigram and elegy.[6]

The developed love-imagery of the Roman elegiac poets can be studied at its simplest stage as early as Horace. Indeed, Horace's short poems of love and invitation are often far more effective than the verbose meandering of Propertius and Ovid. Though Horace seems to have despised the love-elegy as a medium and the "new Callimachus" who practiced it, his odes are full of subtle love symbolism. Love for him is a military campaign (in which, in later life, he felt too old to engage); it is the sacking of a city with torches, ropes, and arrows. And, at the end of a successful campaign, he hangs up his arms in the temple of *Venus marina* (*Odes* 3. 26). Very aptly are love-offerings made to Neptune and Venus, gods of the sea, for the vagaries of love are like the sailing on a moody sea. But for Horace, too, love is an intoxication, a bondage, a facile cruelty, a living under a spell. A maiden like Barine (*Odes* 2.8) is somehow in league with the spirits of darkness and exercises a malign influence on all the men, young and old, around her, incorrigibly perverse and beautiful. But the days of love soon fade and old hags like poor Ibycus' wife, Chloris, should no longer join in the sport of youth; she is a damp cloud stifling the shining stars (*Odes* 3.15).

Perhaps one of the most striking of Horace's love poems is the ode to Lyde (3.28) to celebrate the *Neptunalia*. It is noon, and the day seems to pause like a bird in flight. Horace begs Lyde to bring down a good wine from the consulate of Bibulus, "the Tipsy." And as they begin to sip their wine, Horace and Lyde engage in a charming love duet: Horace sings of Neptune and the Nereids; Lyde replies with a song of Venus and Night—all powers associated with the love of men and maidens. The poem ends with the key word *nenia*—for the tone of the entire piece is a simple, almost childlike song, a gay tune of love and carefree celebration on the day of Neptune's feast.

The main tension in Tibullus' poetry centers about the pleasure and the security of the *foedus amoris*, "the pledge of love" (1.5.7, 1.9.2.), and all the things of life which threaten to tear him away from it—war, duty, death.[7] "I am dragged off to war" (*ad bella trahor*) he cries (1.10.13.), when he would prefer to be on the battlefield of love, fighting "the wars of Venus" (1.10. 53ff.), the sweet "quarrels" and "battles of love" (cf. 1.1.74, 1.3.64). For the most part, however, the love symbolism in Tibullus is associated with images of sleep and peace, the security of "the wonted couch" and "the tender bosom," while the chill rains and wind moan outside (1.1.44-47). Love is a game that begins as Night yokes her chariot and streams across the sky (2.1. 87-90). At other times for Tibullus, love is a sweet torture (1.5.5, 2.1.80), the lover's life is like a spinning whiptop (1.5.3-4), like a war captive (1.1.55), or a hunted animal (1.6.4-5). The chains of love[8] are a familiar image in the *Garland of Sulpicia* (3.11.14-15, 3.12.8), and the separation of the lovers, Sulpicia and Cerinthus, because of a boar hunt (3.9),[9] seems to bind them all the more closely when the poet (who speaks for Sulpicia) utters the prayer:

> Whatever girl steals my love, I pray
> She may be caught and torn by beasts.
> Do leave the hunting to your father,
> And come back quickly to my breast.

For Tibullus, like Catullus, clothing-symbolism is regularly associated with love, and especially the naked foot (1.3.92, 1.5.66) and the uncombed hair (1.3.91). In the *Garland of Sulpicia* (3.8) the scene of Sulpicia dressing breathes an atmosphere of almost religious awe: she is almost to be worshipped, recalling as she does the grace and costume of the gods.[10]

But some of the most moving passages of Tibullus are filled with scenes of death and the pyre and the ambiguity of the world beyond the grave. But this is not to be attributed to self-pity or to a neurotic death-wish. Like Catullus, he was terrified of being cut off in love by the "night of perpetual sleeping." In addition, Tibullus seems to have written a good deal of his poetry either while he was seriously ill or else faced with imminent death on the field of war.

He should not be accused of abnormality for facing the ugly things of life, the labors of war and the effort to make a living (1.1.1-6), or for dreaming of a lost Golden Age when men lived in innocence (1.10.1-12). Rather this probing into the mystery of man's iniquity represents the most profound area of his thought.

Tibullus' death-imagery deserves closer analysis. Death first appears with covered head, *mors adoperta caput*: 1.1.70, like a blackclad Roman matron following the funeral procession to the grave. Almost as though he were writing in a delirium, the poet sees himself on his deathbed, then the sad procession with weeping boys and girls (1.1.65-68); or, again, he sees the pyre burning with his body (2.4.45-50), or his sister and mother pouring the ritual perfume on his ashes as they tearfully collect them for burial (1.3.5-8). This somber scene, which underlines the fundamental seriousness of Tibullus, is unsuccessfully imitated by the so-called Lygdamus (3.2.9 ff.). As though in an invalid's dream, we see the very inscription on his tomsbtone (1.3.55-56), and we see him transported to the world beyond the grave (1.3.57-82). All the Roman poets were fascinated by the problem of portraying the Descent into Hell, the *descensus Averno*,[11] but with each one the poetic tone is correspondingly different. With Catullus it was the mock descent of Lesbia's bird, as hough to lighten the fear of death and to exorcise the terrors of the *iter tenebricosum*, that "darkling road." With Horace it is the Hades of Sappho and Alcaeus, the holy place that resounds with the strains of the Aeolian lyre (*Odes* 2. 13.21-40). For Vergil the descent symbolizes the intuition of life's meaning, the penetration of those ancient oracles which foretold Rome's glory within the cyclic process of time. For Tibullus, however, it is a lovers' paradise, where cassia and roses bloom, and men and maids sport on an ever-fertile earth. Two sections there are to Tibullus' Hades: the Elysian fields, wherein Venus is supreme (1.3.57-66), and the Place of Sin covered with black night and washed by dark streams (1.3.67-82). The *scelerata sedes*, the Abode of the Wicked (1.3.67), exists for those who have slighted Love. Though most unreal, Tibullus' conception is a charming one and original in its way. The poem closes with a picture of Delia, chaste and dutiful, waiting like an anxious schoolgirl for Tibullus' return. The dawn he prays for, when Delia will run to meet him as he returns from death and from war, beautifully expresses the deep longing which is the central theme of the elegy (1.3.89-94). It is a longing for peace and for love, for a release from the sickness of the flesh. But it does, in a sense, suggest that Tibullus has resolved his conflict, that the crisis is past. The fear of sickness and of death, the fear of separation from mother and sister and Delia—all of these somehow find their resolution in the poem. I have weathered the storms, the poet seems to say; death and annihilation no longer hold any terrors for me. With the final prayer for dawn the spectre of black Death is finally banished.

The dominant polarity of Tibullus' poetry, love and death, is, as we have seen, inherited from Catullus but it has been substantially enlarged and extended. Tibullus, too, has his own poetic landscape, a dream-world where love imperceptibly passes into sleep and sleep into death. But Hades for him is by projection another age of Saturn, it is a new Venus-land where the *foedus lecti*, loyalty in love, is the only criterion of good and evil. For if Tibullus was weak in health and cowardly in war—though we are not to stress the biographical force of these details too strongly—he was loyal, brave and strong in the *proelia amoris*.

It should also be noted that Tibullus' poetry is remarkably religious. Both the poet and Delia are devotees of Isis (1.3.23 ff.); and though he is extremely superstitious, often resorting to sorcery (1.2.41 ff.; 1.5.11-12, 47 ff.; 1.8.17 ff.), he is nonetheless a sincere follower of the traditional Italic cults (cf. e.g., 1.1.11 ff.; 2.1; 2.5). This deeply religious aspect of Tibullus' elegies reflects, I feel, his youthful sincerity and good breeding. His loves are intimately bound up with his beliefs as well as his emotions. He shows a straightforwardness here that is far removed from the sophisticated sensuality and religious cynicism of Propertius.

From the point of view of imagery and symbolism, Tibullus' second book shows a distinct impoverishment, as do the other poems of the corpus, those of Lygdamus, the *Garland*, the *Panegyric* and the brief epistolary poems of Sulpicia (3. 13-18). In Lygdamus we see the symbols of the pyre (3.2. 9 ff.), Hades (3.5.21 ff.), and death (3.3.35-39), and the literary dream now becomes the stuff of an entire poem (3.4). But the imagery, now, is tired and dull, and the dream-narrative technique, to be used so effectively by Propertius, seems like a rhetorical exercise (cf. 3.4, especially lines 61-80) in the manner of the Roman *suasoria*. Sulpicia's *billets d'amour*, however, are quite good for all their brevity. The two birthday poems have for their theme the separation of lovers by the "ill-timed journey," *non tempestiva via*, on the occasion of Sulpicia's birthday (3.14-15). The imagery is quite well-chosen: Sulpicia sees herself *abducta*, almost abducted by force (3.14.7-8); her only comfort is, typically, to be a chilly stream, *frigidus amnis* (*ibid.* 4). One has the impression that the poems which deal with Sulpicia's illness (*Garland* 3.10, and *Sulpicia*, 3.17) carry overtones of the love-sickness theme, the *morbus taeter* of Catullus; the real sickness is love,[12] a disease for which there is no medicine, as Propertius says (2.1.57-58); its only cure is the presence of the beloved. Thus Sulpicia's fever (*me nunc vexat corpora fessa calor* 3.17.2) is not only real, it is also symbolic. And thus she is pained at the thought that Cerinthus can bear her troubles with heart unmoved (3.17.6). Sulpicia's verse is as charming as it is transparent, but it is frail and all too brief.

Propertius is one of the most difficult and frustrating of all Latin poets. Highet has penetratingly written of his angularity and "obliquity," and has attempted to explain his annoying pedantry as well as his almost capricious abruptness.[13] My own view is that Propertius is, frankly, a very uneven poet. What is good deserves a place among the best of Latin literature, but he too often yielded to the temptation of writing when he had nothing to say.

The tone of his poetry varies greatly: from sensual passion to dull, morbid melancholy; from tongue-in-cheek whimsy to that mythological shorthand through which he sometimes communicates. All throughout, however, there is a tone of bravado and even vanity, bred of the facility, and virtuosity of which he was so conscious. *Aspice me*, "look at me," he says (2.34.55-58),

> Meagre is my patrimony; in my family line,
> No forebear ever triumphed after battle.
> And yet, see what a king I reign at banquets
> Over bevies of young maidens, by reason of that wit
> Of mine that you so make light of!

Propertius is, in short, an insufferable prig, and this view is, I think, confirmed by the bold comparison of his fame with Homer's (3.1.31-36), or at least the mention of himself alongside of Homer, Aeschylus, Callimachus, Vergil, and Catullus (2.34.31 ff.). Though we are not perhaps to press this poetic self-apotheosis too closely, it remains true that there is no more blatant appeal for fame in all ancient literature.

His poetry is difficult to analyze from the viewpoint of imagery; it is, predominantly, the poetry of statement, often written in an abstract way. It is almost as if he used the obscure tales of Hellenistic mythology as a substitute for symbolic expression. His most successful technique, however, is the dramatic vision or the dream-tale; of this we shall have more to say farther on. There is no recognizable poetic landscape, but the central source of his imagery is still that Venus-mystique of which I spoke earlier. "No time," he says, "is long enough for love" (1.19.26): this is the general theme of much of his verse. There are the usual images of "the irksome slavery" (1.5.19), the "mistress's yoke" (3.6.2), the sweet captivity of love (3.11.1-4). But in Propertius' development of the symbol of the wounds (3.21.32) and the battle (2.1.13) of love, I detect a faint trace of what has been called sado-masochism. Both elegies 3.8 and 4.8 deal with Cynthia's severe beating of Propertius, and both poems go into detailed descriptions of the blows and wounds, the bites, scratches, and torn clothing. It is the first time that we find such a prolonged treatment in Western literature. Indeed, I am not sure whether the passages which deal with the Spartan women wrestling and boxing (3.14.3-14), and the oriental wives' practice of suttee (3.13.15-22), are not to be analysed along the same lines.[14]

But Propertius' forte is in the technique of elegiac narrative, especially the dream-narrative. Elegy 3.3 is more in the Hellenistic mythological tradition; Propertius is wafted off to Mount Helicon where Apollo and Calliope speak to him, and the Muse finally washes his face with "water from Philetas' spring" (3.3.51-2). Elegy 3.6.1-20 tells us the story of one of Propertius' dreams about Cynthia. He dreamed, he says, that Cynthia was shipwrecked and was near drowning in the Ionian Sea; as she is sinking she remorsefully confesses all her lies to Propertius. The poet, watching from some lofty rock (*ibid.* 19-20), prays to Neptune and the Dioscuroi, when suddenly he sees a dolphin coming to Cynthia's aid. He had just been about to jump in and swim after her when his dream is over, and he wakes up in terror. The poem is merely a whimsy, but it resembles what we today would call an anxiety dream and, in a sense, a wish-fulfillment dream insofar as Propertius seems to feel that Cynthia deserved some sort of punishment for her faithlessness to him. In any case, the unity of the dream imparts to the poem a psychological tension which we often miss in so much of Propertius' poetry.

The same sort of technique can be seen in 2.29, which might be entitled "On Visiting Cynthia Asleep." It would seem to be a later version of the theme which we also find in 1.3. The elegy breaks up naturally into two parts. In the first (2.29.1-22), Propertius tells how he wandered alone and somewhat drunk through the streets, until he met a strange crowd of naked boys with torches and arrows—obviously the *Amores* or *Cupidines*, the *amorini* of Hellenistic art. Putting a noose about his neck they lead him to Cynthia's door and there leave him. In part 2 (23-42) it is already morning and Propertius goes up to Cynthia's bed; the description of her beauty as she awakes is quite charming, and the poem ends as she leaps from bed, puts on loose sandals and rebuffs the lovelorn poet. The poem (or pair of poems) is undoubtedly one of Propertius' best, and it is proof that he could be, when he wanted, both brief and effective.

The longest and most striking of the dream-poems is elegy 4. 7, the apparition of Cynthia's ghost. Cynthia's shade, *umbra*, appears at the head of Propertius' bed as he sleeps, in a horrid form marked with the ravages of death and the pyre. She chides him for sleeping, reminding him of their love. She accuses her slave Lygdamus of poisoning her in collaboration with a certain Nomas, and two of her former maids, Petale and Lalage, have been tortured for showing affection for their departed mistress. She rails against Propertius' new love, a girl named Chloris, and begs him to burn all the poems he wrote in honor of Cynthia. Finally before vanishing, she gives him a verse to carve as an inscription on her tomb in Tibur on the banks of the river Anio. With the threat that soon he will be hers in death, she departs from the poet's embrace.

Despite the tedious length of Cynthia's address to Propertius, and the rhetorical tone that recalls the style of the Ovidian *Heroides*, the apparition-poem is a fairly successful one. But was Cynthia really dead or is the portrayal symbolic?[15] If she was really dead, it is hard to imagine the audience for which the macabre poem was intended. Why the accusation of her slave-boys Lygdamus and Nomas? What is the meaning of the charge (4.7.77 f.) that the poet should burn his Cynthia-poems? And why must Propertius place the inscription on her tomb? The ultimate answer is a difficult one, but there are fewer difficulties in the way if we simply assume that the poem is not an historical account, but a symbolic vision in the manner of other death-poems like Tibullus 1.3.53ff., and Propertius 2.13. Even Lygdamus has an uninspired bit of verse on his own death, in the Tibullan corpus 3.2.9-30. In Tibullus, Lygdamus, and the earlier Propertian piece (2.13), there is a vision of the pyre, the cremation ashes and the funeral inscription. What Propertius has done in the *Apparition of Cynthia*, if we may so entitle elegy 4.7, is merely projected a vision of *her* death in the elegiac manner, even though it is unusual for the poet of elegy to portray any other death than his own. At the same time the poem is not meant to be completely humorous. What seems clear is that the references to the poisoning by the slaves, and to Propertius' new mistress together with the charge that he should now burn his Cynthia-collection—all this points to the suspicion that Cynthia is very much alive. But whether the poem was written to amuse or to shock her, whether it ultimately symbolizes the "death of the heart," the death of their love affair, we shall never know. It is in this whimsical sort of writing that Propertius is at his best.

Two final poems may be considered here, the comic narrative 4.8, and the elegiac epitaph of Cornelia, 4.11. In the dramatic style of 4.8 Propertius again shows his power. As the story develops (it was not, perhaps, entirely fiction), Propertius plans a dinner-party at Rome with two young girls of dubious reputation, Phyllis and Teia; his alleged purpose, of course, is to punish Cynthia. In describing Lanuvium the poet cannot resist mentioning the local monster, a "fasting serpent" that dwelt in a dark cave and had to be fed by *virgines castae* if the farmers wished their harvest to be good. Cynthia, apparently squired by a wealthy new lover, goes down by carriage, as though she were going to worship at the Lanuvian shrine of Juno (4.8.16). On her return, however, Cynthia rolls into Propertius' banquet like a storm-wind, beats servants, girls, and her lover. Like a conquering general she imposes her own terms of surrender, and finally, before the lovers are reconciled (as one would expect), she purifies the entire household with fresh water and fire. Venus' temple had been desecrated by these "alien girls," *externae puellae*; only after a ritual purification could an armistice be established.

Of the elegiac lament on Cornelia, the wife of Paullus Aemilius Lepidus, little remains to be said. It is, of course, a strict sepulchral elegy or epitaph, and not a lament: it is the dead that speak and not the living. But it is also a *laudatio funebris*, recalling the so-called *Laudatio Turiae*,[16] in the form of a testament. Symbolically (if not in actual fact) it is also a tomb-inscription: "On this stone it will say that I was espoused to one man" (4.11.36) — a verbal monument to the purity and devotion of her life. But it should be noted that the dominant image of the poem is that of fire. There is the torch of marriage (*ibid.* 33), and the torch of death (*ibid.* 10), the fire that sets the funeral pyre ablaze. And between the two, she says (*ibid.* 45-46):

My life was constant and without blame; nobly
Did we live—between the torch of marriage and of Death.

For the symbol of that blameless life was, it would seem,
the very fire of Vesta which virgins tend in white linen robes
(*ibid.* 53-54). It is this fire, suggestive of devotion, religious
constancy, warmth and light, that gives a sacred quality to
the sad ashes, which, Cornelia prays, will be borne to heaven
to the dwelling place of all her noble ancestors (*ibid.* 100-
102). Despite the shortcomings[17] of the poem, it remains
one of the most moving elegies in literature.

But the Latin poet whose works stand at the summit of
symbolic creation is Vergil. As I have suggested earlier, it
will always be difficult to give a final estimate of his poetic
achievement, partly because we are at times distracted by
his borrowings from Homer, Hesiod and Theocritus, and
partly because it is difficult to grasp fully his quiet, meditative,
subjective tone. Even in the *Aeneid*, his work reveals an
enormous imaginative scope, and, compared with the *Iliad*
and the *Odyssey*, the *Aeneid* extends its range into theological
dimensions which go far beyond the primitive thinking of
Homer. Theology and philosophy, of course, do not make the
poet. But in Vergil they are part of the total symbolic fabric.

Experience has taught us not to go to the excesses of scholars of the school of Dunlop, Drew, and others who attempted to allegorize the *Aeneid*, or to interpret it almost like a
roman à clef.[18] It still remains true that there are many levels
of complex poetic symbolism deeply imbedded in its composition. As Walter Wili has pointed out,[19] the *Aeneid* is
above all a religious epic, achieving its aim in an extremely
subtle way. Some of the poem's complexity, on the symbolic level, has been clearly demonstrated by Victor Pöschl;[20]
and his analyses will leave a lasting mark on Vergilian criticism, even though we may not always accept his sometimes
over-subtle combinations.

There is, in the *Aeneid*, a peculiar fusion of past, present and future time. As Norman De Witt once wrote;[21] "Personal suffering has begun to furnish a key to the mysteries of the life of man.... The present finds itself reflected in the past." This time-fusion is at the heart of the poem. If in the character of Aeneas, Vergil put something of his own ideal self, he also embodied an image of Rome and of the ideal Roman. His canvas is at once personal and epic. But the *Aeneid* is much more than the story of the founding of Rome—so "great a task was it to found the Roman race" (*Aen.* 1.33). It is an episode in the eternal cycle of human existence, according to the pattern which Anchises sketched for Aeneas in the Sixth Book.

According to Anchises' revelation, the tragedies that happened in the past, will happen eternally. But Vergil can only portray a limited portion of world history, even though in the portion we have it all. His story unfolds like the narrative frieze that Aeneas saw in the temple of Juno at Carthage. Like Vergil's own poem, the frieze is a *pictura inanis*: it is not life. And yet in this storied frieze is the *Projektion der Gegenwart* that Norden spoke of: *sunt lacrimae rerum et mentem mortalia tangunt*, "it reveals the tragedy of life, and (in it the story of) our mortal lot deeply touches the soul" (*Aen.* 1. 462). This is Vergil's summary of his own poetic creation at least as he would wish it to be; we will find in this sombre tale something of our own tragedy, the sadness of human existence.

In Aeneas, then, are embodied all the fortunes of Rome, all the historic grandeur that she hoped for and, to an extent, achieved. Time present and past are, symbolically, fused into one. But besides the mythic and the historical levels, there is still a third. For in Aeneas Vergil is also proposing to us an *utile exemplar*, as Horace said of Homer's Odysseus, *quid virtus et quid sapientia possit*.[22] Aeneas is a grand-scale projection of the Roman Everyman, the ideal *sapiens*, who conquers all the malignant powers within himself as well as above and below the earth, wresting himself free from the ultimate temptation. Indeed, the opening storm and its stilling sets the stage for the entire poem: for it is Aeneas' destiny to quell the forces of chaos and conflict and unify them in his final dedication.

At the very centre of the narrative frieze is the Descent into Hell, the turning point and focal book of the entire poem. We can be easily deceived into thinking that this is a mere imitation of Odysseus' Descent in the eleventh book of the *Odyssey*. But for Odysseus, the Descent is simply another adventure set in the panorama of his voyages. It is almost for him, and for us, a kind of Cook's Tour. But though Vergil has borrowed the incident and the setting, he has totally transformed its meaning. It is clear that for Aeneas only in the realm beyond time and space does the meaning of human existence become clear. Hence what was for Homer a mere satisfaction of curiosity or, perhaps, an artistic *tour de force*, becomes in Vergil completely integrated in the structure of the epic and in the development of Aeneas' character.

Nathaniel Hawthorne in his *American Notebooks* has this entry for the period 1842-1843:[23]

> The human Heart to be allegorized as a cavern; at the entrance there is sunshine, and flowers growing about it. You step within, but a short distance, and begin to find yourself surrounded with a terrible gloom, and monsters of divers kinds; it seems like Hell itself.... The gloom and terror may lie deep, but deeper still is the eternal beauty.

Here, in Hawthorne's reverie, we have a clue to the symbolic meaning of the Sixth Book. In it Vergil incorporates the result of his own heart's searching and introspection, but Aeneas is not to receive it by meditation but by a descent to the place that holds the answer to the riddle of life, of birth and of death. It is a return to the womb of humanity. Dante, too, felt the force of the symbol, when he transformed the Descent into the entire book of the *Inferno*. Again the image implies the anxious probing, the search for the ultimate reality. But much more in Dante is the *Inferno* a portrait of the depths and terrors of the human heart, documented, as it were, by examples from history and literature. In Vergil it is rather a mythic representation of introversion and mystic, religious intuition.

This is not to deny that the final revelation of the *Descensus ad Inferos* comes as a sad disappointment. Here, apart from the terrifying figures or distracting shades, Aeneas receives the apocalyptic vision of Rome's—and of man's— destiny from the Anchises-figure,[24] which recalls the Jungian symbol of the Sage, the feeble human creature who enjoys surpassing wisdom. It is the focal scene of the entire *Aeneid*, and holds the clue to the problem of the time-fusion. The tone and atmosphere prepared, the vision speaks:[25]

> First a spirit does sustain the heavens, the earth,
> The shining circlet of the moon, the Titanian
> Star, and in them this spirit nurtures all
> Within, diffused throughout the mass, and moves
> These members mingled in its mighty frame.

And he concludes with the doctrine of the eternal rebirth:[26]

> So diversely do we suffer, all the shades,
> And then pass to the wider spaces of Elysium;
> Some few enjoy those joyful fields, until
> The length of wheeling Time absolves the stain
> Deep dyed, and leaves behind merely the ethereal
> Essence and the spirit's simple flame.

The tone and setting convey perhaps more than the words themselves. Vergil's peculiar mixture of Stoic and Pythagorean eschatology embodies all of the hard-won Roman wisdom and pathos. Here indeed is the tragedy of life, the *lacrimae rerum*. It brings merely the slender expectation that the monotonous cycle of existence, *longa dies perfecto temporis orbe* (*Aen.* 6. 745), will ultimately issue in some permanent achievement, in the attainment, at least by some, of the *laeta arva* of Elysium. Thus Rome's glory is only a minute particle within the cycle of the universe. And by an interpenetration of planes, the story of Rome can be seen as an image of man's development on earth.

Some scholars have felt that the most serious artistic defect of the *Aeneid* is the weakness of its central character.[27] So often Aeneas appears as a mere spectator of events, and when he does participate, he seems lifeless and inhuman. His reactions are very often studied and not spontaneous, and his frequent tears, especially in the first six books, suggest a psychological inability to cope with the role into which he has been thrust. It is only rarely that we get brief glimpses into the tender and more human aspect of his character: in his love for his father and for his son, in his love for Dido, in his fatherly pity for the young warrior Lausus whom he is unwillingly forced to kill (*Aen.* 10.815-832). But these rare flashes of humanity and tenderness show rather the submerged portion of Aeneas' personality and the direction in which his character might have developed had it been allowed to grow. But man's character evolves through the succession of his free choices, the free expression of his personality within the limits of his environment. But Aeneas is not truly free;

> If destiny let me lead my life alone,
> And solve my problems in my own way—

he freely admits to Dido (*Aen.* 4. 340-341). And once more in the Underworld, before Dido's mute ghost he makes his protest (6. 460-462):

> It was not by my will, my queen, that I left
> Your shores. The overmastering law of god

> Drove me—that same law which now makes me walk
> Through this land of shadow and dark night,
> This thorny ground.

But from here on the inner voice of protestation is heard no more. Aeneas steels himself to fulfill his destiny.

The problem of Aeneas' character is crucial for our understanding of the meaning of the poem. In character portrayal Vergil had none of the virtuosity of the Greeks. All of his characters in the *Aeneid*, men and women alike, represent facets of himself. He is in general unable to portray objectively—except perhaps in one case, the character of Dido. But to say that Aeneas suffered from the limitations of Vergil's own temperament is surely to solve no problem. Again if one were to meet Aeneas in the real order of things—in the Forum or on the rostra—he would discover a disturbed visionary, a paranoiac with delusions of grandeur, or a religious fanatic. But this would not be literary criticism. And it would overlook the entire theological and symbolic dimension which Vergil has carefully built into his poem. There is a change in Aeneas' character from Troy to Hades and from Hades to Latium. And yet Aeneas is not allowed to develop naturally; to develop, as the Peripatetic School would say, his ἕξεις, or habits, in accordance with his φύσις or nature. And this is because Aeneas has no φύσις or nature in the true sense: he is for Vergil a messianic figure, the bearer of a sacred trust, the symbol of Rome's dedicated role in the present cycle of man's destiny.[28]

The whole of the *Aeneid* is, in a sense, a descent into the Heart; it is a record of the poet's profound vision and his ultimate commitment. It is ironically fitting that Aeneas, at the end of the Sixth Book, should emerge by way of the Ivory Gate, the Gate of False Dreams.[29] Apart from the mythological reference, these lines reflect Vergil's view of artistic presentation and of his own poetic genius in particular. For like the narrative frieze on the temple of Juno at Carthage, Vergil's poem is merely a *pictura inanis*. It cannot be more than a symbol of life's tragedy. Nor could the Sixth Book be anything more than a pale imitation of the profound experience which Vergil is trying to communicate. Thus, with his profound philosophic reticence he is fully aware that his creations are but *falsa somnia*, "lying dreams," imaginative reconstructions of life and not life itself. They cannot deliver the whole of the mystery. Nor can they substitute for the experience of the human condition from birth to death. Indeed, the poem itself was left unfinished, as though it could never, however perfect, fulfill the poet's highest intentions. The last word, fittingly, was left unsaid.

FOCAL SYMBOLS IN HORACE'S POETRY

No work on Horace can ignore the sound philological acquisitions of the past. E. Fraenkel's *Horace*,[1] for example, stands as the culmination of many centuries of labor. In these pages, however, I should like to explore more of the symbolic levels of Horace's poetry along the lines we have laid down in the previous chapters.

Horace's *Satires* represent some of his earliest work, and yet they possess an amazing maturity and originality. He is closer than Juvenal to the sources of Italic *satura*, perhaps because he had Lucilius before him while he wrote; his use of stock-characters and broad, dialogue style recalls the antique buffoonery that combined community fun with chastening criticism. There seems to have been almost a religious, ritual element in the primitive *satura*, as though public exposure of faults would invoke the gods' blessing on man, his crops and his beasts. Indeed, some of these elements are still reflected in Horace's "conversation pieces," the "sermones." But with a craftsman's eye and hand he has transmuted the ancient genre into poetic symmetry and beauty.

The explicit theme of the first satire is man's general discontent (cf. lines 1-3 and 108-109), and the suggested remedy. Despite the apparent conflict between the two levels of the poem, the theme of discontent and the theme of avarice, Fraenkel, among others, has shown that from the point of view of source-criticism there is no need to postulate with Gercke, Kiessling-Heinze, and others, a patchwork combination of different Cynic diatribes.[2] Now it would appear that symbolic analysis lends support to Fraenkel's view. The poem opens with the Cynic theme of μεμψιμοιρία, "destiny-blaming,"or man's universal dissatisfaction with his lot, and Horace confirms this with a sort of vocational catalogue, a list of different walks of life (4-12). In each case the common cause of discontent is anxiety, lack of security, uncertainty of the future; thus the importer (*mercator*) and his ships of merchandise, the old soldier with his battle wounds, the farmer, the barrister. But the image of the world-stage (15-22), so unique in Latin literature,[3] reduces all these ways of life to a common denominator. They are all roles in a great cosmic drama, all equally unimportant, equally managed by the great *entrepreneur*, Jupiter. Man's instinctive hesitation in changing his role, even when Jupiter allows it, suggests that his dissatisfaction is not at all connected with his *persona* as such, with the mask he has to wear in life. It is rather something deeper, from which all men suffer independently of their external differences.

After a transition (25-27), which contains an important food symbol—

As coaxing teachers give their charges cakes—

Horace proceeds to another vocational catalogue (28-40). But here there is a new element: what is common to soldier, seaman, and stingy innkeeper is the obsessive accumulation of money. Nothing, no season of the year, keeps them from their efforts. Indeed, the "torrid summer-heat," *fervidus aestus*, which fails to give them pause is symbolic of the passion which consumes them. Here again, all suffer from insecurity, and to allay the pangs they engage in a relentless pursuit of money, in a contest to outdo all others, *ne sit te ditior alter*. The pursuit of wealth here becomes a substitute, a security symbol with which they hope to satisfy their anxiety.

What critics have missed is the theme of basic insecurity which is at the heart of the entire poem. The following section, the longest (41-100), is in dialogue form, a relic perhaps of the ancient *satura*, and here Horace trades quips with a stock character, the miser, who will be the butt of all his banter. As the inner compulsion of the miser is laid bare, we see the basic insecurities which are at its root: fear of hunger, fear of sickness, fear of losing friends and relatives. It is a relic of man's primitive precarious existence. And Tantalus in Hades becomes the archetype of this insecurity (68-69), forever snatching at the water and the grapes that he can never reach. This is the miser, and, by implication all men who pursue the world's goods as a substitute for inner peace and security. Like Tantalus, they are all the more tortured by frustration; they do not see that they have a thirst they cannot satisfy.

Horace begins now to weave in amusing anecdotes: that of the self-applauding Athenian miser Ummidius (64-67), slain by his slave girl (94-100), to show how ridiculous the pursuit of wealth can become. Finally, the portrait of the sick man begging in vain for the doctor to cure him (80-85) becomes symbolic of the entire disease with which the miser is afflicted. It is a moral one, for so far as loved ones are concerned, he might as well be dead.

In a brief transitional passage (101-107) which prepares the way for the close, Horace touches on the metaphysical problem of the mean and extremes. The ultimate answer, he suggests, lies in the "mean" which exists in reality, *est modus in rebus*, to act as a rational guide for men. The mean is a kind of structure which men can recognize—just as though there were clear boundary lines laid down, *certi denique fines*, (106) into which right living could naturally fit. Like a piece of land, moral rectitude can only exist within these lines, these *fines*: it may not overlap or fall short in any way (107). And this solution reminds us of "human nature," *humana natura* (75), that is pained when deprived of its due, and of the earlier reference (49-51)

> If a man lives within nature's bounds, what matter
> Whether he ploughs a hundred or a thousand acres?

We must recognize "nature's bounds," that is *humana natura* the way man has been made. For only by such an awareness with an attempt to live in accordance with it, can we allay the fears and anxieties which, in Horace's view, obsess the majority of mankind.

The satire closes with two significant contrasting images: the chariot race and the banquet. Men are like actors in a play; they are like children learning their ABC's, or slaves of one master carrying unequal burdens. But those who wrongly try to satisfy their insecurity by pursuing wealth are like charioteers in the Circus, with all the destructive tensions that are set up in their constant effort at competition (*superare... festinanti... instat*). The excitement of such a life—for many liked the Circus—is merely a projection of our anxiety and frustration. Rather, the image which Horace commends is that of life as the calm banquet at which men are not competitors but equally enjoy the food offered them, and, at the end leave the table content and satisfied. Here at last, in the full table, is the focal symbol which Horace seizes to express the joy all men seek in life. The Horatian banqueter is full but, living within the "bounds of nature," not to excess. Thus we can see the relevance of all the food symbols throughout the poem: the teachers who inspire confidence with little cakes (25-26), the bread of the slaves (45-48), the purchase of a modest fare (73-75), the food of Tantalus (68-69). Thus the images of food and drink furnish a clue to the real theme of the satire. In the drama of life man, to be happy, must play the role of a banqueter, keeping his mind on the "certain bounds" within which happiness alone lies; secure in this conviction, he can experience a limited but true enjoyment of life, and then make his exit modestly, "when his term is over," *exacto tempore.* Through Horace's imagery we can glimpse a profound intuition of the meaning of life, and man's search for security becomes the unifying message of the poem.

Horace's own search for security was made considerably easier by the benefactions and friendship of Maecenas. For Horace, Caius Maecenas took the place of a second father, and the poet's emotional attachment to the Roman statesman is at the heart of much of his poetry. This sincere feeling will help us to understand somewhat more fully the charming ninth satire on the Bore, *Ibam forte.* For although the piece is a bit of dramatic whimsy, it should be noted that the longest single section of the poem is devoted to the Bore's request to be introduced to Maecenas (43-60). As Horace reminds him, Maecenas' household is a *domus pura,* an almost untranslatable expression, "a house of utmost sincerity." The Bore has completely misunderstood the inner spirit which binds all of Maecenas' circle together: it is ultimately friendship in its highest sense, and the shared admiration for good things in art and literature. But the Bore is the embodiment of all the traits that Horace most disliked: he is a poet on the make, an ambitious climber, he can both sing and dance (presumably, for Horace, both together suggest vulgarity), writes poetry hastily and in great quantity, and is ignominiously involved in litigation. In direct contrast with Horace's well-bred shyness in the great man's presence (*Sat.* 1. 6. 56-7; cf. Terence, *Phormio* 281-4), the Bore intends to scale the walls of Maecenas' affection by brute force (*Sat.* 1. 9. 54-60). Thus the Bore is, symbolically, Horace's exact opposite, a kind of Jungian "shadow-self," a malign *dibbuk* or *Doppelgänger* conjured in the satire and then finally destroyed by the mock-epic theophany of Apollo (77-78). The conclusion is like the miraculous endings of episodes in the Greek or Roman novel, where the heroine is saved by a fantastic *deus ex machina*. The Bore is a unique creation, and it is a complete misunderstanding of the technique to try to find his historical counterpart. For the historical counterpart is, by inversion, none other than Horace himself. They are like Dr. Jekyll and Mr. Hyde. For, even though the piece is almost pure whimsy, there is an underlying thread of seriousness. The Bore is all that Horace is not— and yet perhaps what Horace, *per impossibile*, might have been if he had not been sheltered by the *domus pura*, where each one, rich or poor, has his place, and where the bond of unity is love and not ambition.

The meaning of Maecenas' friendship is developed by Horace in another way in the fifth Satire, the Journey to Brundisium, but we shall reserve this for the following chapter. A further variation on the same theme can be found in the second book of Satires, *Sat.* 2. 6, published after Maecenas had comfortably settled Horace on the Sabine Farm. The structure of the satire is quite subtle. Its setting is really within Horace's own consciousness, as he reflects on the different episodes which characterize his double life. It may be divided into three (or four) parts:[4]

City and Country are sharply contrasted as symbols of anxiety and tranquillity. From the calm of green fields and running brooks Horace turns to the pushing mobs on the Roman streets. Like the chariot race at the end of the first satire, everyone is fighting to get ahead in life: one must "insult those who are too slow" (28). The very Esquiline is bleak and dark (32-33), because it suggests the nagging business that Horace is unwillingly involved in. The thought of Maecenas is his only comfort (32), though in the busy atmosphere of Rome he sometimes feels out of place in the great man's entourage (41-58). Gradually, as we follow Horace's thoughts through a kind of interior monologue, we are back in the country again (59-65), amid simple food and pleasure. There is the image of the modest banqueter (68), that recalls the close of the first satire; it recurs like a leitmotif in the two dinner-scenes in the Fable of the City Mouse and the Country Mouse. The fable which follows, however, is not so much an actual event as a kind of day-dream within Horace's mind as he pictures himself absorbed in the anxieties of the city (60-61). The fable of Cervius is a story within a story, like a dream within a dream.

It is difficult to discover how far Horace has modified the fable as he had learnt it. In all likelihood the original folk-tale concerned a field-mouse and a house-mouse, the *mus domesticus* and the *mus agrestis*, that compared the advantages and disadvantages of their different ways of securing food.

But Horace has changed the domestic mouse to a *city* mouse, in order to develop the theme of the earlier part of the satire, the opposition between Rome and his country estate. Surely no commentary can do justice to this masterpiece of poetic fable, nor would we want philological pedantry to destroy its charm. At the same time, it is not out of place to suggest some possible interpretations of the Fable. If the Country Mouse is Horace, it would seem natural to take the City Mouse as Maecenas. Maecenas would constantly be trying to bring Horace to Rome. Further, there may be a slightly sinister note in the Country Mouse's remark that his rustic home will at least keep him *tutus ab insidiis* (117), "safe from attacks." This may be a possible reference to the "attacks" which lurked in the background of Maecenas' political attachment to Octavian, even if we have no record of a serious breach until later on. Even the Molossian hounds may perhaps be taken to represent some disturbing element at Rome which tended to make Horace's relations with Maecenas sometimes unpleasant. Horace would have no part of politics. It may be that this pushes the evidence too far, but the *insidiae* of the last line, so casually mentioned, is a strong word and ought not perhaps to be taken lightly.

The city with its rushing business and its "attacks," the country with its "nights and banquets of the god"—and all through, the banquet-image assumes an importance—adequately illustrate the polarities of the satire. Indeed, they embody the two dimensions of Horace's own character, inner and outer, security and anxiety. For if on one level the two mice represent Horace and Maecenas, on another they represent two sides of Horace himself. Thus the satire presents an exploration of a problem which remained with him to the end of his life.

Before discussing the imagery of Horace's lyrics, I should like to indicate how Horace's family and friends play a symbolic role in his poetry. It is a known fact that Horace never expressly refers to his mother. The three human beings who are the objects of his strongest affection are his father, Maecenas, and Vergil. Vergil is, of course, his friend (*Sat.* 1. 5. 44), the "very half of my soul" (*Odes* 1. 3. 8).[5] But Horace's attitude towards his father and Maecenas was of quite a different order. It may be said that no other Greek or Roman poet shows such an attachment to his father as does Horace, and his awareness of his rise from humble origins is everywhere at work.[6] It is to his father that he attributes the inspiration for writing satire (*Sat.* 1.4.105ff.); in writing satire, he is not only expressing a decision to avoid the faults he criticizes, but he is also making his father's words live again. To his father's advice and to the education his father's sacrifices made possible, Horace seems to attribute all his later success (*Sat.* 1.6.71-96). As psychologists would say, the father-image is very prominent in Horace's poetry; it embodies, in a sense, his superego.

Now what is most interesting about *Sat.* 1.6, directed to Maecenas, is the way Horace associates his devotion to Maecenas so closely with his love for his father. And this would be logical; for Maecenas became a haven of security for Horace after Horace's father had passed away, and he took the place of Horace's father in the encouragement of the poet's talent. Thus Maecenas and Horace's father are both closely connected in Horace's imagination; both function, in his poetry, as symbols of security and protection, and each becomes, in different ways, a source of poetic inspiration. One might almost say that Maecenas filled the role of a father-image for Horace.

When we consider Horace's lyric poems, it becomes clear that his entire poetic landscape is based upon the Italic countryside, with a few ventures into the streets of Rome. The brief, simple joys of life in the Sabine hills represent by metonomy "the short span of life," the *vitae summa brevis* (*Odes* 1.4.15). There is the poignant beauty of the murmuring springs, grapes, ripening on the vine, the luxuriant plane trees, the winds that dissipate the threatening thunderheads (*Odes* 1. 7. 15)—indeed, all the smells and sights and sounds of spring.[7] Horace's landscape is deeply emotional, and all the images of beauty tends to summon up the dissolution of death. Romantic attachments between boys and girls suggest the brevity of youth and love,[8] and even religious ritual, so often connected with a spirit of rustic gaiety,[9] may perhaps be linked in the same emotional context. And at the edge of this landscape, as it were, lies the sea. In a playful mood, Horace uses it like Semonides of Amorgos, to suggest the moodiness of women (*Odes* 1. 5), but more often it is associated with man's self-destructive intrepidity,[10] the desire for escape,[11] and, in general, with the unpredictable storms of life.[12]

But Horace's country sky is often overcast with more immediate symbols of death. First of all there is sickness, always in Horace associated with a certain, inner malady of soul.[13] One can often detect, even in Horace's joy at the prospect of wine or a supper with his friends, in his vaunting of his prowess as a lover, in his awareness of his poetic gifts, a certain inner restlessness and anxiety perhaps arising from the reflection that all is passing, that "we are but dust and shadow" (*Odes* 4. 7. 16). Indeed, Horace sees his poetry as a kind of incantation whose purpose is therapeutic:[14]

> Come now, the last of all my loves
> (For I shall never love another),
> Come learn these verses and then sing
> With your compelling voice. Black anxiety
> Is by sweet song allayed.

This black anxiety appears in the grisly form of Lady Death, pale, knocking her foot relentlessly at every door, and in the eschatological symbols of Charon, Orcus, and the *imag-*

ines of Tullus, Ancus, and other long dead heroes of old.[15] These need not, for Horace, represent details of actual belief; rather, they are poetic transformations of his own real terror and horror of the grave.

Horace's imagery becomes clearer if we see it as a polarity between the simple, country joys of spring, and wine, and friendship on the one side and the grim auguries of death on the other. His poetry is full of chiaroscuro, in the sense that even the things dearest to him can somehow remind him of their loss, and the soft, bright clouds of his Sabine countryside are always shot through with threads of ominous grey.

Against this general background, we may now examine the imagery of some of the lyric poems in more detail. In *Odes* 1. 9, *Vides ut alta*, the setting is adapted from Alcaeus, LP 338:

> Zeus is raining: from the heavens
> A mighty storm descends. The streams
> Of water are stiff.....
> Defy the storm! Set up the fire;
> Mix sweet wine (don't stint!), and then
> Put a soft pillow behind your head.

For Horace the setting is a cozy room, from which snow-capped Mt. Soracte is visible. The six strophes are neatly divided, according to sense, in 2:2:2; and the two centre strophes more clearly state the poem's message. It is "let the gods care for the rest" (9), and "never mind what the morrow may bring" (13). Horace attempts to rid us of the nagging anxiety with regard to all the imaginable ills that are beyond our control: the future, old age, death. The wine and the hearth, the warmth of a happy company drinking around the fire, become symbolic of the present peace and security which Horace seeks to erect as a bulwark against the uncertainties of life. The poem opens with the picture of Soracte in the icy distance, and dwells on it for its own sake; Soracte stands for all the things which the warmth of the fireside is meant to dispel. Thus, by a natural metonomy it seems to embody the chill that grips us in the face of the anxiety and uncertainty of human existence. Thus, in a sense, Soracte is old age, and death, and all the grim thoughts that Horace would banish from his mind by the cask of four-year-old wine.[16]   In the third section of the poem, the mention of "peevish old age," *morosa canities*, brings up another symbolic scene, the gay lovemaking of the youths and maidens of Rome, which acts as a counterpiece to the more staid and reflective happiness of Horace and his companions in the second strophe. The very absorption of the young people in their childish fighting over bracelets and love pledges tends to make us forget the grim realities of the earlier part of the poem—just as in life they would distract the young man from the moroseness of thoughts about approaching death. The vivid excitement of the final scene of the lyric contains the germ of the poem's message: absorb yourself in the delightful, childish excitement of the world we can see and touch, so that you will not think about the fearful anxieties that life may still have in store. It is, indeed, a poor and unsatisfying message; but it is expressed in a craftmanship which is superb.

Another poem which is deceptively simple and elusive is *Odes* 3. 13, *O fons Bandusiae*.[17]   Horace may here be celebrating some local rustic festival, such as the *Fontanilia*, when sacrifices were offered in honor of the spirit of the springs. The name of the spring was apparently taken from one, in the vicinity of Horace's native Venusia; it possesses for him a special power, an almost personal *numen*, and is therefore worthy of veneration. To it is due the sacrifice of a kid cut off in its prime (with poignant overtones, perhaps, of human death), and the sacred atmosphere of the spring is, for Horace, manifested in its cool seclusion, a peace which the strife of life, the heat of the Dog Star, cannot affect. But the peace and calm which Horace projects into his spring is also the peace which is productive of his greatest poetry. For Bandusia will become known because he will sing of her, *me dicente*, and her running rills will speak forever in his poetry. Thus the spring is intimately associated with Horace's own awareness of his poetic creativity. The symbolic transformation of Bandusia into an objective, animistic force, intimately associated with Horace's own powers of poetic contemplation, is the real source of the poem's power. Psychologically speaking, the *fons Bandusiae* is for Horace truly a Pierian spring.

The tone of the Bandusia poem is closely connected with many of the other pieces in which Horace expresses pride in his poetic craftsmanship, as for example, *Odes* 1. 32 and 3. 30. In all of Horace's references to his own ability, beginning with the earliest in *Sat.* 1. 4. 39-40,[18] there is always an element of uncertainty. It is as though Horace sensed he was not as great as he might have been; yet there is always a supreme sense of achievement and self-conscious bravado, as though he would have said: What other Latin poet has done what I have done? Hence, as we shall see, the imagery he uses to describe his own poetic achievement very often conveys mixed, whimsical overtones. There is an ambiguity of tone which reflects conflicting attitudes in his appraisal of himself.

There is a similar ambiguity in Horace's references to the gods and to traditional Roman belief. Horace's only definite statement of his position, in his Epistle to Albius (*Epist.* 1. 4. 15-16), is expressed in such a comic, ironical way that we cannot take it seriously:

> Imagine every day that dawns your last;
> Then you will love the extra hours you have.

> An when you want a laugh, come visit me:
> A sleek, fat, well-kept pig of Epicurus' sty.

There is, as we shall see, a peculiar ambiguity in Horace's use of animal symbols in reference to himself. Again, another Epicurean pronouncement, which is a paraphrase of Lucretius, 5.82, occurs in *Sat.* 1.5.100-104, at the close of the Journey to Brundisium:

> Let the Jew Apella put faith in that; I can't.
> For I was taught that the gods lead a carefree life,
> And that nature's marvels do not come from them—
> As though they angrily send them down from heaven's roof.

The almost childlike introduction of "I was taught" *didicimus*, may suggest that there is not a completely confident conviction that the gods have naught to do with men. Even *Odes* 1. 34, the so-called "conversion" ode, with its theatrical epiphany would seem to be ambiguous in tone. The fact is that, though scrupulous in matters of moral behavior (*Sat.* 1.4.129-143), he was a "stingy devotee of the gods," *parcus deorum cultor*; and yet, his brave show of disbelief was perhaps somewhat disingenuous; he only wished he had more secure grounds for his protest, *nulla mihi religio est* (*Sat.* 1. 9. 70-71), "I'm not a church-goer." The Jewish people, on the other hand, become symbols of pious credulity;[19] but that this implied good-natured banter rather than real contempt is perhaps closer to the truth. In religion, as in so many other areas, Horace wavered. His remark on his personal philosophy can be taken as deeply characteristic (*Ep.* I. I. 14-15):

> I'm not committed to swear by any master:
> Wherever the storm blows, I'll follow along.

He thus oscillates, he admits (*ibid.* 16-19), from one extreme to another.

There is a further type of image in Horace, which has not been completely understood. It is what we might call the "nonsense-symbol," and one which we are more familiar with from the writings of authors like Edward Lear and Lewis Carroll, or Kafka and Mann. The nonsense-symbol is one that seems incongruous, or even ridiculous, even though it occurs in a context that is otherwise straightforward or serious. There are a number of these in the *Satires* and *Epistles*. Horace speaks of himself as an excitable bull with hay about its horn (*Sat* 1. 4. 34), as an old wheezing horse (*Epist*. 1. 1. 8), as a fat, glistening pig (*Epist*. 1. 4. 16). Again, he portrays his book of *Epistles* (and this is, in a sense, himself) as a promiscuous young slave-boy sent out to satisfy the lusts of the market place (*Epist*. 1. 20).[20]

More obvious nonsense images occur in the *Odes*. There are two mock-apotheosis symbols in *Odes*. 1. 1, and 2. 20, based apparently upon the picture the ancients had of the way in which a human being becomes a god, rising to heaven to be deified, changing into another, purer form.[21] Thus in *Odes* 1. 1. 29-30, 35-36:

> The ivy that crowns the poets' brows
> Puts me among the gods above....
> And if you count me among the lyric bards,
> I shall strike my head against the stars.

Thus the picture is of Horace rising to heaven to join the blessed lyric poets of antiquity among the celestial spheres—only to knock his head against the vault of heaven. The "knock" is enough to bring Horace's poetry back to reality. There is another mock-apotheosis in *Odes* 2. 20, where the poet envisages himself taking leave of his bodily form and rising up to heaven in the form of a swan—a poem that has aroused such unfavorable comment on all sides.[22] But critics have misunderstood the whimsical mixture of the nonsense imagery in an apparently serious context. The poet sees his dead body, surrounded by mourners and ready for the grave. In mock-seriousness he tells how Maecenas will make the solemn invocation, *quem vocas, dilecte Maecenas*, (6-7) over his body, but his spirit has already been released, and Horace feels himself, as he rises up, turning into a swan, in an apotheosis of his poetic genius, soaring precariously like Icarus. Thus he imagines himself telling the mourners to leave "the empty burial"—for the real Horace has taken flight and has been transmogrified into a celestial bird. Despite a number of real difficulties and ambiguities, it is an ingenious joke, an almost blasphemous parody of Roman ritual. But this paradox is peculiarly Horatian, and what the commentators have missed in all these images is their common element: the nonsense symbol involves a peculiar form of self-expression, a mixture of self-deprecation and egotism. It is Horace's attempt to express an awareness of his distinct poetic talents, at odds somehow with the pragmatic Roman world around him. There may also be present an element of *superstitio*: Horace feels self-conscious or even guilty at praising himself, and his self-esteem is transformed into whimsy, lest perhaps the gods be offended. In any case, the nonsense-symbol reflects a cynicism which masks Horace's conflicting feelings; it is as though he were trying, unconsciously at least, to hide from himself, if not from the gods, his true sentiments. And it is this confusion which emerges in the incongruous symbol.

It would seem, then, that Horace's peculiar sort of self-mockery is found, in varying degrees, in the many whimsical images which we find throughout his poetry. It is present, to an extent, in the opening stanzas of *Odes* I. 2, *Iam satis terris*, though there the mood soon changes to a serious one. We find it in the serio-comic 2. 13, *Ille et nefasto*, in which Horace immortalizes the tree that nearly sent him to join Sappho and Alceaus in the realm of Proserpina. There is a similar tone in *Odes* I. 22, *Integer vitae*; for, after a somewhat sombre introduction, he leads us into a trivial tale:

> Once wandering carefree in my Sabine woods,
> And singing of my Lalage, a wolf appeared
> But fled from me though I was unarmed—.

But surely this is no real wolf. Horace himself describes it as a monster, and Roman literature has many references to mysterious wolves that appear and vanish.[23] It is simply Horace's way of saying that he has become a creature of special powers (and he attributes this more immediately to his love of Lalage and his "pure life"), such that neither heat nor cold nor anything on earth can any longer hold any terror for him. Love has made him immune.

The same sort of treatment and imagery may be seen in the famous ode to Pyrrha (*Odes* 1.5), *Quis multa gracilis*. Horace is imaginatively watching Pyrrha, a former flame, embrace a slim young man in a summery grove. All is smooth sailing now, but soon the storm will come; Horace himself only barely managed to escape. For (13-16)

> There on the temple wall
> A votive tablet shows how I hung up my clothes,
> Soggy, to the potent god of the sea.

Such tablets were either painted or done in bas-relief, and they would illustrate the cure or favor that had been granted by the god, or, in the case of a healing, they would show exactly what part of the body was affected by the cure. In the case of shipwreck—and we still find examples of crude paintings of this type in some European shrines today— there would be a portrait of a man being saved from a foundering ship or something similar, with perhaps some sign of the god's intercession. But what exactly is the meaning of the poem? As a bit of whimsy, we ought not to examine it too minutely: it is a tuneful bit of fluff, on how delightful life and love can sometimes be, when even minor tragedies are amusing. But the final image of shipwreck would suggest that all is not so clear as it would seem at first sight. Let us examine the imagery a little closer. First of all, there is throughout an atmosphere of remotely sexual symbolism: the grotto, the perfume, the roses, the sea. Next, in the "skinny boy" who is Pyrrha's current flame, Horace sees himself before experience made him wiser. Pyrrha, like the unpredictable sea,[24] makes a shipwreck of all who are attracted to her. Pyrrha, the *femme fatale*, is like Homer's Sirens whose sensuous song lures sailors to their doom. Or she is like a stormy, untamed sea; there is something perilous even in making an attempt to sail.[25] To what then does the shipwreck refer? Is it simply Pyrrha's unfaithfulness, her habit of moving on to new conquests before her lovers are ready to give her up? Rather, so far as Horace is concerned, shipwreck would perhaps have been some permanent involvement, even marriage—with a temperamental woman. Horace, too, had almost been her victim and is thankful to have escaped. But after a serious line and a half (*me...indicat*), the offering of soaking garments comes almost as a blasphemous intrusion after the reverence of the "sacred wall" and the "votive tablet." The actual humor here escapes us, and it is incongruous that these should be the thank-offering at Poseidon's shrine. But like the other nonsense-symbols, this too is a mask for conflicting feelings. Here, we come to the deeper point of the poem. It is that Horace, in his attititude towards women is uncommitted; when involved almost to the point of shipwreck—at least with the lady Pyrrha, if she is real—he just managed to escape unscathed, still a free man, unmarried. Though the poem is whimsy, it hides a serious truth. Horace's airy attitude towards shrines and gods is analogous to his attitude towards women and marriage. And the final blasphemous joke reflects his ambiguous feelings, just as the incongruous portrait of his Parthian victory over Pyrrha hides perhaps a fear of ultimate defeat.

But the sea also becomes for Horace a metonymy for man's courage and intrepidity. In his beautiful *bon-voyage* ode to Vergil (1.3), the danger of Vergil's trip to Greece becomes universalized: it is now a tiny epic on man's courage in the voyage of life. Man's achievement is measured by his daring, his rebellion, his tempting the very gods. All mythology is fitted into this pattern of man's history on earth: fire on earth (Prometheus), air (Daedalus), even Hell itself (Hercules). The four elements are thus comprised: for the water is the element in which Vergil is making his voyage. All these heroes of old are symbols of man's ultimate courage, bringing in its wake evil and self-destruction. Horace had perhaps in mind the first *stasimon* of Sophocles' *Antigone* in which the chorus sings of man's rise from earth to struggle with the elements, with Death and with Sin. But Horace is not so optimistic. Even though he is partly whimsical, the thematic statement of the poem is clear from the last few lines:

> Mortal though he is
> For man, nothing is impossible.
> We even quest for heaven—in our folly.
> And our sins never let the bolts
> Of Jove lie idle.

It is then man's eternal questing that has made him what he is: foolhardy, courageous, even evil. Sin and courage are, for Horace, two aspects of the same virtue. More clearly, perhaps, is the theme stated in the lines: "We even quest for heaven—in our folly." Heaven is the ultimate and impossible limit of man's journey, and his dissatisfaction leads him to ultimate glory. But on a second level this ambiguous line may mean: "We seek even heaven—what folly!" Thus man's ultimate desire for apotheosis—for a habitation among the stars according to the *Dream of Scipio*—is his worst folly. The tension within man, dissatisfaction and achievement, are

for Horace, precisely his claim to glory. There is no immortality beyond the grave.

The sea assumes another symbolic role in the epistle written about the year 20 to Bullatius (*Epist.* 1.11). Here the
call of the sea is an attempt to escape from the anxieties that
eat man's heart, but his dash across the seas to view the pal-
aces of kings changes merely his geography, not his soul.
We must not seek happiness in chariot or in ship. "What
you seek," says Horace "is right here." It is *ratio* and *pru-
dentia*, a true awareness of oneself and the ability to bear
life, as it is, with calm forbearance. The quiet of Italic cities
and the bustle of Asia and the Aegean isles become opposite poles in Horace's ultimate struggle with himself. He
does not say that we should not travel; actually we enjoy
it and refuse to give it up, spending our leisure time in stren-
uous activity (*strenua inertia*). The point is that all of us
must solve the ultimate inner conflict before we set out for
a change of environment: it is really ourselves that we are
trying to change. Thus the poem, as so many of Horace's,
is a poem of decision; Horace takes his stand, at least on
the ideal poetic level, on the side of self-awareness, as opposed
to extrovert activity, as the solution to the inner anxieties
of man.

This duality, which emerges especially in Horace's later
work, the *Epistles,* which are indeed more introspective, is
seen again in his letter to young Celsus Albinovanus (*Epist.*
1. 8), one of the poets in the cohort of Tiberius on his diplomatic mission in Armenia. In the last line of the poem, Horace delivers a sort of oracular riddle: "As you bear your
fortune, Celsus, so will we bear you." If Celsus is calm in
accepting life and himself so others will accept him; if he is
unhappy and discontented, so others will be discontented
with him. But in urging Celsus, Horace is in reality reflect-
ting his own conflict: the melancholia and depression that

he is suffering (*ibid.* 7-12) is rooted in the torment of not doing what he knows is right. Thus it is that our relations with others are indeed a function of our entire attitude towards ourselves, and towards the entire human condition. It is typical of Horace to express a profundity in whimsical language.

Thus we have seen now that this oscillation we find in Horace's poetry is an expression of his own internal conflict. Town Mouse and Country Mouse, Epicurean and Stoic, Lalage and the Wolf, the ecstatic release of wine amid pleasant companions versus the austere probings of the heart, denial of the gods versus the anxious hope of immortality: all these are the poles of his conflict. The solutions suggested in Horace's poems are never decisive, but always tentative and ambiguous.

In conclusion, it is clear that the focal symbols in Horace can yield important clues to the ultimate meaning of his poetry. In this chapter in an effort to be brief we have stressed one type of symbolic dimension: the scale of ambivalent and conflicting feelings about life, love, poetic achievement and death. This dimension can ultimately be traced back to the meditation which Horace embodied in his first satire (I. I. 1-3):

> How is it, Maecenas, that no one's happy with his lot?
> Whether it came by choice or destiny, no matter;
> We are always praising other people's lives.

It was this unending quest, *ut contentus vivat*, to be happy with his lot, that expressed itself symbolically throughout the entire span of his creative work.

This was the tension which we find in various forms from the earliest days of the *Epodes* down to his latest *Epistles*. In the end, Horace seems to have found what he sought. As he wrote to young Lollius (*Epist.* 1.18.104ff.),

> As often as the stream Digentia
> Refreshes me, that chilly brook from which

The town Mandela drinks, wrinkled with cold,
How, think you, do I feel, how make my prayer?
May I keep all I have—or even less;
May I live out my span as the gods may will.
I hope I've food and books to last the year;
I pray I won't be a slave to the passing hour.
But all I need to ask of Jove (who gives
And takes away) is to grant me life and strength:
A tranquil mind I can myself provide.

There is no more attractive prayer in all antiquity. It is a fitting epitaph to a life given to the poetic exploration of the universe.

VIII

HORACE AND HIS FRIENDS: BRUNDISIUM

DESPITE THE VAST AMOUNT OF ERUDITION THAT HAS
grown up around Horace's *Iter Brundisinum* (*Sat.* 1. 5), we seem
to be no nearer to a solution of many of the problems which
it raises.[1] Even if we pass over, for example, the identification of some of the places mentioned on the journey, there
is the problem—admittedly not an important one—of de-
termining the exact number of days Horace and his party
required to reach Brundisium. Indeed, though many plod-
ding scholars have retraced Horace's footsteps along the steaming roads of Italy, no agreement has yet been reached.
Some, like Orelli, allowed for as many as seventeen days—
a very leisurely pace. Most scholars have calculated fifteen
days;[2] and some would compress the trip into thirteen days.[3]
The historian Gibbon, who was familiar with at least part
of the actual terrain, saw no reason why it should take
more than twelve.[4] My own view is that the slowest pace

of all, seventeen or fifteen days, would fit in better with the mood of the poem. But on this point one cannot but feel that, in the absense of any certain clue from the text itself, doubt must remain.

Much more important, however, is the problem of the dramatic date of the poem, and intimately connected with this is the question of the poem's ultimate meaning and significance. In the past, scholars have interpreted the poem historically, and have based their solutions on an identification of the important diplomatic mission (28; *missi magnis de rebus uterque*) in which Horace, indirectly, was involved. Only three historic occasions have ever been seriously considered: 1. The Pact of Brundisium (probably in early October 40 B. C.); 2. Maecenas' mission to Athens as Octavian's personal envoy (in Autumn or Winter of 38 B. C.); 3. The Peace of Tarentum (early Spring, 37 B. C.) Let us consider each of these occasions in order.

The Pact of Brundisium (early October 40, B. C.).[5] This was the great reconciliation between Octavian and Antony which was to result in Antony's marriage with Octavia and in a fresh partition of power among the triumvirs. The struggle against Sextus Pompeius was thenceforward to be their common care, and Octavian, on his part, consented to an amnesty of all those who had joined Antony from the disbanded armies of Brutus and Cassius. Now if we may rely on the account of the meeting as reflected in Appian (*Civil War* 5.64), the delegates chosen by Octavian's soldiers were Asinius Pollio as a friend of Antony, C. Maecenas as a confidant of Octavian, and L. Cocceius Nerva as a man who would be acceptable to either side. It is interesting to note that the only difference between Appian's delegation and the one mentioned in Horace is that instead of Asinius Pollio as Antony's friend, Horace has C. Fonteius Capito. At any rate, because of the early date of the pact, most scholars—but not L. Desprez and E. Shuckburgh—tend to rule out this occasion as the historical kernel of Horace's satire. For Horace could hardly have become so friendly with Maecenas before the year 38, or, just possibly, the latter part of 39 B. C.[6] And Horace himself seems to suggest that the journey of *Sat.* 1.5 was not the first diplomatic mission of this nature (cf. 29: *aversos soliti componere amicos,* "used to reconciling friends who are estranged"). But the presumption all along has been that all the details that Horace gives us are to be taken as belonging to a *single* historical context —and this is precisely the position which I propose to question.

Maecenas' Personal Mission to Athens (Autumn/Winter, 38 B. C.).[7] Antony was residing at this time at Athens with his wife Octavia, and Maecenas was dispatched from Rome to confer with him on Octavian's behalf and once again to solicit his support against Sextus Pompeius. Those who support this occasion assume that Maecenas would sail to Greece from Brundisium and that he would be accompanied to the point of his embarkation by his *docta cohors.* One difficulty, however, is that Appian, our only source for this diplomatic mission, makes no mention of other delegates, and, since Maecenas' *démarche* was not apparently in the nature of a reconciliation, other delegates would not strictly be necessary. At any rate, many scholars have accepted Maecenas' mission as the occasion of the satire, chiefly because of their conviction that the journey described by Horace was made in the autumn or winter.[8] On this view, of course, the assumption is that Horace and Vergil would accompany Maecenas only as far as Brundisium (*finis chartaeque viaeque*); Maecenas, Nerva and Capito would continue on to Athens, but this detail could, in the poem, be discreetly passed over. It seems clear that, from an historical point of view, this occasion is the least suitable for Horace's poem.

The Peace of Tarentum (Early Spring, 37 B. C.).[9] Here our sources are in substantial agreement that Antony and Octavian were reconciled largely through the mediation of Octavia. Though Dio mentions no delegates by name, he does say that the triumvirs at first presented their grievances through friends. Plutarch gives us a charming picture of Octavia, who was heavy with Antony's child, running on ahead to meet her brother as he approached Tarentum in the company of Maecenas and Agrippa. But how is such a meeting to be reconciled with Horace's account? There is no reason to suppose that Octavian or his party made the journey to Tarentum by way of Brundisium. And to fit Horace's picture one would have to suppose that Maecenas and his party of delegates travelled separately from Octavian and took the incredibly roundabout way by the Via Minucia, as it has been called, to Brundisium. Some scholars have seized on Plutarch's suggestion, differing here from Dio and Appian, that Antony first sailed to Brundisium and, when the people refused to receive him there, proceeded around to Tarentum. But this detail seems to be out of its logical historical context, and must belong to the account of the negotiations of 38 B. C. —and so Tarn and Rice Holmes have taken it.[10]

And yet, notwithstanding these difficulties, most scholars have attempted to link Horace's journey with the Peace of Tarentum, chiefly I think, on the conviction that the *Iter Brundisinum* was made in the spring; for thus the night on the canal, with the croaking frogs and the gnats, would be more plausible.[11]

From the historical evidence, when all is said, even if we could logically exclude hypothesis 1 (40 B. C.), it is difficult to choose with any certainty between 2 (38 B. C.) and 3 (37 B. C.). And when we study the actual poem, the clues Horace gives us about the season of the year—the frogs and gnats on the one hand, and the rains and the fire on the other—would appear to be contradictory. After considering the various views, Palmer sums up the case for 2:[12]

> The chilly evening and the fire of branches with leaves on, vs. 81; the heavy rains, vs. 95; these suit autumn better than early spring.

And Gow puts the case on behalf of theory 3:[13]

> The choice between these views turns on the question whether frogs croak loudly (see 1.14) in Italy in the fall of the year. On this topic, I have made enquiries from some distinguished naturalists who are well acquainted with frogs in general and with those of S. Italy in particular. They agree that—though a frog may give an occasional croak a late as August, frogs do not croak in concert except from about February to April, i. e., in the breeding-season and for some weeks afterwards (see *Class. Rev.* 1901, p. 117). This fact seems to show conclusively that Horace must have travelled in the spring.

These are the reasons, such as they are, that have convinced many scholars. And yet, if we accept the spring theory, how are we to explain the fact that Maecenas and his party go to Tarentum by way of the circuitous sea-coast route, instead of taking the Appian way directly from Beneventum through Venusia to Tarentum? All the sources seem to suggest that Tarentum was the appointed place of the meeting, and even Plutarch's remark about Antony's ships skirting the coast, even if we do not reject it with Tarn and Rice Holmes as we should, would not alter this fact.[14]

If we accept theory 2, Maecenas' mission to Athens, it is easier to explain why Brundisium was the end of the journey for Horace. But we are still faced with the difficulty of reconciling the presence of the frogs and gnats with the colder weather. And, as I have suggested, it would seem that the nature of Maecenas' mission would not require the presence of other delegates. To sum up: the list of the delegates fits the first reconciliation (of 40 B. C.); the actual route of the journey along the sea-coast to Brundisium would suit Maecenas' voyage to Athens (of 38 B. C.); and the season of the year would most plausibly fit in with the Peace of Tarentum (of 37 B. C.), And as the bewildered scholar turns from one theory to the next, there is the gnawing doubt that this after all is poetry and not history; our author is Horace, not Livy or Tacitus.

A further complication arises if we are to take seriously Porphyrion's statement: "In this satire, Horace is competing with Lucilius"; *Lucilio hac satyra aemulatur Horatius*.[15] For if Horace is throughout consciously imitating Lucilius' *Iter Siculum*, there would be further reason to doubt the historicity of some of the details. One incident is surely suspicious: the *agôn* between the two buffoons, Sarmentus and Cicirrus, and their joke about the *equus ferus* would seem to depend upon Lucilius' joke about a rhinoceros in his third book.[16] It is tempting to look for more parallels, and one suspects that that much more *aemulatio* might be in evidence if we had more of Lucilius' text.

In view, then, of the meagerness of our historical sources, and considering what seem to be in Horace conflicting details, can we be sure that the poem is completely historical? [17] May it not be that the satire is a poetic fiction, a composite picture perhaps of journeys made at different times and bound together as a *jeu d'esprit* in imitation of Lucilius? In composing such a piece, Horace could have taken details from any one of Maecenas' missions, even from those in which he was not personally involved. On such a journey the typical things would happen: the party would be troubled by gnats and frogs, Horace would suffer from dysentery[18] and Vergil from stomach ulcers or merely indigestion. And, recited before Maecenas and his friends sometime before the year 35 B. C., in a version perhaps a little fuller than the one we now have, the poem would be amusing precisely because of its fusion of fact and fancy. And further, from Maecenas' point of view, the prudent use of fiction in such a delicate matter would be further proof, if any were needed, of how completely trustwortly Horace could be in connection with that more serious side of Maecenas' life, his political relations with Octavian.

In any case, I feel it is a useless task to attempt to assign any specific dramatic date to the poem, or try to sort out those details that might be (a) historically true, (b) pure fiction, or (c) imitations of Lucilius. We are dealing with poetry, as I have said, and not history. But I believe that perhaps much more may be said of the poem on a symbolic level. V. D'Antò, however, has gone too far in suggesting that the scene between the two buffoons Messius and Sarmentus is Horace's portrayal of the conference between Antony and Octavian.[19] If the symbolism is there, it would certainly have been understood by Maecenas or his friends, and as an implied criticism of the *imperator* and future *princeps* the poem would surely have been politically dangerous and prejudicial to Horace's newly found patronage. Nonetheless I think that it is precisely in a symbolic interpretation that the real significance of the ninth satire will begin to emerge.

I think it may be said that the predominant feeling of the poem is the unfailing good humor and friendship of Horace and his party against the background of the charming Italian countryside. And this becomes all the more striking despite the minor inconveniences which the travellers suffer on their way. Again, it should be noted that the longest single incident of the entire poem is the banquet held in Cocceius' country house near Caudium (*Sat.* 1. 5. 50-70); it is here that, after the mock *pugna* of the two frowsy epic warriors, Horace concludes: *prorsus iucunde cenam producimus illam* (70),

"we had a most delightful time prolonging that supper."
Now the mood of this central episode sets the tone of the
entire poem. The delight here, *iucunde*, recalls the delightful
friend, *iucundo amico*, of 44; and this is surely generic, referring to the entire party and not merely to Vergil. Here
I think, we touch upon the meaning of the entire poem:
it is an *Iter iucundum*, the "Happy Journey of Horace and
His Friends." It is a kind of Epicurean mock-epic celebrating
the life that Horace led under the aegis of Maecenas. There
are suggestions of the epic style all throughout, and instead
of the usual heroic episodes, we have the changing landscape
of southern Italy, the little private jokes, the illnesses and
inconveniences shared in common, some games, a skit between
clowns in the spirit of the Italic *satura*, and even love (though
here it is the cynical adventure with the "deceitful girl" of
Trivicum). And the whole, charming tale comes to an abrupt
close with a note of skepticism about the role of the gods
in this world of men adapted from Lucretius, *On the Nature
of the Universe* 5. 82 and 2.1194-5:

> Let the Jew Apella swallow that, I can't.
> For I've learnt that the gods lead a carefree life;
> And if we see some natural wonder, we are sure
> It is not the gods who send it down from heaven
> In token of their wrath.

Thus Horace's Journey fulfills all the best traditions of an
Epicurean life of carefree friendship, *solutis legibus insanis*,
"with insane laws abolished." But it is a Roman Journey
and over it all presides Maecenas, typically busy about some
political business which does not in the slightest impinge
upon the party's gaiety. He is ever "excellent Maecenas,"
optimus Maecenas (27),[20] and it is clear that he is the entire
cause of the trip, as well as of all the privileges accorded to
his diplomatic equipage. This then is the charm of Horace's
mock-odyssey: the various incidents, which Edward Gibbon

found so trifling, form a poetic symbol of the transient happiness which Horace felt as a member of Maecenas' privileged circle. It is the closest Horace ever came to epic, and it therefore shares all the ambiguity of tone which Horace felt when he toyed with the idea of writing in a more serious genre.

There still remain, it must be admitted, certain small details in the poem which convey an air of historicity and hence may present some difficulty against the view which I am here proposing. One of these is the unexplained departure of L. Varius Rufus, *flentibus amicis*, "leaving his friends in tears" (93). Why did Varius leave the company at Canusium and why were they so grieved? This surely would seem to reflect an actual incident familiar to Maecenas' circle, which took place either on some journey or under other circumstances. It may be that our text of the satire has been abridged at this point.[21] But the apparent authenticity of this episode, whose significance and context has now completely escaped us, need not force us to abandon our position with regard to the poem as a whole.

To sum up, therefore, it would seem that earlier analyses of the *Journey to Brundisium* have stressed the historical element to excess. All throughout the poem there are parodies of the epic style, as in the description of night (9-10) in the battle of the comic warriors; there is perhaps a parody of mythological poetry in the fire at Beneventum (71-76), when

> our bustling host
> All but burnt his house toasting pigeons
> Too skinny over a fire. Soon Vulcan slipped
> Abroad and spread through the old kitchen
> And well nigh caught the roof.

But in the final jest, the miracle of the burning incense at Egnatia, is the clue to the entire poem. For now we see that the emphasis is on pleasures and hardships shared, the gay banquet scenes, the intimacies of friendship (43-44),

> Ah, what joy, and what embraces then!
> Nothing to me compares with a delightful friend—

all this suggests that the poem is a kind of mock-epic celebrating in Epicurean style the joys of the Maecenatan circle.
This was the *domus pura*, the house without guile of *Sat.* 1.9,
friends at the banquet of life, oblivious of the gods. There
is still the zest for life and love, so characteristic of the *Satires*;
in the later *Epistles* the banquet would become a poignant
symbol of old age and death. Then he would write (*Epist.*
2.2.213-216):

> If you cannot learn to live, then leave it to those
> Who can. You've played, eaten, and drunk enough.
> It's time to go. Don't let our children laugh
> And jostle us, who perhaps have drunk too much,
> And join in our carouse with better grace.

LIFE A DREAM: THE POETRY OF PETRONIUS

PETRONIUS ARBITER IS CHIEFLY KNOWN AS THE AUTHOR OF that curious and sometimes scatological novel, the *Satyricon*. That he is to be identified with the Master of the Revels of Nero's court who enjoyed a rather theatrical suicide in A. D. 66 is most likely, there being very little serious evidence to challenge the traditional point of view.[1] But he has also left us a very striking collection of lyrics and short elegies which will repay serious study, since they are quite modern in their poetic technique.

We get a brief glimpse of Petronius' talent for symbolic composition in the brief and unfortunately corrupt fragment 84 which begins *O litus vita mihi dulcius*. Following the most commonly accepted text, we may translate:

O shore sweeter than life! Ah sea!
How happy I am that I can come straightway
To the land I love.

> Ah, lovely day !
> This is the country spot where once I used
> To rouse the water-nymphs with swimming-stroke.
> Here is the spring's pool. There the weeds that the sea
> Washed up. Here the sure haven of my silent hopes.
> I have lived. And no meaner fate can ever destroy for us
> The blessings of time past.

The setting is somewhat ambiguous, but it would seem to be as follows. An old man returns—at least in reverie—to the scenes of his childhood, to the country lake of Italy where he used to swim as a boy. As he thinks of the joys he had, the quiet pool suddenly becomes a kind of symbol of the peace and security he has finally achieved in old age. He is happy in the remembrance of Time Past. Almost as in *The Lake* of Lamartine, the spring and its cool basin stand as a permanent token of happiness that cannot be destroyed. Despite the obscurities of the poem, it is masterly in its brevity.

But perhaps Petronius' greatest power may be seen in his use of dream-symbolism. In that beautiful elegiac poem, *Lecto compositus* (frag. 99 Baehrens), a young man in his first sleep is awakened by Amor tugging him by the hair. "How can you, my servant," says Cupid, "lie alone?" He leaps up and dashes out into the night with bare feet and tunic ungirt; then, bewildered by the various streets, he stands stock still like a wandering madman; he can move neither forward nor backward. Suddenly he is aware that

> Silent are men's voices and all street sounds;
> Silent the song of the birds and the noise of faithful
> >   watchdogs.
> I of all men stand alone,
> And I am afraid of sleep.
> Great lord of Desire, I am at your service (11-14).

It is like an anxiety dream or a dream of wish-fulfilment. But all at once in the silence of the night, passion yields to a philosophic awareness of man's fundamental loneliness. The conclusion is ambiguous: *sequor imperium, magne Cupido, tuum* (14); but the stark picture of the pathetic, bewildered sleep-walker is unforgettable.

Petronius' most interesting dream poem is frag. 30 (Bue-cheler; frag. 121 Baehrens), *Somnia quae mentes ludunt*. It is easy to hazard the guess that it occurred in one of the lost sections of the *Satyricon*; a similar poem, in fact, may be found in § 128. The ostensible theme of fragment 30 is that dreams are merely a continuation of the day's activities—in Freudian terminology, the "day's residues." In translation:

> Dreams that trick the mind with flitting shadows,
> Come not from the shrines of the gods or powers of heaven.
> Each man makes his own. For when sleep presses
> On the body crushed with weariness, then the mind
> Can play without burden, pursuing at night whatever
> Occurred by day. The man who makes towns tremble
> In war, and destroys unhappy cities by fire,
> Sees spears and routed hosts and dying kings
> And plains flowing with shed blood. Lawyers
> See statutes and law-courts, and gaze in terror
> On a judge's bench that is merely within the heart.
> The miser buries his wealth, discovers treasure.
> The hunter shakes the woodland with his pack.
> The sailor saves his ship or, drowning, grips it.
> The courtesan writes her lover; the adulteress yields.
> The drowsing dog barks at the spoor of the hare.
> The wounds of the unhappy perdure through the hours of
> night.

On a superficial reading of the poem, the theme seems almost a commonplace of the sort found frequently in literature with an Epicurean tinge. For the Epicureans attempted to combat the view held by the superstitious masses and encouraged by the Stoics, that dreams could be communications from the gods. Indeed, the second century dream writer, Artemidorus of Daldis, incorporating what seems to have been Stoic material, taught that in addition to dreams prompted by bodily needs there was a true class of prognostic dreams due to divine influence: the "theorematic" or vision-dreams, which embodied a clear indication of the future, and the allegorical or obscure dreams, which required expert interpretation.[3] Stoic dream theory, as reflected particularly by Posidonius, seems to have had an important influence on Christian allegorism chiefly through the writings of Philo Judaeus. For Philo utilized Stoic theory in his attempt to explain the three types of dreams which occurred in the Old Testament, the divine, the angelic and the non-divine.[4]

It is logical to suppose, then, that our poet is attempting to refute this prophetic theory of dreams, and, for this reason, he takes only such examples which would readily fit his case. The instances are obviously tailored to picture continuations, or possible continuations, of the day's activity. He does not treat, as do other theoreticians, the body-need dream, the fantastic allegorical dream or the theophany type of dream, which poets like Sappho, Tibullus and Propertius could describe so well. But, it is precisely this selectivity, among other things, which arouses suspicion that the poem may have a level of meaning which is not completely on the surface, though not irrelevant to the Epicurean view of life.

As we begin reading the first line, it is not immediately clear that the *somnia* which trick the mind are *night* dreams in the literal sense. Before the meaning becomes specified the associations of "vague fancies" and "pretenses," which can be attached to the word *somnia*, seem very present. Again, they deceive the mind "at the time of hovering shadows," or "by means of flickering shadows," perhaps like the "images of things," *rerum simulacra*, that flutter through the air in Lucretius 4. 32. Further, can the "shadows," *umbrae*, mean "ghosts"? Indeed, it is not completely clear what it is that each man makes for himself until we come to the "sleep" and "weariness" of the succeeding lines, and then it becomes obvious that the poet is dealing with the prophetic theory of dreams and, perhaps, the practice of incubation.

Thereafter, the sequence of the various dream narratives is clear: the soldier, the orator, the miser (at least as a type from the mime), the hunter, the sailor, the women of ill repute. The dreams are of the sort that one would today call wish-fulfillment dreams and, at least in the case of the terrified orator and drowning sailor, anxiety dreams. A modern Freudian analyst might perhaps tend to see more, especially in the sacking of cities, the plain flowing with blood, the hunter and his hounds, the sinking sailor and the unfaithful women. But these images are familiar enough from ancient accounts of dreams, as we find them, for example, in the Hellenistic papyri and especially in the *Dream Book* of Artemidorus. The pathetic little line on the barking dog—in Lucretius, incidentally, the dog wakes itself up—should not, I feel, be deleted, nor should *latrat* ("barks") be changed to *lustrat* ("follows" the tracks of). The detail would seem to have been a regular Epicurean topic, to show the affinity between animals and men, and is similarly developed by Lucretius.[5]

But it is the ambiguity of the final line, *In noctis spatium*, ("The wounds of the unhappy," etc.) that suggests an entirely different reading of the poem. What is meant by the "wounds" and who are the unhappy? One possibility that occurs is that the lines refer to those who are in sorrow, or otherwise ill. Or, again, because of the previous reference to lovers and their ladies, we may legitimately think of the "wounds of love"; the image is frequent enough in the elegiac poets. Hence physical pain, moral affliction, the pangs of love—all seem possible. But still we are not sure whether the line is intended to refer to a type of dreamer not previously mentioned, or is meant to be a summary of all the types of dreams that have gone before. After the mention of the dog, we should have expected the list to be complete. It is this final possibility, that the last line sums up the entire poem, which presents an entirely new dimension in imagery. For all of the dreamers that the poem describes are all in search of happiness in one form or another, aptly symbolized by the hunter and the courtesan; and thus all might be described as "unhappy" and suffering from "wounds." In this way, the final line of the poem, "The wounds of the unhappy perdure through the hours of night," would resume the meaning of the entire fragment. Dreams merely continue the unhappy quest of our conscious lives; in the Epicurean view, they are symbolic of man's pursuit of happiness without benefit of providence. Like hounds we too merely bark at the hare's scent.

Thus a further nuance suggests itself. If dreams are merely a prolongation of what we do by day—and, indeed, the poet speaks of the dream activity almost as though he were describing men's daily lives—Petronius may be hinting, though not expressly stating, that all these absorbing interests are, in a sense, mere dreams, *somnia*. This would bring us back to the ambiguity we noted in the first line, where *somnia*, "dreams," could have the suggestion of "idle fancies." Hence what the sailor, the courtesan, the warrior do in their dreams is hardly less substantial than what they do in the light. If this suggestion is correct, the poem would have two levels of meaning. On the first level, it would represent a fairly straightforward case against the prophetic theory of dreams as supported by the Stoic school. This would confirm the impression we get from the poem quoted in § 128 of the *Satyricon* as well as the slighting reference in § 10 to "dream-interpretations," *somniorum interpretamenta*. But I cannot escape the impression that on a second and more poetic level the fragment would seem to be saying something about the dream quality of life: that the most absorbing interests of men, their passions and ambitions, are little more than dreams.

JUVENAL: THE CRITIC WITH A SMIRK

GOOD SATIRE IS A DIFFICULT TECHNIQUE IN ANY AGE. Because of its restricted point of view, the audience it reaches is very limited, and, like comedy, with which it has always been associated, it soon becomes dated. It is hard for good criticism not to be local and concrete. Satire has so wide a range and exists in so many media that it is not useful to essay a definition. It is not strictly a genre; it is best described by discussing the various authors, or artists, who have attempted it and by indicating their divergent points of view. In the broad sense, it is a critique of behavior, but, when all is said, it is not different from all other types of human criticism. There is always some selectivity with resultant distortion. There is always the witty portrait of men's behavior, in whatever field, with obvious disapproval, and with, perhaps, a suggestion of the ideals or standards from which the satirist feels men deviate. In perhaps no other artistic area is moral truth conveyed through falsification as it is in satire. Whether in prose, verse, music or the visual arts, satire maintains a precarious existence between the ideal and actuality. And somewhere there is the prophet with a smile (Horace's *ridentem dicere verum, Sat.* 1.1.24f.) —or at least a smirk, Juvenal's *rigidi censura cachinni* (*Sat.* 10.31). Whether satirists are serious social reformers matters little; it is at least the medium in which they would express themselves, or some facet of their creativity. For those of a certain temperament, their very "anger writes their poetry," as Juvenal so candidly admits (*Sat.* 1.79). They enjoy being angry, and their intolerant, distorted view of reality caters to their disposition. But apart from the literary or artistic dimension of satire, one always suspects the vicious, or "Juvenalian," satirist of being disingenuous. While we perhaps enjoy the vicarious experience of *Schadenfreude*, we are aware that to write a satirical novel or poem, is surely not the most immediate or most practical way of influencing and controlling human behavior.[1] The end of good satire is, perhaps, itself; it is its own reason for existence.

The tone of Juvenalian satire is particularly hard to maintain. Juvenal lives within the confines of a narrow poetic world, a world of sharply contrasted colors, sounds, and smells; indeed, all its stimuli are provocations to frustration, bitterness, and disgust. It is a universe of distrust and suspicion, in which a man is ever at war with the gods and even virtue is not what it seems. There is something tainted about all our natural, human instincts; everywhere we are being dragged down by visible proof of man's kinship with the beast; we must constantly do violence to ourselves to correct, chide, castigate.

For Juvenal even the arts are suspect: they breed sensuality and pamper luxury. Government officials are often masters of depravity hiding under the cloaks of Roman *severitas.*

Men's worship of the gods is either hypocritical or deluded. Human ambition is a snare; power, wealth, fame, beauty— there is a canker of corruption in all of them. There is peace only in retreat: retreat from the steaming, stinking metropolis to the simple fare and unimaginative life of the country. This is Juvenal's world, the product of anguished brooding and discontent. It is a warped vision—but it has, oddly enough, become the stuff of poetry.

THE FIRST SATIRE

Juvenal's first satire[2] grapples with the problem of his vocation as a critic of *mores*; but it is a program rather than an apologia, though it does contain elements of both. It is also a poem of self-revelation and decision. There is first of all an ambiguous prologue (1-21) —ambiguous because the exact tone of the attack on contemporary poets is unclear— and this serves to introduce us to the poet in the petulant manner of the Cynic diatribe. In any case the stage is set, and Juvenal's urgent, strident voice begins to make itself heard. Then follows the famous *pompa*, a kind of Juvenalian mock-procession, through the steaming streets of Rome, of murderers, blackmailers, debauchees, and pimps (22-72). Here are the leading characters of the pageant; some come by palanquin and sedan-chair, others walk alone or with bodyguards, jostling the others as they move. After an interlude of a few lines (73-95), the scene will change to the queue of miserable clients outside a wealthy patron's door (95-126), and then in rapid succession to those other keyhole glimpses of the Rome of Juvenal's indignant nightmare which form so much of his charm (127-146).[3] There is an attractiveness even in the pathetic grubby figures of the mob fighting in formal togas for a miserable pittance. And there is something grand in the vice that provokes such magnificent anger. Finally, the conclusion (147-171) contrasts the dangers of writing satire under the Emperors with the *simplicitas*, the straight-forwardness, of republican Rome, and comes to a quiet end with Juvenal's mock-promise to speak only of the dead. An exaggerated picture, surely, for the reign of Nerva, Trajan and Hadrian.[4] But historical distortions aside, what is the poetic meaning of this veritable hotch-potch, this *farrago*, as Juvenal so aptly named it?[5]

Juvenal's chief trick here is the procession, the queue, the list. On one level it is a pageant; on the other it is as though he were composing a legal indictment, a *libellus accusatorius*, listing crimes to be delated to the magistrates. Thus the focal scene of the entire poem is contained in the great *pompa vitiorum*, the mock-procession of Rome's great (22-72). Their idle shuffling through the crowded streets assumes the proportions of a triumphal procession or, if you prefer, of a funeral cortège moving out of Rome's gates to the city of the dead. Indeed, the figures that march before us are both alive and dead. And there Juvenal stands, like a *delator* with note-book,[6] *medio quadrivio*, right at the centre of the cross-streets. Like a Greek choral figure, his vision is all-pervasive, he alone is innocent and uninvolved. And what *quadrivium* is this? It is the intersection of two *viae* somewhere close to the Roman forum, at the heart of Rome. It is the symbolic centre towards which all types of evil converge. Indeed, it is not irrelevant to recall that ancient cross-roads and cross-streets possessed a sacred character; even in Roman times, they were associated with a special *numen*, with the *lares compitales*. It is thus a fitting, symbolic vantage point from which the poet can watch and fill his fat note-books, *ceras capaces*.

To this centre, this gathering-place of vice, all roads lead—and, in particular, the Latin and Flaminian ways (61,171).

And Juvenal, in promising to mention in his *libellus* only those whose dust is buried along these roads—there is here an ironic reference to the proverb "Speak no evil of the dead" —implies that men do not essentially change, and that the sins of the fathers, of those buried there, like the Scipiones and the Scaevolae, are still vigorous in their sons who are alive in Rome. Juvenal therefore sees a continuity between Lucilius and himself in raising a voice against depravity. And as he proceeds he becomes aware that the vices of Rome, that *uberior vitiorum copia* (87), a "fine, rich supply of sin," are the culmination of her history. Degeneration, like a mysterious putrefaction, has set in. It is hard to conceive of things ever becoming worse: "every vice has reached its peak," *omne in praecipiti vitium stetit,* (149.)

But in all this we have the impression that the satirist's indignation springs, in part, from an insecurity within his own soul, from the disturbing awareness that he too, Juvenal, if not actually guilty, is made of no sterner stuff than those who would risk prison "to be something" (73-74). As the psychologists would say, his oral aggression is a protective mechanism. But Juvenal's melancholy reference to the dust of the Roman ways, over which so many victorious legions tramped, surely suggests that he is concerned not with individuals but with the common disease, and that his canvas is a wider one in which he seeks to explore the very source of all weakness and malice, the very heart of man.

It is precisely in this way that the first satire is revelatory. Juvenal's anger is fierce because he can glimpse within himself impulses to the very vices whose indictment he so bitterly draws up. And there is a certain attraction about his portrait of vice, because he himself has felt its seduction. But it is a poem not only of exploration but of decision. For the *indignatio* which is the fountainhead of his verse stands as proof to the world and to himself that he will have no part in the pageant of viciousness. He has taken his stand and made his decision at the crossroads.

THE THIRD SATIRE: ROME'S MORAL COLLAPSE

In his third satire, a picture of Rome's moral collapse, Juvenal retains a relic of the ancient dialogue form of the *satura*, although, it is true, Umbricius is merely a *persona* or mouthpiece for the poet himself.[7] Umbricius' going into retirement, is a symbolic gesture of despair; he is going alone to the Sibyl, to the fountain of truth and the prophetic source of Rome's ancient greatness. And, almost as though he were leading a funeral cortège, he stops outside the *Porta Capena* to pronounce a kind of *laudatio funebris* on the death of a once great city. Umbricius and Juvenal halt at the grove of Egeria, sacred with the memories of Rome's dim past. And even though in the aside,

Here, where Numa held his nightly rendezvous—

he suggests that the seeds of Rome's corruption had been sown in the mythological past—the grove is the most fitting place for Umbricius' farewell discourse. The violation of the native tufa, *nec ingenuum violarent marmora tofum*, suggest the violation of Rome's ancient mores and traditions by the influx of foreign blood. For this is Umbricius' theme: the city's moral collapse brought about ultimately by the steady stream of non-Italic immigrants.[8]

After establishing the setting (1-20), Juvenal allows Umbricius to speak for the rest of the piece. In 21-57 Umbricius suggests the reasons why he is disgusted with the general lack of morals in Rome; next, in 58-125, is his diatribe *adversus Graecos*. In 126-301 he sketches the general conditions of the poor Romans of good blood who are forced to live as paupers in the tenement districts in a "competitive poverty," *ambitiosa paupertate.* Then, after a short digression on the rise of crime in the city (302-314), Umbricius draws his discourse to a close (315-322).

The logic of Umbricius' speech is difficult to grasp. It is not composed by the rules of rhetoric, but its emotional tone and general direction are clear. Juvenal is on to a favorite theme: the source of Rome's moral degeneration. The ultimate source of the cancer is the uninhibited immigration of foreigners, especially Greeks, Jews, and Orientals, and the rise in population, Juvenal implies, has forced the native born Romans, the *ingenui Romani*, to live in filthy, overcrowded conditions. It is a typical search for the scapegoat, the *bouc émissaire.* Rome has now become a Greek city (61), wherein there is no more room for the trueborn Roman (162-163):

> Long ago the slender sons of Romulus
> Should have formed ranks and marched away.

The central theme of the satire can be found in the long passage that deals with the tenements of Rome (190-231). The scene is laid in a teeming *insula*, an "island" or block of cheap flats in the heart of Subura, the slum-area of the city, where Umbricius seems to have lived. Despite the imminent danger of collapse, the landlord's agent, the *vilicus*, cheerfully tells them all to sleep in peace as he hides a crack in the wall (194-196). There is a macabre touch in the verb *dormire*, "sleep." But the image of the collapsing tenement is crucial for the meaning of the entire poem. For, says Umbricius (193-194),

> We're keeping up a city, for the most part,
> Propped on a slender strut.

The crumbling, decaying tenement stands for the entire city precariously propped on a slender support. And the imminent physical collapse is only a symptom of the deeper corruption that is within.

Indeed, the entire area around this imaginative *insula* in Subura becomes the setting for the rest of the accidents which Umbricius describes, the fires, the nightly terrors, the cracked skulls and assaulted passersby. It is Umbricius' final indignity to be pummelled by a street bully, who recalls Achilles only by his drunken wallowing on the pavement. Thus does Juvenal, by a single stroke, suggest how far Roman standards have fallen. The epic battles of antiquity have become drunken street brawls between respectable Romans who play Hector to swaggering foreigners.

But the tale of Rome's degeneration, symbolized in her noisome, over-crowded tenements, becomes in Juvenal's hands exciting in the telling. There is a fascination in putrefaction, and to have captured this is not the least part of Juvenal's peculiar genius. And yet, there is a final irony: one wonders how Umbricius can bring himself to leave such an exciting city for the dull solitude of Cumae to become the master of a single lizard. There is an ambivalence here whose solution is suggested in the last few lines.

The closing lines are like an ancient σφραγίς or seal (315-322), which helps us to authenticate the poem and more closely to identify the poet. It also suggests a further interpretation of the satire. The author has a country seat that was perhaps also his birthplace, in the municipality of Aquinum, not far from the shrines of Diana and Ceres Helvina. Here I think the meaning of Umbricius as the poet's voice, his *persona*, becomes clear. There is both parallelism and contrast between Umbricius' poetic retreat to Cumae and the poet's to his Aquinum. Umbricius' absolute withdrawal is the ideal, Platonic retreat, which the poet himself cannot attain. He is still tied to Rome, and it is only on occasion that he can come back, in haste, to be refreshed: "As often as Rome lets you return," says Umbricius. For Juvenal belongs to Aquinum, but he must live at Rome.[9] And Umbricius is the *persona*, the mask, under which he can give vent to the feelings he sometimes has. The division of his life between Aquinum and Rome represents the partial solution to his conflict—the conflict between introvert and extrovert, between participating in life, with all its imperfections, and being merely a passive, contemplative spectator. From the security of his country haven, in the presence of his rustic goddesses, he can watch the city he loves collapse under the weight of its decadent but fascinating way of life. Hence the conflict in the poem mirrors a conflict within the poet's soul, and, on this deeper level, the dilemma is not solved but ends in compromise.

But even the external conflict presented by the poem hides a more subtle issue. For though "the Orontes has long been flowing into the Tiber," it is not so much the Greeks and the Orientals who are ruining the city. Rather, the vigorous stream of Italic blood is running dry, and the "slender sons of Romulus," *tenues Quirites*, themselves bewildered, are at the mercy of every charlatan that comes along. Inability to assimilate the foreigner is in itself a symptom of internal degeneration. Rome's disease is of her own making, and is incurable. In any case, this conflict between the internal and the external is at the very heart of the poem, and it is only in the lay figure of Umbricius that the dilemma is, symbolically at least, resolved. Once again the explicit message of the poem seems simple and straightforward; yet its implied theme strikes deeper, at the very source of all human inability to achieve.

THE TENTH SATIRE: HOW SHOULD WE PRAY?

No one any longer takes serious Ribbeck's view that the tenth satire is not from the hand of Juvenal. Yet his skepticism has forced scholars to reexamine the style and thought of the later satires in a new light.[10] The theme of the tenth is more philosophical, not to say more religious, than the earlier ones; it could almost be considered as a poetic transformation of a treatise *De votis notissimis*, on the "most popular prayers," and on the proper petitions we should make to the gods. The title that has been traditional since Samuel Johnson, *The Vanity of Human Wishes*, is most misleading; for it would ignore the fact that Juvenal's poem is written in a profoundly religious context; it is like a formal sermon.[11]

The theme of the poem is *vota*, the prayers of petition, *cunctis notissima templis* (23), that are the best known in Roman temples. Juvenal, here the poet-priest, the *poeta-vates*, sets the scene before the shrines of favorite gods, watching deluded men and women come, offer their prayers and then leave behind wax-tablets inscribed with their requests.

> Can our prayers then be superfluous or destructive,
> Those prayers we leave in wax on the laps of the gods ?[12]

Far from being an interpolation, as Knoche has thought, these lines contain the proposition and theme of the entire piece. There is a subtle irony in leaving our requests "on the laps of the gods"; and the use of the verb *incerare*, "to smear with wax," makes the action at once vulgar and superstitious. The scene and the setting are again explicitly resumed in the last section of the poem, "In Praise of Beauty," where the distracted mother makes specific requests for her children at the shrine of Venus (289-219), and, most clearly, in the concluding passage where the poet takes it upon himself to tell us what we should pray for (354-356). To give us something to ask for, Juvenal suggests with a waspish irony, as we offer our "prophetic sausages" to the gods, to "pray for a sound mind in a sound body." The poet is here like an elderly sacristan who has long overheard the prayers of those who visit his shrine, or has read the messages they have left scribbled on potsherd or wax tablet. But scholars in general have missed the tone of the poem. Cynical and worldly-wise it may sometimes be, but it is fundamentally religious. Juvenal's prophetic message is at once serious and enlightened.

Most important for the understanding of this theme is the difficult digression on Democritus and Heraclitus (28-53). We must of course consider these two philosophers not as they really were but as Juvenal uses them, symbolically, in his poem. For him they stand for two views of life, though both based on philosophic reflection: the way of tears and withdrawal as symbolized in Heraclitus, and that of censorious laughter, the way of Democritus. It is a dilemma very similar to that which we saw in the third satire: the problem of withdrawal or participation in the life of the creative poet. It is the way of Democritus, the way of aggressive criticism— to tell Fortuna to go hang herself (53-54)—which Juvenal makes his own. It is thus wrong to characterize his work as a remorseless, vindictive misanthropy; underlying the banter and the bullying is the message of prudence:

> Had we but prudence, Fortune, you would lose
> Your power. It is we who make you a goddess
> And place you in the heavens (365-366),

lines which are not to be deleted with Knoche.[13]

What can easily be overlooked in the satire is the delicate tension that exists between human prudence and divine power, *numen*. For Juvenal is at pains to show that there are only two poles to be considered in the problem of existence: the gods and ourselves. He wishes to eliminate all vague talk of a third force, *Fortuna*, or Sejanus' goddess, the Etruscan *Nortia*. What man's own ingenuity does not effect comes from the will of the gods—except that in Juvenal's doctrine the gods can be malign (7-8,111), by granting at man's request precisely what they know will harm him. If man is really "dearer to the gods than he is to himself" (350), Juvenal falls into a serious contradiction with the doctrine of the divine malignity. But we are not perhaps to press him here too closely. Indeed, the whole satire, as a *reductio ad absurdum* of the various goals men think important, resists logical analysis. To say that some men have lived longer than they wished, that physical beauty has led some astray or that power, wealth, and eloquence have often brought destruction in their train—this does not normally deter men who would desire these blessings in moderation. Must men always go to extremes? Surely it is not Juvenal's teaching that men are pushed to the edge by the very malice of the gods. Rather, the satire is not a logical or rhetorical brief, but a poetic meditation on the mysteries of the human heart. Its most intense desires are fraught with danger; and the pomp and allure of the external world are not all that they seem.

In view of this, then, what is the meaning of the poet's final recommendation? For what are we to pray? We have the ambiguous line (356):

> Pray to have a sound mind in a sound body.

Despite its surface simplicity, it is not really clear what the ine means. For if we are to take Juvenal's entire meditation seriously, would it be safe even to pray for a sound mind in a sound body? We may note that a similar phrase is used in Seneca's tenth letter to Caius Lucilius, that modest knight who has become immortal as his master's sounding-board. Seneca bids his disciple to reconsider his method of praying, to dispense the gods from answering all the detailed requests he had formerly made, and simply

> Ask for a good mind, good health of soul
> and then of body.

What this would here appear to mean is the general physical and spiritual vigor to lead a virtuous life; for Seneca then goes on to discuss the ways in which Lucilius might become "free of all desires," *omnibus cupiditatibus solutum*; a suggested means is to ask the gods for things one would not be ashamed of having one's neighbor hear. Yet in Petronius, it should be noted, the phrase *bonam mentem bonamque valetudinem* becomes a mere toast at a banquet.[15] It would seem there to be the equivalent of so many modern expressions used before drinking, all harmless, non-committal and almost meaningless.

The meaning of the line in Juvenal, therefore, still remains a problem. Is its connotation the banquet-cliché of Petronius or the generalized Stoic prayer of Seneca? In Seneca, however, we are not forbidden to pray, provided we are not subject to the whims of passion; whereas in Juvenal the doctrine would suggest complete abandonment of all petition. I had once speculated whether the line, "Pray for a sound mind in a sound body," had been interpolated. The entire context would indeed be happier without it. For one thing the change of verbs and persons is abrupt: "So that you might ask," *ut tamen poscas....* "One should pray," *orandum est....* "Pray for a brave heart," *fortem posce animum*; and the transition would perhaps be smoother if we could delete the offending line. But the change is not convincing. The solution must be that he poet himself did not feel that his final recommendation contradicted his previous doctrine. In the first place, in the "sound mind in sound body" he is merely using, like Seneca, what seems on the surface a harmless, non-committal formula. The request is vague and generalized and commits one to nothing; in any case, it does not request anything by which the passions may be gratified. In Seneca, too, at least by implication, the prayer is for a mental and spiritual health which will minister to the pursuit of Stoic virtue. And it is this line that Juvenal develops. The sound mind and body is nothing less than the virtue of the Stoic sage, without desires, without passion, without ambition. It is the Choice of Heracles again: toil and pain instead of pleasure.

But granting this is the meaning, is this doctrine seriously proposed? Can the author of these vicious satires seriously suggest to his readers that "not to know anger," *nesciat irasci*, is the true path to virtue? There is a contradiction here which offers us another insight into Juvenal's soul. The doctrine is candidly presented, but not by one who pretends to have attained the ideal. The poem is really another record of conflict. Juvenal does not present himself as a Stoic saint; far from it. He has presumably desired wealth, riches, power, length of days and all the rest. But all this has only brought more pain and anguish. Thus the poet here attempts to point to the intuition presented in the final lines: the polarity between human reason and the divine power. And yet the satire offers no easy solution, even though the catastrophe that attends men's folly is so vividly drawn. It stands as the embodiment of an anxious, still unresolved conflict, with the bare glimpse of an ideal, though perhaps unattainable solution at its close. No other ancient author has made us so aware of the torture and anguish of the moral dilemma, and of man's disgust and indignation at the irreconcilability of reality with the ideal.

DIALOGUE OF THE POET AND HIS WORLD

IT HAS NOT BEEN OUR INTENTION TO MAKE A COMPLETE survey of all the images and symbols to be found in ancient poetry, but rather to explore certain lines of development in some of the more familiar Greek and Roman poets. It has been our aim to open up what may be a new avenue into the ancient poetic imagination, relying always, so far as possible, upon the sound acquisitions of the past. Despite the widely different areas we have been forced to enter in discussing ancient symbolism, one theme remains constant: it is the gradual growth and progressive deepening of man's awareness of himself as he attempts to grasp, in poetry, the meaning of the universe. For in discussing the symbol we are touching on the deepest stratum of man: I mean his "transactional" function of assimilating the facts of the external world and his struggle to communicate and express this to others. But in another, and quite related sense, we are touching upon man's ability to overleap the sensuous barriers of his environment and project himself into the transcendent, without being able to give a satisfactory account—again in symbols—of what he is doing. Intimately allied with these two functions in the creation of symbols is man's faculty of moral dynamism: an awareness of a moral dimension in reality in which his own existence is deeply involved. For, indeed, one of the persistent themes of ancient Greek and Latin poetry is a certain striving for moral equilibrium between man's highest ideals and lowest instincts—a conflict which lies at the very heart of man's cultural growth. To express the world, to express the transcendent and the moral dilemma, these are the three chief functions of the symbolic process. The development of this process in the Greek and Latin poets is only one small aspect of man's spiritual history. But it is a most important one. The great "forest of symbols" which Baudelaire saw will always remain with us, ever luring us further into the mystery and poetry of the universe.

I have attempted to show, from an admittedly limited point of view, that there is no violence, no unnatural leap, in the passage of time between Homer and modern poetry. Despite the countless changes, and these must not be ignored, there remains the eternal dialogue between the poet and the world, between the artist and the men and women to whom he feels compelled to speak. We do not perhaps, like Augustine, think of poetry as an incantation to heal the serpent's bite. But the human situation, man's painful immersion into the world of reality, remains today very much as it was in ancient times, and it is of this that the true artist speaks and has spoken since civilization began.

But to the dialogue of literature the critic as well as the audience must come without presuppositions, with (as the phrase goes) one's defenses down. There must at least be an initial good will, a willingness to engage in the conversation.

For every competent poet in the ancient as in the modern world has a vision, his own tragic vision, which he is eager to share with his fellows, not so much perhaps to impose a dogma as to enjoy the comfort of having a listener. It is this symbolic conversation, this dialogue, which is perhaps the essential joy of poetry, the "harmless pleasure" which Aristotle speaks of. And provided the poet shares with us his limited vision of life in such a way as to involve and to draw us into the dialogue, I may not dictate the words he is to use, much less the rhythm of his communication. It is one of the ways by which we realize, to a greater or less degree, the meaning of our existence.

NOTES

CHAPTER ONE

1. For an excellent survey of modern communication theory see Colin Cherry, *On Human Communication: A Review, a Survey, and a Criticism* (Studies in Communication published by the Technology Press of Massachusetts Institute of Technology: 1957) with bibliography up to date, 308–23. For the general problem of symbolism in literature, see P. Wheelwright, *The Burning Fountain: A Study in the Language of Symbolism* (Bloomington, Indiana, 1954); see also W. K. Wimsatt, Jr., and Cleanth Brooks, *Literary Criticism: A Short History* (New York 1957) especially 583–609 and 699–720, with the bibliographies cited. For a discussion of some of the earlier literature, see L. J. Austin, *L'univers poétique de Baudelaire: Symbolisme et symbolique* (Paris 1956) especially 63ff. Very valuable is R. B. Onians, *The Origins of European Thought* (Cambridge University Press, 2nd. edit. 1953); and for a preliminary study of symbolism in the Fathers of the Church, see H. Musurillo," History and Symbol: A Study of Form in Early Christian Literature," *Theological Studies* 18 (1957) 357–386.
2. The *Geschichte der Autobiographie* was first published in 1907; the English edition, *A History of Autobiography in Antiquity* was translated by E. W. Dickes in collaboration with the author. (London 1950)
3. Especially his revised, third edition, London 1953.

CHAPTER TWO

1. Among the most important works in this area are Walter Porzig, *Die attische Tragödie des Aischylos* (Leipzig 1926); C. M. Bowra, *The Heritage of Symbolism* (London 1943), *From Virgil to Milton* (London 1945) and *The Greek Experience* (London 1957) pp. 103–122, "Myth and Symbol"; Gilbert Norwood, *Pindar* (Berkeley 1945); R. F. Goheen, *The Imagery of Sophocles' Antigone* (Princeton 1951); Viktor Pöschl, *Die Dichtkunst Virgils: Bild und Symbol in der Aeneis* (Innsbruck and Vienna 1950). One should also consult J. Dumortier, *Les images dans la poésie d'Eschyle* (Paris 1935); E. A. Havelock, *The*

Lyric Genius of Catullus (Blackwell 1939) which marked a completely new departure in the criticism of ancient poetry; Richmond Lattimore, *The Poetry of Greek Tragedy* (Baltimore 1958), a most original approach to the specific poetic contribution of each of the three Greek tragedians. Of immense value in this direction are F. R. Earp's two painstaking studies, *The Style of Sophocles* (Cambridge 1944) and *The Style of Aeschylus* (Cambridge 1948); cf. also J. Svennung, *Catulls Bildersprache: Vergleichende Stilstudien* (Uppsala Universitets Arsskrift 3; Uppsala 1954).

2. In *Homeri Opera*, ed. T. W. Allen (Oxford, 1931) V, 157. The translation is from F. L. Lucas, *Greek Poetry for Everyman* (New York 1951; repr. Boston: Beacon Press 1956)241.

3. Sappho, Fr. 31 (Lobel–Page), on which see the commentary in Denys Page, *Sappho and Alcaeus: An Introduction to the Study of Ancient Lesbian Poetry* (Oxford 1955) 4–18.

4. Fr. 53 Diehl, *Anth. lyr. graec.* 2 (Leipzig 1925).

5. See the discussion by Page, *op. cit.* 19–33, and the remarks of Gilbert Highet in *Poets in a Landscape* (New York 1957)13, 253–4. Highet shrewdly follows Page's interpretation of Sappho's poem, but I cannot quite agree with his views on Catullus 51.

6. In translating the Greek λεπτόν ("fine," "thin," "small") by *tenuis*, Catullus has perhaps widened the connotation of the "flame" of love; *tenuis* suggests "effeminate" and sometimes approaches the meaning of its cognate *tener*.

7. See the text of R. A. B. Mynors, *C. Valerii Catulli Carmina* (Oxford 1958)35f. with his *apparatus*.

8. Vergil, *Aeneid* 6.724 ff. And see the classic discussion of this turning-point in Aeneas' character by R. Heinze, *Virgils Epische Technik* (Leipzig 3rd. edit. 1915) 275–280.

9. This possibility was first suggested by Miss A. K. Lake, *Class. Rev.* 51 (1937) 53–55. W. C. Helmbold attempts an unconvincing refutation in his otherwise excellent study, "Propertius IV. 7: Prolegomena to an Interpretation," *University of California Publications in Classical Philology* 13 (1949) no. 9, 333–44.

10. Most helpful in this area has been H. J. Rose, *The Eclogues* of *Vergil* (Berkeley 1942) especially Chapter 6 "Vergil and Allegory," 117–38. See also the survey of the literature by T. E. Wright in M. Platnauer, *Fifty Years of Classical Scholarship* (Blackwell 1954)310–11, 333–34, and the bibliographical survey by G. E. Duckworth, "Recent Work on Vergil (1940–1956) *CW* 51 (1958) 123–26 (the *Bucolics*).

11. For a classic example of the rhetorical fallacy in poetic analysis one may read Alcuin's dialogue *On Dialectic* (in Migne, PL, 101.951–976): here the two speakers, Alcuin *magister* and Carolus Magnus discuss the use of the Aristotelian–Ciceronian *Topica* in their analysis of Vergil; see especially cols. 968–72. For a note on the sources of the *Dialectic* and its companion dialogue *On Rhetoric and the Virtues*, see E. S. Duckett, *Alcuin, Friend of Charlemagne: His World and His Work* (New York 1951)113–14, with the bibliography cited. For the most part, medieval and Renascence technique was based on an analysis of the so-called Figures of Speech and Figures of Thought, especially as they were found in the *Rhetorica ad Herennium* 4.18–69 and Quintilian, *Inst. Orat.* 8 and 9. The result was that, just as many poetic and rhetorical pieces were composed by following the rules set down in the medieval *Poetriae*, or manuals, so too criticism often consisted in locating and identifying the various rhetorical devices and figures. See for example the outlines of the manuals composed in the twelfth century by the Oxford scholars Geoffrey of Vinsauf, John of Garland, and others in J. W. H. Atkins, *English Literary Criticism: The Mediaeval Phase* (Cambridge 1943; repr. London 1952) 91ff. For the fortunes of classical rhetoric through the Middle Ages and the Renascence, see also Ernst R. Curtius, *European Literature and the Latin Middle Ages* (transl. W. R. Trask, New York, 1953), especially 74–78, 145–66, and elsewhere. It may, however, be noted that one of Curtius' own faults was a tendency to look on poetry as a kind of rhetoric; with the result that many of the examples he quotes are seen to be good rhetoric but very bad poetry; this problem has been touched on in part in my review of his book: *Thought* 29 (1954) 435ff. But it would seem that only if poetry could be taken as a kind of rhetoric — for rhetoric was thought to be a science allied to dialectic — might it find a place in the medieval world-view. St. Thomas, for example, lists the whole realm of speculative knowledge as a part of the cardinal virtue of Prudence; in this sense, Prudence would include Dialectic, Rhetoric, and Physics: *Summa theologiae*, II–II, q. 48: here literature and poetry would appear to be included under Rhetoric; see St. Thomas Aquinas, *Summa Theologiae*, transl. by the Fathers of the English Dominican Province (3 vols., New York, 1947) 2.1400. St. Thomas discusses the literature of the Bible in general under the question of prophecy, and here his treatment of the prophet's use of symbolism in the expression of his prophecy is perhaps the closest to the modern discussion of the creative imagination; see his

De veritate, q. 12, art. 7, ad 5, and in the English translation, *Truth*, translated by J. V. McGlynn (2 vols., Chicago 1953) 2.143. In the patristic period, the general allegorical method of interpreting the Scriptures was applied to Vergil by Fulgentius in his *Continentia Virgiliana* (6th century); see Atkins, *English Literary Criticism*, 22f. But a more objective method was suggested by St. Ambrose, developed from Aristotle's *Metaphysics* (the doctrine of the causes) and not from his *Rhetoric*. Whereas St. Augustine in his *De doctrina christiana*, Book 4, had recommended the rhetorical analysis of the Scriptures, even to the use of the classical figures, Ambrose suggested an entirely new technique. In a letter to a certain Justus, apparently a fellow bishop of Italy, written about the year 381, Ambrose gives his reply to the query whether there was rhetoric in the Scriptures. The sacred writers, he teaches, composed "not by art but by grace" (*non secundum artem... sed secumdum gratiam*); see *Epist.* 8, Migne, PL 16.950–954. Ambrose therefore suggests four categories which attempt to analyze not rhetorical form, but content. They are: (1) the external cause of the text, that is God; (2) the substance, or material meaning of the text; (3) the purpose or intention, that is, the reason why this particular statement should be written down; and (4) "definitions" or prescriptions, statements which may be taken as embodying a command or God's direct statement. For these Ambrose uses four Greek words: αἴτιον, ὕλη, ἀποτέλεσμα, ὅρος; he then proceeds to apply his method to Exodus 16, the story of the Manna in the desert. Ambrose has obviously adapted the Aristotelian doctrine of the four causes, efficient, material, final and formal; but his approach is strikingly close to some modern analytic techniques.

12. See for example E. E. Sikes, *The Greek View of Poetry* (London 1931) 95; W. D. Ross, *Aristotle* (5th ed., London 1949) 278; A. W. Gomme, *The Greek Attitude to Poetry and History* (Berkeley and Los Angeles, 1954) 53ff. See also G. E. Else, "'Imitation' in the Fifth Century," *Class. Phil.* (1958) 73–90.

13. *Encomium Helenae* § 9, ed. by O. Immisch (Berlin 1927). See also H. Diels, *Die Fragmente der Vorsokratiker*, 6th ed. by W. Kranz, (Berlin 1952)2.288–294, with the critical apparatus on B. 11. 9, 290. Cf. Sikes, *The Greek View of Poetry*, 29–31, and the note on the passage by M. Untersteiner, *The Sophists* (transl. by K. Freeman, New York 1954) 130, n.94. Gorgias' description of poetry and its effects (similar, in some ways, to the more modern theory of *Einfühlung* or empathy) should not be restricted to tragedy as such, as A. Gudeman,

Aristoteles περὶ ποιητικῆς (Berlin and Leipzig 1934)165, seems to take it. It is unfortunate that E. F. Carritt, in his admirable book *The Theory of Beauty* (5th ed. London 1949), did not discuss the Gorgianic theory in his treatment of empathy, 273ff. The debate on the authenticity of Gorgias' *Encomium* seems not to have been abandoned; cf. Diels-Kranz, 2.288.

14. Cf. also Horace, *Odes* 4. 11. 35–36: "by song black anxiety is allayed" (*minuentur atrae / carmine curae*). Cf. Diels–Kranz, 1.468. 19: "The Pythagoreans use the art of medicine to cure the body and music to cure the soul." On the application of this theory to literature, see R. Kassel, *Untersuchungen zur griechischen und römischen Konsolations-literatur* (*Zetemata*, Heft 18), Munich, 1958, 4–5. On the use of incantations in healing, see also Sophocles, *Ajax* 581–2, *Trach.* 1000, *Oed. Col.* 1194; cf. Aeschylus, *Agam.* 1019–1021.

15. *Epistle* 231 to Darius (ed. Goldbacher, CSEL, 1911) 3–4. The letter to Darius, a court-official of Valentinian III, was written about A. D. 429.

16. See the discussion in Kassel, *Untersuchungen*, especially on the influence of Stoic philosophy on the growth of Condolence–literature, *op. cit.* 17 ff.

17. The immediate reference is perhaps to the Phaeacians' love of feasting, the lyre, the dance, clean clothing, and baths; *Odyssey* 8.248ff.

18. *Poetics* 9, 1451^b 5–10, and see the commentary by A. Gudeman, *Aristoteles* περὶ ποιητικῆς (Berlin and Leipzig 1934) 206–7.

19. On ancient theories of the imagination, see M. N. Bundy, *The Theory of the Imagination in Classical and Mediaeval Thought* (Univ. of Illinois Studies in Language and Literature 12, Urbana 1927); cf. also W. D. Ross, *Aristotle* (London 1949)142–45. See the discussion in note 11 above.

CHAPTER THREE:

1. On the Greek pastoral, see E. A. Barber in *Fifty Years of Classical Scholarship*, 223 ff., with the additional remarks by B. Otis in *CW* 49 (1956) 149–52. A. S. F. Gow, *Theocritus*, 2 vols. (Cambridge 1950) together with his edition of the pastoral poets in the Oxford Classical Text series, and his translation, *The Greek Bucolic Poets Translated with Brief Notes* (Cambridge 1953) have made a substantial contribution to our comprehension of pastoral poetry. As an introduction to Eng-

lish pastoral, W. W. Greg, *Pastoral Poetry and Pastoral Drama: A Literary Inquiry with Special Reference to the Pre–Restoration Stage in England* (London 1906) is still very valuable. W. Empson, *Some Versions of Pastoral* (London 1935, repr. 1950) contains some acute insights into the broader problem of pastoral conventions and the ultimate aesthetic function of the pastoral genre. That the bucolic element in a poem should be derivative is not necessarily an indication that it is a poor poem; but one must always analyze the pastoral element to see how far it has been successfully transformed. Apart from pure pastoral poetry, one may detect traces of the bucolic symbol in the Roman elegiac poets, and occasionally in Horace's lyrics.

2. There is a dispute on the exact locale that Vergil has imaginatively used as his background; see Rose, *The Eclogues of Vergil*, 45ff. with the vast literature there cited.

3. In Terence the scene is always laid in Athens or Attica. The same is mostly true of Plautus, though we find, in addition to those mentioned in the text, settings such as Sicyon, Epidaurus, Epidamnus and Calydon. For a discussion, with the literature, see G. E. Duckworth, *The Nature of Roman Comedy: A Study in Popular Entertainment* (Princeton 1952) 82ff. On change of scene, see the brief remarks by W. Beare, *The Roman Stage: A Short History of Latin Drama in the Time of the Republic* (London 1950)267ff.

4. See his "Note on Contaminatio," *ibid.* 100–04. Cf. also Duckworth, *op. cit.* 202–8, and the Index, *s. v.*

5. This is not to deny the strict conventions that separated the *fabula palliata* from the *fabula togata*; see Beare, pp. 120–128, and, on the decline of the *palliata*, Duckworth, *op. cit.* 68–72. For a general discussion of Athenian New Comedy, see Katherine Lever, *The Art of Greek Comedy* (London 1956) 186ff.; cf. also T. B. L. Webster, *Studies in Menander* (Manchester 1950) and K. J. Dover's article in *Fifty Years of Classical Scholarship*, esp. 105ff. with the review by P. W. Harsh in *CW* 49 (1956) 125-26. On the *Dyskolos*, see Jean Bingen, *Menander: Dyscolos. Critical Edition* (Leyden 1960) bibliography, XII–XIV.

CHAPTER FOUR:

1. For a general discussion of the ethical views of the Homeric poems, see M. I. Finley, *The World of Odysseus* (London 1956)119–57. And for the problem connected with the abnormal theological views of

the *Odyssey*, in contrast with the *Iliad*, see D. Page, *The Homeric Odyssey* (Oxford 1955)168–69. On the symbolism associated with the idea of Fate, see Onians, *The Origins of European Thought about the Body, the Mind, the Soul, the World, Time and Fate* 390–94, with the literature there cited; on the image of the weighing of the Κῆρες see *ibid.*395ff. On the *Iliad* and *Odyssey* as group-expression, see E. M. W. Tillyard, *The English Epic and Its Background* (London 1954) 36–9. For a sound discussion of the Homeric simile, with bibliography, see Michael Coffey. "The Function of the Homeric Simile," *Amer. Journ. of Philol.* 78 (1957)113–32. For further suggestions on Homeric imagery, cf. Cedric Whitman, *Homer and the Homeric Tradition* (Harvard Univ. Press 1958).

2. The fortunes of this "archetypal Ulysses" are most interestingly developed by W. B. Stanford, *The Ulysses Theme: A Study in the Adaptability of a Traditional Hero* (Blackwell 1954); cf. especially his remarks on pp. 37ff., and 279f.

3. Apparently the theme of the Choice of Hercules was, in fifth-century Athens, a regular subject for the rhetorical ἐπίδειξις. At the banquet depicted by Xenophon in his *Memorabilia* 2. 1. 21–34, Socrates paraphrases an exercise taken apparently from a work of Prodicus of Ceos entitled *The Seasons*. Here Hercules is forced to choose between an immodest woman named Eudaimonia (Happiness) and a chastely severe Arete (Virtue) and St. Basil in his Sermon 22 (or *Address to the Youth*) 5. 11–14, uses the story of Xenophon as an example of the philosophic value of pagan Greek literature. See my article, "A Note on the Two Ways," *Folia* 9 (1955)102–6; cf. also *St. Methodius: The Symposium* (Ancient Christian Writers 27, London and Westminster Md., 1958)185, with the literature there cited. On the Hesiod passage, see Wilamowitz's sound discussion in his edition, Ἡσίοδος Ἔργα (Berlin 1928)74–75, and cf. his *Sappho und Simonides* (Berlin 1913)169–71. Hesiod's image of the second or Silver Age of the world as a babe in the arms of its mother is a very striking one, but perhaps insufficiently developed: *Works and Days* 127-31. For the image of Eros, "looser of limbs," see *Theogony* 120.

4. As early as 1921 in his *Psychologische Typen* (1st ed. 1921; Zurich, 1937)315ff. Jung thought he recognized an archetypal pattern in the "transition from the service of Woman (*Frauendienst*) to the service of the Soul (*Seelendienst*) particularly in the apocalyptic Christian work *The Shepherd* attributed to Hermas (second century), in Dante's *Commedia* and in other secular and Christian literature. Jung's

hypotheses were taken up, for example, by Maud Bodkin in her *Archetypal Patterns in Poetry* (Oxford 1934)174ff.

5. See the listing of the papyri fragments by Roger A. Pack, *The Greek and Latin Literary Texts from Greco–Roman Egypt* (Ann Arbor 1952) nn.73–75.

6. On Archilochus' independence of thought and *"heroische Nacktheit"* I can add very little to the long analysis by H. Fränkel, *Dichtung und Philosophie des frühen Griechentums: Eine Geschichte der griechischen Literatur von Homer bis Pindar* (Amer. Philol. Assoc. Monograph 13, New York 1951)182–207. In Archilochus there is a clear emergence of the personal, subjective lyric—what Fränkel has called "the primary data of the Here, the Now and the Ego." *Ibid.* 206. See also Bruno Snell, *The Discovery of the Mind: The Greek Origins of European Thought* (tr. by T. G. Rosemeyer, Blackwell 1953)49ff. Among the older studies, the most penetrating is J. A. Symonds, *Studies of the Greek Poets* (2 vols. in one, New York n. d.)1.279-280.

7. It is perhaps not by accident that Alcaeus is never mentioned by pseudo-Longinus, and only once by Demetrius, *On Style*, § 142; see Henrietta V. Apfel, *Literary Quotation and Allusion in Demetrius περὶ Ἑρμηνείας (De Elocutione) and Longinus περὶ Ὕψους (De Sublimitate)*, (Diss. Columbia University 1935). Alcaeus' fragments more than once remind us of the gulf that separates ancient and modern poetry. Fränkel recognizes Alcaeus' limitations as a poet, though he believes "he often transforms the raw material at hand into real poetry," *op. cit.* 265. For Alcaeus and Sappho, one must now consult E. Lobel and D. Page, *Poetarum Lesbiorum Fragmenta* (Oxford 1955)=LP; and D. Page, *Sappho and Alcaeus: An Introduction to the Study of Ancient Lesbian Poetry* (Oxford 1955). For the general bibliography, see J. G. Griffith, "Early Greek Lyric Poetry," *Fifty Years of Classical Scholarship*, 38–70; G. M. Kirkwood's bibliographic survey in *CW* 47 (1953–54)33–42, 49–54; and the annotations of W. M. Calder, *CW* 49 (1956)120-21.

8. Alcaeus fr. 326 (LP) and cf. the discussion of E. Fraenkel, *Horace* (Oxford 1957)154ff. Without the knowledge that Horace was imitating Alcaeus, it is hardly clear from Horace's text that the ship is an allegorical one. Indeed, Horace's poem seems a poor one; apart from the clever transposition of Alcaeus' idea into Latin metric, it is hard to see what Horace has contributed from a poetic point of view. For a general discussion of the Ship of State image and its implications, see Page, *Sappho and Alcaeus*, 179–97. Page feels that

"the evidence at present available indicates that the allegorical interpretation is certainly to be applied" to LP 6 and 326 (our present fragment), but that LP 73 remains doubtful. Interpretation has become clearer with the discovery of the ancient anonymous *Commentary on Alcaeus' Poetry* (now, in the Lobel–Page edition, frag. 306) especially in one of the more legible portions of it, frag. 14. However, the poem which the *Commentary* here presupposes is no longer extant, but judging from the commentator's remarks, it must have made a comparison between a decayed and ancient vessel, ready to be scrapped after many voyages, and a diseased old ἑταίρα or courtesan, at the end of a long career. See the discussion in Page, *op. cit.* 195ff.

9. See Pöschl's brief note in *Die Dichtkunst Virgils*, 254 n. 1.

10. See the brief discussion, Page, *Sappho and Alcaeus*, 121. The interpretation of the fragment ultimately derives from Himerius, *Orations* 1.16.

11. See the translation and commentary in Page, *Sappho and Alcaeus*, 88-96.

12. LP 132; cf. Page, *op. cit.* 131.

13. For a discussion of this Lesbian rivalry, see Page, *op. cit.* 133-40. The different households that vied for the favor of the girls seemed to have been a combination of a finishing school and a literary salon. The atmosphere, difficult to recapture, developed from the peculiarly sheltered condition of women in many parts of the ancient world. But compare also the rivalry of the girls reflected in Alcman's *Maiden Song*, with the commentary of Page; *Alcman: The Partheneion* (Oxford 1951)64-68. Cf. also U. E. Paoli, *Die Frau im alten Hellas* (transl. by L. and H. Rudiger, Bern 1955) especially on the "cloistral existence" of women in the Greek world, 9-14.

14. It is clear from the well-known hymn to Aphrodite (LP 1; Page, *op. cit.* 3ff.) that the theophany Sappho prays for in the first line has occurred frequently in the past. "What is it *now*?" Aphrodite asks, "Whom *now* am I to persuade?" There is a note of impatience in the twice repeated "now" that is most delightful. In the festival poem, LP 2, Sappho describes Aphrodite's mystic presence among her votaries: Aphrodite invisibly pours out nectar, which they drink as wine. In this poem especially we catch a glimpse of the two levels of Sappho's religious vision. See Page's dilemma, *op. cit.* 18 and 43.

15. *Pindar* (Sather Classical Lectures, vol. 19, Berkeley and Los Angeles 1945). For a survey of the literature, see G. M. Kirkwood in *CW* 47 (1953)51-54.

16. Simonides, frag. 37 (Diehl). and cf. Hesiod, *Works and Days*, 286ff. On Aristotle's *Hymn to Virtue*, see also D. E. W. Wormell in *Yale Classical Studies* 5 (1935)57ff.

17. Frag. 5 (Diehl).

18. The verb used here is ἀμαυροῦν meaning to "darken," usually referring to light.

19. Frag. 6 (Diehl).

20. Frag. 13 (Diehl). It is interesting that Dionysius of Halicarnassus, *On the Arrangement of Words* 26, quotes this as a piece of poetry that greatly resembles prose. For the translation, see F. L. Lucas, *Greek Poetry for Everyman*, 260–261. H. Fränkel refers to it as "the first Madonna image in Greek literature": *Dichtung und Philosophie des frühen Griechentums*, 407. See in general his shrewd analysis of Simonides' achievement, *ibid.* 391–419. See also the remarks of J. A. Symonds, *Studies in the Greek Poets*, 1.331.

21. Frag. 58 Diehl. It is quoted by the first–century writer, Apollonius Sophista, in his *Homeric Lexicon* 101.18 (ed. Bekker, Berlin 1913). For the Greek text see Page, *Alcman: The Partheneion* (Oxford 1951) 1.161. See also W. Schmid and O. Stählin, *Geschichte der griechische Literatur* 1. 1 (Munich 1929)462; H. Fränkel, *op. cit.* 229, n. 19.

22. See Page, *op. cit.* ⁻59–62.

23. For the idea, compare also the fragment once attributed to Sappho (52 Bergk: E. Lobel, *The Fragments of the Lyrical Poems of Sappho*, Oxford, 1925, 72) beginning "The moon is set," and now omitted from the new Lobel–Page.

CHAPTER FIVE:

1. Some of the more specific studies that have dealt with the problem are Goheen, *The Imagery of Sophocles' Antigone*; B. M. W. Knox, *Oedipus at Thebes* (New Haven 1957); and Richmond Lattimore, *The Poetry of Greek Tragedy*. My own brief article in the *Am. Journ. of Phil.* 78 (1957)36-51, was subjected to a critical analysis by Harsh, *Am. Journ. of Phil.* 79 (1958)243-58. For the literature on Sophocles in general, see Webster in *Fifty Years of Classical Scholarship*, pp. 71-95, with the review by Gerald F. Else in *CW* 49 (1956)121-5. See also J. C. Opstelten, *Sophocles and Greek Pessimism* (transl. by J. A. Ross, Amsterdam 1952); S. M. Adams, *Sophocles the Playwright* (*The Phoenix* Supplementary Volume 3, Toronto 1957); Kirkwood, *A Study of*

Sophoclean Drama (Cornell Studies in Classical Philology 31, Ithaca 1958), with his bibliographical study, "A Review of Recent Sophoclean Studies," *CW* 50 (1957)157-72.

On Aeschylus, in addition to Webster's survey cited above, see H. J. Mette, "Literatur über Aischylos für die Jahre 1950 bis 1954," *Gymnasium* 62 (1955)393–407; and McKay's bibliographical survey in *CW* 48 (1955)145-50, 153-59. To these should be added J. D. Denniston and D. Page, *Aeschylus: Agamemnon* (Oxford 1957).

On Euripides, there is a perceptive essay in Gilbert Norwood, *Essays on Euripidean Drama* (Berkeley and Los Angeles 1954) 1–51 ("Towards Understanding Euripides"); for the literature, see H. W. Miller, *CW* 49 (1956)81–92.

2. See 244, 348, 419–20, 680, 693–4, 718, 737, 755, 836 and elsewhere.

3. See Barbara H. Fowler, "The Imagery of the *Prometheus Bound*," *Amer. Journ. of Phil.* 78 (1957)173–184, presented as one chapter of an unpublished dissertation, "*The Dramatic Imagery of Aeschylus.*" Miss Fowler's conclusion is that just as disease was presented by the ancients as a μοναρχία of a single power, and health as an ἰσονομία, so the imagery of the play foreshadows the future harmony that will result from the compromise between Prometheus and Zeus.

4. For a good discussion with bibliography, see J. A. Davison, "The Date of the *Prometheia*," *Trans. of the Amer. Philol. Assoc.* 80 (1949) 66–93.

5. A. O'Brien–Moore, "Madness in Ancient Literature" (Diss. Princeton, Weimar: 1924)101–14, stresses the preternatural source of Ajax's madness, but explains that its root lay in "his false apprehension of the external world through faulty perception, a faulty perception which Sophocles explains as directly due to Athena"; 113. Sophocles' analysis of the daemonic role in Ajax's derangement is extremely subtle. And it is in some such way, he suggests, that the "heavenly *Atē*" operates upon men's passions. Thus indeed did the gods destroy Ajax: *Ajax* 1253-4. See the discussion in C. H. Whitman, *Sophocles: A Study of Heroic Humanism* (Cambridge 1951)78f.; Lattimore, *op. cit.* 66–68. On the unity of the play, see H. D. F. Kitto, *Form and Meaning in Drama* (London 1956) 196-8.

6. On Deianeira's fundamental guilt, see the very sound discussion by Bowra, *Sophoclean Tragedy* (Oxford 1947)126ff.; I cannot agree with Whitman's criticisms, *op. cit.*, pp. 114–15.

7. See Bowra's comment on the freedom which the act of vengeance brings: *Sophoclean Tragedy*, 257–58.

8. On the symbolism of Philoctetes' Bow, see Whitman, *op. cit.* 182
For an interesting though more fanciful discussion, see Edmund Wilson, *The Wound and the Bow: Seven Studies in Literature* (London 1952) 244ff., where Wilson develops André Gide's theory that Philoctetes represents the artist in conflict with the world, in the spirit of Baudelaire's *Albatros* and Thomas Mann's *Tonio Kröger*. In Gide's closet-drama, *Philoctète*, first published in 1898, Neoptolemus, Odysseus, and Philoctetes represent three stages of morality: that of the credulous child, the self–enlightened morality of the man of duty, and, in Philoctetes, the self–determined ethos of the poet–philosopher who is above the slogans of the mob. Indeed, Philoctetes becomes almost a projection of Gide's own self–centered ideal; the moralist and artist, whose criteria in ethics as well as in art are independent and individual. For Gide, too, the afflicted warrior takes on almost a mystical meaning, whereas for Wilson, Sophocles' play is a parable which suggests the absolute importance of the artist in society, despite the repugnance men may have for him as a person.

9. See especially Goheen's moderate "Postcript," *The Imagery of Sophocles' Antigone*, 101ff.

10. The problem is perhaps a dead question now, but I cannot believe that the passage extending roughly from 904 to 913 (it is difficult to detect the join) is really from Sophocles' own hand. The passage was suspected by Goethe, because of the motivation "that is quite unworthy and almost borders on the comic": *Conversations of Goethe with Eckermann* (transl. by John Oxenford, London: Dent, 1946) 178, for March 28, 1827. Goethe was, however, anticipated by A. Jacob, *Quaestiones Sophocleae*, 1821. Since that time it would appear that most Sophoclean scholars tend to reject the passage. And the decisive factor has perhaps been not merely the change in motivation reflected in the lines, for this might be attributed to hysteria at the imminence of death, but also the closeness of the actual Greek to Herodotus 3. 119, the speech of Intaphrenes' wife to King Darius. But it should be noted that the peculiar psychological twist in the passage, which tends to shock us in the mouth of Antigone, is precisely suitable in the Herodotean story. There Darius, after imprisoning Intaphrenes with all his children and relations, allows his wife to plead for the life of only one person. When the woman cleverly pleads for her brother on the grounds that she can always get another husband and other children, Darius is so impressed by the argument that he grants her the life of her brother as well as her eldest son.

For a discussion, see Page, *Actors' Interpolations in Greek Tragedy* (Oxford 1934) 86–90; Bowra, *Sophoclean Tragedy*, 95; Kirkwood, *op. cit.* 163–6, with the references there cited. Kirkwood is one of the most recent to rehabilitate the passage. But that the passage is a borrowing, at least from the traditional story of Intaphrenes, I have no doubt; that it was taken from the Greek of Herodotus I am inclined to believe, on the analysis of the text made by Page, *op. cit.* Whether or not the present passage replaced an earlier one of less psychological interest, it is my view that it was added during a later revision—a revision which ultimately was used for the fair copy placed in the Athenian archives by order of Lycurgus. It would not be the place here to reopen the discussion, but it may be that the old theory of F. Schneidewin came close to the mark: that our present text of the *Antigone* is a revision made for a posthumous performance of the play produced by Sophocles' son Iophon.

11. See 295, 303, 1045–7 and elsewhere. For a discussion, see "The Money Sequence" in Goheen, *op. cit.* 14–19.

12. One of the best analyses of the Choral ode on *Atê* is by F. J. H. Letters, *The Life and Work of Sophocles* (London 1953)81–87. Letters points out that before we emend the text of this ode we must be able to understand the basic symbolism. Particularly illuminating is his discussion of lines 601–602: "the hope (of the house of Oedipus) is being mowed down now by blood–red dust, by lack of reason and the Fury that rules the mind." I think that Letters has convincingly shown, once and for all, that the better reading here is the original one of the MSS, "blood–red dust" κόνις, and not "blood–red chopper" (κόπις), an emendation suggested by Jortin and followed by most editors. For just as the dust storm, which the Guard calls "the heavenly plague," cut off the light of the sun, so too did *Atê* in the play achieve the destruction of the Theban house—a heavenly dust, indeed, like the bloody dust that covered the corpse of Polyneices. The symbolism of the Choral ode is violent, but vivid and perfectly in keeping with the play's poetic texture. The "heavenly plague" of the dust storm, however, which the Guard describes in connection with the second burial of the body (417–420) is surely a natural phenomenon created by Sophocles to enhance the mysterious atmosphere surrounding Antigone's discovery. It carries certain symbolic overtones, but I cannot feel, as some commentators do, that it was the dust-storm, preternaturally caused by the gods, that brought about the first burial of Polyneices' body; see Adams, *op. cit.* 49, where he cites

Sheppard in support of the view he himself had advanced earlier, in *Class. Rev.* 45 (1931)110-11.

13. For a brief note on the final Choral "tag," see Adams, *op. cit.* 58. For Kitto, this "wisdom" consists in the understanding of the operation of Dikê, Retribution, in the universe; see his *Form and Meaning in Drama* (London 1956)176–78, and *Sophocles: Dramatist and Philosopher* (London 1958)40-41. I have discussed Kitto's theory of Greek Tragedy in the *Amer. Journ. of Phil.* 79 (1958)79–84.

14. For a critique of my point of view, see Harsh, "Implicit and Explicit in the *Oedipus Tyrannus*," *Amer. Journ. of Phil.* 79 (1958)243-58, with the literature there cited. A more extensive analysis of the symbolic levels of the play may be found in B. M. W. Knox, *Oedipus at Thebes* (New Haven 1957). There is also a very nuanced discussion of the play against the background of Sophocles' poetic imagination in Lattimore, *The Poetry of Greek Tragedy* 81–102. For Sophocles according to Lattimore, "drama comes first: in what puzzles or disturbs the coherent interpretation of complete drama, or at least stands unaccounted for in the economy, we may look for the poetry" (p. 8). Lattimore traces the poetic themes of foundling, mountain–spirit (that is, child of the mountain Cithaeron), murder, manhunt, and tyrant; see the conclusions on 100–1. This is very close to my own approach to the play.

15. For a discussion of the term *pestis*, see Caelius Aurelianus (whose work is ultimately based on the Greek doctor Soranus, of the second century A. D.) *On Acute Diseases*, edited by I. E. Drabkin (Chicago 1950)1. 12, 8, where he quotes the definition of Asclepiades (first century B. C.).

16. It is curious that there is very little similarity between Sophocles' plague and the one described by Thucydides; the only details that they really have in common are the existence of fever (*O. T.*, 25, 191; cf. Thuc. 2.49.8) and the numerous unburied bodies spreading contagion (*O. T.*, 180; cf. Thuc. 2.50). There is little evidence in Thucydides for any concomitant epizootic, blight, or puerperal sepsis. We do find an instance of puerperal fever as a concomitant of an epidemic in the Hippocratic work *Epidemics* 1.16, ed. W. H. S. Jones (Loeb Library, 1939, vol. i). For the fullest modern discussion of the medical problem, see Page, "Thucydides' Description of the Great Plague at Athens," *Class. Quart.* 47 (New Series 3) (1953) 96-119. Page comes to the conclusion that the Athenian plague was a peculiarly virulent form of measles; for this, of course, he must make

a selection from Thucydides' confusing and contradictory symptoms, and his view has not yet won general acceptance. The older view, that it was a typhus epidemic caused by ship–borne rats and aggravated by the poor living conditions during the Peloponnesian War, is defended by Sir William P. MacArthur in *Class. Quart.* 48/4 (1954) 171–74. For an attempt to date the *Oedipus* from the details of the plague, see the article by Knox, *Amer. Journ. of Phil.* 77 (1956)132-47, but his opinion must, I feel, be revised in view of Sophocles' use of poetic symbolism in his portrait of the plague symptoms. For Sophocles' use of medical language, see Knox, *op. cit.*, pp. 141-42 and *passim*, esp. the Index *s. v.* "Hippocrates." It becomes clear that the concept of disease and its cure is deeply interwoven in the entire fabric of the play.

17. On the Greek concept of *miasma* or defilement, see Erwin Rohde, *Psyche: Seelencult und Unsterblichkeitsglaube der Griechen* (9th ed., 2 vols., Tübingen 1925)2. 75ff. See also M. P. Nilsson, *Geschichte der griechischen Religion* (Munich 1941) 1. 83–84; W. K. C. Guthrie, *The Greeks and Their Gods* (London 1954) *passim*, and on the *Oedipus* in general, Bowra, *Sophoclean Tragedy*, 169-73, with the passages there cited.

18. On other latent imagery implicit in these lines, see Knox, *op. cit.* 140-41, where he points out the medical overtones of the words used.

19. On Oedipus the helmsman, see also Knox, *op. cit.* 112–13.

20. For the various possibilities, see Liddell–Scott–Jones, *s. v. πίπτω*.

21. See the fragment of Empedocles cited in Diels–Kranz[6], B98, 3, in *Fragmente der Vorsokratiker* 1. 346. 21, and see Liddell-Scott-Jones, *s. v. λιμήν*. On the Freudian interpretation of the play, see the remarks of Knox, 3–5, with the notes, 197–98, But the apriorism of the Freudian position is its chief flaw, even if it added anything to the play's interpretation. On the connection between the symbol of water and fertility, see Onians, *op. cit.* 272ff.

22. Cf., for example, *Antigone* 569, though the reference is contemptuous; and see Liddell–Scott–Jones, *s. v. ἀρόω* (to plough) and its cognates. See also the remarks of Knox, *op. cit.* 113-15. One might also note here the ceremony of carrying the Plough in Alcman, *Partheneion* 61ff., with Page's commentary on the passage (Oxford, 1951) 78-79. This might very well be a Spartan fertility symbol.

23. See Callimachus, fr. 572 (Pfeiffer, I, 401, with literature cited).

24. See Helmbold, "The Paradox of the *Oedipus*," *Amer. Journ. of Phil.* 72 (1951)293ff.

25. Polyneices is said to "flee the darkness of his mother" (that is, his mother's womb) Aesch., *Seven Against Thebes* 664.
26. Cf. also Knox, *op. cit.* 111-12. On the possibility of foot-symbolism in the play, see 182f., but the evidence is not convincing.
27. In Euripides' *Hippolytus*, the bull, though sacred to Poseidon, (*Hipp.* 44-5) is the instrument of Aphrodite in the final destruction of the young hero (*Hipp.* 1214ff.). Here it is a portent of power and mystery. On the sacred nature of bulls as associated with cults in the ancient world, see Jane E. Harrison, *Themis: A Study of the Social Origins of Greek Religion* (Cambridge 1927)151ff.; Nilsson, *Geschichte der griechischen Religion*, 1.197–200; Charles Seltman, *Wine in the Ancient World* (London 1957) 50-53.
28. See also Knox, *Oedipus at Thebes*, 177 and note.
29. On this see Nilsson, *op. cit.* 1.206f.; and on the symbolism of Zeus' scales, see Onians, *The Origins of European Thought*, 397–400.
30. As the lines stand, the address to the citizens of Thebes—is this seriously meant to include the audience?—can hardly be put into the mouth of the Chorus–leader, and thus the ancient Scholiast taking his cue perhaps, from the recurrence of the lines 1524-5 in Euripides *Phoenissae*, has assigned them to Oedipus. If the lines must be accepted, this would appear the only reasonable position. It has been adopted by many scholars, including Hartung, Blaydes, Wilamowitz, Pohlenz (*Die griechische Tragödie*, Göttingen 1954, p. 215) and E. Fraenkel (*Agamemnon*, 803-4). But this is the only extant play of Sophocles that ends with trochees instead of anapaests, and the shocking grammatical inconsistencies suggest the hand of a stop-gap revisor rather than that of the master. To continue emending the text ingeniously (as has been done by Martin, Musgrave, Ellendt, Stanley, and Jebb) seems like an endless game. Hence I must agree with those who have rejected the lines since the time of H. van Herwerden (1851), including F. Ritter, the edition of Schneidewin-Nauck-Bruhn (1910), and A. C. Pearson (1924). Either the original anapaestic ending was deliberately replaced for a later, posthumous performance of the play, or, as I am inclined to believe, it was lost and the gap was unskillfully filled in by some later scholar, who adapted the first two lines from Euripides and labored ponderously through the rest. If this solution seems unsatisfactory, the passage must be abandoned as a *locus desperatus*.
31. Solon's relationship with Croesus (Herodotus 1.26ff.) seems to have been a typical illustration of contrasting ways of considering hap-

piness with a view to revealing the inferiority of the barbarian. Sophocles tends to paraphrase quotations from the pre-Socratics when he is giving an impression of traditional Greek common sense or orthodox morality. For example, when Jocasta describes the anxiety-ridden Oedipus as not judging "the new in accordance with the old" (*O. T.*, 916), she is reflecting another dictum attributed to Solon: "Judge the invisible by what is manifest": Diels-Kranz [6] 1.63.22f., n. 20. It would appear that Laius' unprovoked attack on the traveller Oedipus was a serious offence against the Greek code of courtesy on the road; see the saying attributed to Chilon of Sparta: Diels-Kranz 1.63.33f., n. 17. Creon's character, all through the play, is quite in accord with the Solonic dictum about prudence in speaking (Diels-Kranz, 1.63.21 f.) and especially at the close of the play, his conduct (e. g., in lines 1422ff.) illustrates the saying of Pittacus of Lesbos, "Do not revile the unfortunate": Diels-Kranz, 1.64.13 f., n. 5. On Sophocles' use of the pre-Socratic morality in the *Antigone*, especially in connection with the concept of the Unwritten Laws, see Bowra, *Sophoclean Tragedy*, 99-100, and *passim*.

32. From a non-imagist point of view the play could be considered against the scale of blessing-curse. Implicitly all of Thebes had been pronouncing a blessing on Oedipus and upon themselves, and this is sharply reversed by the catastrophic revelation, in which the Chorus remind themselves of the Solonic dictum. The curse, on the other hand, is what best characterizes Oedipus' life, and once he effectively pronounces it (*O. T.*, 249-251), it begins to have almost a separate existence, remaining irreversible, and operating even despite Oedipus' will and intention (*O. T.* 350ff., 816ff., 1381-82). It is more than a mere dramatic trick, and deeply reflects the primitive religious feelings of fifth-century Athens. Cf. also Nilsson, *op. cit.*, 1.758-59, with the literature there cited.

33. It may be that Sophocles is anticipating the cult of Tychê, which seems to have risen formally to the level of a divinity in the fourth century: see Otto Kern, *Die Religion der Griechen* (3 vols., Berlin 1926-1938) 3.74-80. For a discussion of the passage, see also Knox, *op. cit.* 166-67; H. D. F. Kitto, *Sophocles: Dramatist and Philosopher* 62-63. Kitto sees especially here a polemic against "a certain moral and intellectual arrogance that was seeping into contemporary thought under the influence of the new Enlightenment" (p. 63). Emotionally at least this symbol would appear to be connected with the theme that Lattimore has referred to as that of Oedipus the foundling,

the nature-child or mountain-spirit: see his *The Poetry of Greek Tragedy*, 99ff.

34. For a criticism of this point of view, however, see Harsh, *art. cit.* "Implicit and Explicit in the *Oedipus Tyrannus*," *Amer.Journ. of Phil.* 79 (1958)244 and *passim*.

35. For an alleged parallelism between the *Coloneus* and the *Prometheus Bound*, see S. M. Adams, *op. cit.* 160–61. On the meaning of the play, see also Kitto, *Greek Tragedy*, 400–1.

CHAPTER SIX:

1. Cf. Cyril Bailey, *Titi Lucreti Cari De Rerum Natura libri sex* (Oxford, 1947)1.66–72, with the literature cited; and see the sound remarks in Sikes, *Roman Poetry* (New York, n. d. [1923])161–72, and *Lucretius: Poet and Philosopher* (Cambridge 1936) especially 129. These remarks should be set against the entire background of Roman didacticism in poetry, which is thoroughly analyzed by Sikes in *Roman Poetry*, 27–31, 172ff., and *passim*. For a discussion of the source of some of Lucretius' imagery, see Agnes K. Michels, "Death and Two Poets," *Trans. of the Amer. Phil. Assoc.* 86 (1955)160–79, especially 160–71.

2. On Catullus' imagery, see especially J. Svennung, *Catulls Bildersprache*: *Vergleichende Stilstudien* (Uppsala Universitets Arsskrift 3, Uppsala, 1945) with the bibliography pp. vi–ix. There is a good survey of recent Catullan studies by R. G. C. Levens, in *Fifty Years of Classical Scholarship* 284–305. See also Highet, *op. cit.* (New York 1957) 3–44,with the notes.

3. Frank O. Copley, *Gaius Valerius Catullus: The Complete Poetry* (Ann Arbor 1957)46.

4. See the penetrating comments by Highet, *op. cit.* 25–27. For a commentary, we must still rely heavily on W. Kroll, C. *Valerius Catullus* (2nd ed., Leipzig and Berlin, 1929)129ff.

5. See Highet, 17–18 with the notes.

6. The origins of the Latin love elegy would now appear to be a stale and profitless question; for a discussion of the problem, see H. E. Butler and E. A. Barber, *The Elegies of Propertius* (Oxford 1933), Introduction, xxxv–lxii; A. A. Day, *The Origins of Latin Love-Elegy* (Oxford 1938); P. J. Enk, *Sex. Propertii Elegiarum Liber I (Monobiblos)* (2 parts, Leyden, 1946) pars prior, 29–40. It cannot be denied, however, that the Latin elegy, as we have it today, has certain unique

qualities which cannot be found in anything yet discovered in Greek. The first true love–elegy may be said to be Catullus 76, *Si qua recordanti*; for a discussion, see A. L. Wheeler, *Catullus and the Traditions of Ancient Poetry* (Berkeley 1934)170–71, with the literature cited. Wheeler rightly concludes: "Catullus had begun to work into subjective–erotic elegy by way of epigram" (p. 171). Cf. also the remarks of Eduard Norden, *Die römische Literatur* (5th ed. Leipzig, 1954)70ff., with bibliography, 164–65, 177–79; Norden, however, seems to have underestimated Catullus' true poetic genius.

7. For recent bibliography on Tibullus, see Norden, *op. cit.*, 177; M. Schuster, *Tibull–Studien: Beiträge zur Erklärung und Kritik Tibulls und des Corpus Tibullianum* (Vienna 1930); L. Alfonsi, *Albius Tibullus e gli Autori del Corpus Tibullianum* (Pubbl. dell' Univ. Catt. del S. Cuore 13, Milan 1946), with bibliography; J. Hammer, "Tibullus," *Oxford Classical Dictionary* (Oxford 1949); Wright, in *Fifty Years of Classical Scholarship*, 324–26. See also Esther Breguet, *Le roman de Sulpicia: Elégies IV, 2–12 du "Corpus Tibullianum"* (Geneva 1946); L. Herrmann, *L'âge d'argent doré* (Paris 1951); Highet, *Poets in a Landscape* 156–72, with the notes. In particular, on the development of the form of the "song at the mistress' house door" παρακλανσί-θυρον, see F. O. Copley, Exclusus Amator: *A Study in Latin Love Poetry* (American Philological Association Monographs, 1956).

8. In the images of Battle, Chains, Sickness, Death, we have an anticipation of the motifs which were later to occur in the Courtly Love poetry of the Middle Ages. For an outline of these motifs, see A. R. Nykl, *Troubadour Studies* (Cambridge 1944) with bibliography to date; see also the discussion in J. J. Parry, *The Art of Courtly Love by Andreas Capellanus* (New York 1941) Introduction, 3ff. A. J. Denomy, in his penetrating study, The *Heresy of Courtly Love* (New York 1947) tends to underestimate the influence of Latin elegiac love–poetry. The origin of Courtly Love remains a mystery, but the evolution of the symbols and themes of Roman elegy in the peculiar climate of the early Middle Ages should be allowed more weight in any final analysis.

9. On the Hunt theme, see Bréguet, *op. cit.* 294–304, with the places there cited.

10. Cf. also Bréguet, *op. cit.* 282ff.

11. One of the best discussions of the topography of the Netherworld may be found in Franz Cumont's Yale lectures, *After Life In Roman Paganism* (New Haven 1923) especially 70–90, and *passim*. For an

interesting comparative study of the various poetic conceptions of the Afterlife in pagan and medieval poetry, see H. R. Patch, *The Other World According to Descriptions in Medieval Literature* (Cambridge, Mass. 1950), especially pp. 16ff. ("The Classical Tradition") with the vast bibliography cited.

12. See K. F. Smith, *The Elegies of Albius Tibullus* (New York 1913) 417; Breguet, *op. cit.* 305–14.

13. Highet, *op. cit.* 79–82. On Propertius in general, see also Enk, *op. cit.*, and his Propertian bibliography in the *Proceedings of the Cambridge Philological Association* (Cambridge 1952–2) 9–20, and add especially D. R. Shackleton Bailey, *Propertiana* (Cambridge 1956).

14. There is a very searching discussion of symbols of chastisement in Renaissance art, insofar as they were borrowed from pagan motifs, by Edgar Wind, *Pagan Mysteries in the Renaissance* (New Haven 1958) 124ff. I think that there is an anticipation in the elegiac poets of the later motif of "Amor as a god of Death" with certain Platonic, mystical overtones; cf. Wind, *op. cit.* 129ff. Wind, however, does not draw upon the Latin love poets as much as he could.

15. See the article of Miss Lake, *Class. Rev.* 51 (1937)53–55.

16. This great inscription, which still awaits complete reconstruction, is a husband's eulogy of his departed wife, perhaps composed by an historian or rhetorician; for the text, see M. Durry, *Éloge funebre d'une matrone romaine* (Paris 1950) together with the new fragment published by A. E. Gordon, *Amer. Journ. of Archeology* 54 (1950)223–26.

17. Cf. Butler and Barber, *The Elegies of Propertius*, 378ff. Some of the weaknesses in the poem might perhaps be due to the possibility that the length and treatment of the material was prescribed by Cornelia's husband Paullus. Indeed, the poem might be called a *consolatio ad Paullum*, composed by Propertius but placed in the mouth of the departed woman.

18. See A. S. Pease, *Publii Vergilii Maronis Aeneidos Liber Quartus* (Cambridge 1935)23. There are still strong overtones of the allegorical in Guillemin's interpretation of the character of Dido; see A. M. Guillemin, *Vergile poète, artiste et penseur* (Paris 1951)264ff. For a sane reaction against excessive allegorism, see R. Mandra, *The Time Element in the Aeneid of Vergil* (Williamsport, Pa. 1934)172–73, n.317.

19. W. Wili, *Vergil* (Munich, n. d. [1930]) p. 112.

20. *Die Dichtkunst Virgils: Bild und Symbol in der Aeneis* (Innsbruck and Vienna, 1950). Earlier work along these lines had been begun by W. F. Jackson Knight, *Roman Vergil* (London 1944) 111–79, and also,

but without success, by R. W. Cruttwell, *Vergil's Mind at Work: An Analysis of the Symbolism of the Aeneid* (Oxford 1946). It is safe to say that two of the most important books on Vergil since 1900 have been *Virgils epische Technik* by Richard Heinze (3rd ed., Leipzig, 1915) and the commentary of Norden, *P. Vergilius Maro Aeneis Buch VI* (3rd ed., Leipzig and Berlin, 1927). For a survey of the vast bibliography on Vergil, one may begin with Wright, in *Fifty Years of Classical Scholarship*, 307–18, with the supplements of Otis in *Classical Weekly* 49 (1945)154f.; and see the survey articles by Duckworth, "Recent Work on Vergil (1940–1956)," *Classical World* 51 (1958), now reprinted as a pamphlet by the Vergilian Society ([1958] undated and unpaginated).

21. Norman W. De Witt, *Virgil's Biographia Litteraria* (Toronto 1923)127.
22. On Vergil's adaptation of the character of Odysseus, see Stanford, *op. cit.* 128ff. On the adaptation of Achilles, see L. A. Mackay, "Achilles as Model for Aeneas," *Trans. of the Amer. Phil. Assoc.*, 88 (1957)11–16.
23. Cf. *The American Notebooks by Nathaniel Hawthorne*, edited by Randall Stewart (New Haven 1932).
24. See also Robert B. Lloyd, "The Character of Anchises in the *Aeneid*," *Trans. of the Amer. Phil. Assoc.* 88 (1957) 44–55.
25. *Aeneid* 6.724–7.
26. *Aeneid* 6.743–7.
27. See, for example, the discussion in Bowra, *From Virgil to Milton* (London, 1945)60ff. The fundamental view of Aeneas' character was laid down by Heinze, *op. cit.* 271–280, and *passim*. For the more recent discussions, see·the bibliographical notice of Duckworth, *Class. World, loc. cit.*
28. See the remarks of Pöschl, *op. cit.* 65f. (on Roman *Pflichtgefühl*) and 40f. on the three levels of meaning in the *Aeneid*. Cf. also MacKay, "Three Levels of Meaning in the *Aeneid*," *Trans. of the Amer. Philol. Assoc.* 86 (1955)180–89.
29. *Aeneid.* 6.893–9. Norden's view, *Aeneis. Buch VI*, 348, followed, for example, by F. Fletcher, *Virgil's Aeneid VI* (Oxford 1951)101f., was that the exit by way of the Ivory Gate suggested the time of Aeneas' return from the Lower World. Among the numerous studies of the problem, see especially E. L. Highbarger, *The Gates of Dreams: An Archaeological Examination of Vergil, Aeneid VI, 893–899* (Johns Hopkins Univ. Studies in Archaeology 30, Baltimore 1940). For Highbarger, the journey is ultimately a symbol of the soul's expe-

riences. Cf. also Brooks Otis, "Three problems of *Aeneid 6*," *Trans. of the Amer. Philol. Assoc.* 90 (1959) 165–179.

CHAPTER SEVEN:

1. Oxford: Clarendon Press 1957, a book which is based in part on the lectures which Fraenkel delivered as Corpus Professor of Latin at Oxford University. For a general bibliography on Horace, see N. I. Herescu, *Bibliographie de la littérature latine* (Paris, 1943) 169–88; T. E. Wright, in *Fifty Years of Classical Scholarship*, 318–24; G. Radke, "Horaz: Auswahlbericht," *Gymnasium* 61 (1954) 231–48. Cf. also Highet, *op. cit.* 106–55, with notes and bibliography; and the survey by R. J. Getty, "Recent Work on Horace (1945–57)" *CW* 52 (1959)167–88.

2. See the discussion of Fraenkel, *Horace*, 90–101.

3. The image seems to have occurred in the diatribes of the third-century Cynic philosopher Teles, and probably goes back to the earlier Cynics; according to Diogenes Laertius, 8.1.8, Pythagoras used to compare life to a πανήγυρις, or celebration of the great games, at which people have different roles, some competing, others merely watching. On the image in the Middle Ages and Renascence, see Curtius, *European Literature and the Latin Middle Ages*, 138–44.

4. See Highet, *op. cit.* 134; and see also the discussion of the satire by Fraenkel, *op. cit.* 138–44.

5. See Duckworth, "*Animae dimidium meae*: Two Poets of Rome," *Trans. of the Amer. Philol. Assoc.* 87 (1956)281–316. On Horace's friendships in general, cf. L. P. Wilkinson, *Horace and His Lyric Poetry* (Cambridge, 2nd ed. 1951) 53f.; H. Hommel, *Horaz: Der Mensch und das Werk*, (Heidelberg 1950)51–56; Fraenkel, *Horace*, 409, has some penetrating remarks on the difference between the characters of Horace and Vergil.

6. Cf. *Sat.* 1.1.58, 1.4.105ff.; 1.6.6ff.; *Odes* 3.30.12. See the discussion of Hommel, *Horaz*, 14ff.; Fraenkel, 5 ff.(in connection with the *Vita Horati*). As Fraenkel shows, Horace's father was not a tax collector, but a *coactor argentarius*, who was a combination of banker and head-auctioneer, under whom is the *praeco*, who handles the actual auctioning process. One should also compare the sympathetic portrait Horace paints of the poor *praeco* Volteius Mena in *Epist.* 1.7.50–95.

7. Cf. *Odes* 1.4, 4.7, 4.12.

8. Cf. *Odes* 1.9, 2.4, 2.8, 4.11, and *passim.*
9. A good number of country rituals are celebrated in the third book of the *Odes*, for example, 3.13 (Bandusia), 3.18 (Faunus), 3.22 (Diana), 3.23 (Phidyle's sacrifice), 3.28 (Neptune); cf. also 4.11 (on the Ides of Venus' month). The religious atmosphere of these poems is light-hearted; the cults are an excuse for a celebration, and escape.
10. *Odes* 1.1.14–18, 1.3.10–12; *Sat.* 1.1.6. But see E. de Saint-Denis, *La Rôle de la mer dans la poésie latine* (Paris 1935)279ff.
11. Travellers who "dash across the seas change not themselves but merely their location": *Epist.* 1.11.27. This epistle is really a study of the two approaches to reality, by way of the superficial and the external, and (as Horace always attempted) by way of interior values.
12. Cf. *Odes* 2.9.3, 2.10.1ff.
13. Cf. *Odes* 2.2.13–16: "The dropsy grows with self-indulgence." The dropsy is again used as a symbol of spiritual illness in *Epist.* 1.2.34. Thus the "bloated inertia" (*aquosus languor: Odes* 2.2.15) of the man suffering from edema is taken as the analogue of the moral sluggishness of the person unwilling to correct his faults. Cf. also Horace's description of his own illness in *Epist.* 1.8.7–12. There he feels that the doctors can do nothing for his spiritual disorder, a *veternus*, or "sluggishness." Illness is the one dark cloud in *Sat.* 1.5, the Journey to Brundisium; Horace suffers from dysentery and from sore eyes; Vergil from nervous stomach or indigestion. The irony of minor ailments is also suggested in the discussion of Stoic philosophy, *Epist.* 1.1. 105–7; the Stoic wise man can still suffer *pituita*, apparently some mild disorder (like dyspepsia). Useless wealth is compared to *fomenta*, fomentations or poultices: *Epist.* 1.2.52; and this is precisely what Horace's miser asks for in *Sat.* 1.1.82; worries are a "chilly poultice" in *Epist.* 1.3.26; cf. also the *fomenta* which do nothing to alleviate the pain in *Epodes* 11.17.
14. *Odes* 4.11.33–36. Cf. the charms in *Epist.* 1.1.36.
15. Cf. *Odes* 1.4, 2.3, 2.14, 4.17, and elsewhere.
16. On Horace's poetic transformation of the joys of drinking, see Henry Steele Commager, "Wine in Horace's Odes," *Trans. of the Amer. Philol. Assoc.*, 88 (1957)68–80. On the poem, see Fraenkel, *Horace*, 176f.; Highet, *op. cit.* 122f.; Wilkinson, *op. cit.* 130: "The whole scene is a fiction symbolic of old age." However, Wilkinson's correspondences are so close that the poem almost becomes allegorical; the snow on the mountain is equivalent to the snow-white hair (*morosa canities*) of old age, etc.

17. On some of the excessive interpretations to which this poem has been subjected, see E. Stemplinger, "Horaz im Urteil der Jahrhunderte," *Das Erbe der Alten II.* 5 (Leipzig 1921)153. On the poem in general, see Highet, *op. cit.* 145f., and Fraenkel, *Horace*, 202–204. Zumpt, Fraenkel, and others seem certainly right in thinking that Horace transferred the name of a spring near Venusia to a spring not far from his Sabine villa; see Fraenkel, 203, n. 1. This would be further support for the suggestion that the spring was symbolically associated with the entire turn his life took in moving from Venusia to the farm Maecenas gave him. The name, Bandusia, creates a problem; it is uncertain whether it was simply the name of the spring or the name of a nymph. O. Keller, *Epilegomena zu Horaz* (2 parts, Leipzig 1873) 1.233, plausibly derives the name from the Greek *Pandosia*, "generous giver," the name of a number of Greek city states, as well as the word for "harlot": see Liddell–Scott–Jones, *Greek–English Lexicon* (Oxford, 1940), *s. v.* It may perhaps be connected with the Celtic goddess's name, *Bandua*: see W. H. Roscher, *Ausführliches Lexikon der griech. und röm. Mythologie* (Leipzig 1884–90) 1.749–50. In any case, the name is unique in Latin literature; see J. R. Smith, *Springs and Wells in Greek and Roman Literature* (New York 1922) 628–29.

18. Cf. *Odes* 1.32, 3.30, 4.2, and elsewhere; cf. also *Sat.* 2.1.12–13 (his talents not equipped for epic poetry); *Epist.* 1.1.8–9 (the "aging horse").

19. Cf. *Sat.* 1.4.142–143, 1.5.100; 1.9.69–70.

20. Fraenkel is one of the few commentators who have completely grasped the symbolic overtones of the description of the *volumen* of *Epistles*; see his *Horace*, 356–59. For other images, note Horace's description of himself as a charging bull in *Epodes* 6.11–12, or a sheepdog of good breed, *ibid.* 5–8: Aesop's ass who tried to disguise himself in a lion's skin, *Sat.* 1.6.22. Horace identifies himself with a rude Priapus statue on the Esquiline in *Sat.* 1.8. Such animal imagery which comes down from the early Greek Aesopic tradition and is reflected in Archilochus and Semonides of Amorgos, has the advantage of being immediately understood; it establishes the tone of familiar, ironic humor.

21. On this ascent of the soul to the ethereal regions, see S. Angus, *The Religious Quests of the Graeco–Roman World* (New York 1929) 295–320, with the sources cited; cf. also Cumont, *op. cit.* 91ff., and I. A. Richmond, *Archaeology, and the After life in Pagan and Christian Imagery* (Riddell Memorial Lectures, Twentieth Series, London 1950) 13ff.

22. Fraenkel, for example, speaks of the description as "repulsive or ridiculous, or both"; *Horace*, 301.

23. In the song-contest between Damon and Alphesiboeus in Vergil, *Eclogue* 8.95–97, Alphesiboeus tells how he once saw Moeris change into a wolf and vanish into the woods; in the same *Eclogue* 8.52, Damon sings of the change in nature, when the wolf will fly in panic from the lamb.

24. The sea as an image of the moodiness and changeability of woman was first used by Semonides of Amorgos, fr. 7.27–42 (Diehl). For a further discussion of primitive associations between woman and water, see Onians, *op. cit. (supra* Ch. 1, n. 1) 230. In Horace, if we grant that Pyrrha = *mare*, the sea, then there is a whole sequence of ambiguities in the Latin words, with different meanings when applied to Pyrrha or to the sea: cf. *insolens*, "arrogant"; *fruitur*, "enjoy"; *vacuam*, "free", "disengaged"; *fallax*, "deceptive"; *intemptata*, "untried"; *nites*, "gleam brightly." A similar chain of ambiguities occurs in the final or "seal epistle," *Epist.* 1.20, where the Latin words apply equally to the book and to a young slave-boy. Cf. also Horace's letter of introduction to Tiberius on behalf of Septimius, *Epist.* 1.9, where Horace speaks of his efforts as being at once a favor and a playful insolence; he thus excuses his abandoning his accustomed modesty and propriety.

25. The poem is not discussed by Fraenkel, and is only given slight mention by Wilkinson. See Highet, *op. cit.* 127f.; and M. P. Cunningham, "Enarratio of Horace, *Odes* 1.9," *Class Philol.* 52 (1957)98–102.

CHAPTER EIGHT

1. In addition to the general works on Horace's poems, see especially the following useful editions of the *Satires*: J. C. Rolfe (Boston 1901; rev. ed. 1935); J. H. Kirkland (Boston 1902); A. Gow, *Satires: Book I* (Cambridge 1901); E. P. Morris (New York 1909); B. J. Hayes and F. G. Plaistowe (London: University Tutorial Press, n. d.); A. Rostagni (Turin 1948). Cf. also E. S. Shuckburgh, *Augustus* (London 1905) 99 ff.; W. Wili, *Horaz und die augusteische Kultur* (Basle 1948). On the *iter Brundisinum* in particular, see E. Desjardins *RPh* 2 (1878) 144ff.; A. Bischoff, *De itinere Horatii Brundisino* (Landau 1880); H. Duntzer, *Philologus* 55 (1896)416ff.; J. Gow *CR* 15 (1901)117; L. Dorsch, *Mit Horaz vom Rom nach Brindisi* (Prague 1904); G. C. Fiske, *Lucilius and Horace* (Madison 1920), 306ff.; Helena Mata-

kiewicz, "De itineris genere literario," *Eos* 32 (1929) 229ff.; A. Calderini, "Viaggi e avventure di viaggi dei tempi di Orazio," *Le Vie d'Italia* 41 (1935) 498ff.; V. D'Antò, "Il Viaggio di Orazio da Roma a Brindisi," *Rendiconti della Accademia Napoletana*, n. s. 24/25 (1949–1950) 235–55.

2. For example, Müller, Krüger, Palmer, Kiessling–Heinze, Calderini.

3. For example, E. Desjardins, Lejay, Rolfe.

4. For E. Gibbon's essay on Horace's journey, written by him in French at Lausanne in 1763, see his *Receuil de mes observations*: No. iii, in *Miscellaneous Works of Edward Gibbon*, edited by John Lord Sheffield (3 vols., Dublin 1796)3.87ff. Gibbon, who seems familiar with travel in Italy, has Horace arrive at Beneventum on the *sixth* day, though he conceded that the speed of the journey ultimately depended on the urgency of Maecenas' diplomatic mission. But after the party leaves Beneventum, he notes, "we meet with little but obscurity in this part of the route... Father Sanadon [the Jesuit classicist, Noel Sanadon, d. 1733] suspects Horace of having lost his way among his native mountains" (*loc. cit.* 91). Gibbon, by way of explaining why so much of the poem should be about trivial details, suggests that it was perhaps "written to convince his enemies that his thoughts and occupations on the road were far from being of a serious or political nature" (p. 94).

5. See Cassius Dio 48. 28–30, and Appian, *Civil War* 5.63–65, based perhaps on Asinius' lost *History*. For the general background of the period see T. Rice Holmes, *The Architect of the Roman Empire* (Oxford 1928) 1.103ff. and W. W. Tarn, *Cambridge Ancient History* 10 (1934)51ff.

6. See *Serm.* 2.6.40, where Horace tells us that "seven or, rather, eight years" had passed since he was first introduced to Maecenas, and if this satire was written in 31/30 B. C. the introduction could hardly have been earlier than 39.

7. See Appian, *Civil War* 5.92. Indeed, earlier in the same year (38 B. C.), if we may trust Appian 5.78–79, Antony had sailed to the port of Brundisium at Octavian's invitation, but not finding him there, and perhaps disturbed by unfavorable omens, he sailed back again. All the evidence suggests that there must have been much nervous coming and going during this troubled period, and it is difficult to make a connected story out of the different sources. Actually, some older scholars, like Wesseling, whom Heindorf follows, had proposed the abortive meeting of 38 B. C. as the occasion for Horace's jour-

ney. But, as Palmer has pointed out, if we accept Appian's account of all, there is no reason to think that anyone came to meet Antony on this ocassion.

8. So, for example, Schütz, Palmer, Cartault, Kirkland, Morris, Fairclough, Herrmann, Calderini, Illuminati, and, with some hesitation, Wickham and Rolfe.

9. Cf. Dio 48.54; Appian 5.93–94; Plutarch, *Antony* 35.

10. Rice Holmes, *op. cit.* 112f.; Tarn, *CAH* 10.172.

11. So Orelli, Kirchner, Franke, Dillenburger, Ritter, Macleane, Müller, Stemplinger (in Pauly-Wissowa, *s. v.* Horatius), Kiessling-Heinze, Hayes-Plaistowe, Lejay, Gow, Camphell, Rostagni, Fraenkel.

12. In his edition of the *Satires* (London 1883) 172.

13. In his school edition, *Satires: Book I* (Cambridge 1901) 70. Lejay, Latsch, and others suggest that the *udos ramos* (81) must have been still green. But that the size of the *macros turdos* (72) should also be evidence of springtime is too far-fetched, as Cartault and Herrmann have already been at pains to point out.

14. Mr. C. H. Roberts has privately suggested the possibility that Horace's satire may be based on a reconciliation at Brundisium that has not been recorded in our historical sources; for, if there were two such reconciliations between the years 40 and 37 and an abortive one in 38, there may have been more.

15. See his commentary *ad init.*, ed. A. Holder (1894) 255.6 ff. On Lucilius, see E. H. Warmington, *Remains of Old Latin* (Loeb Library 1938) 3.30ff.

16. Lucilius frag. 109–110 (Warmington). It is a question whether *equus ferus* for Horace actually did mean "rhinoceros," as I incline to believe, rather than the usually accepted "unicorn." The meaning "rhinoceros" would fit in better with the rough humor of the two clowns, and would be more reminiscent of Lucilius' Greek expression.

17. Tenney Frank plausibly suggested, in *CPhil* 15 (1920)293, that Horace's Heliodorus (2) is really to be identified with Octavian's Greek tutor, Apollodorus. If this is right, it would seem that a vein of playful fiction enters into the satire right from the first lines.

18. It is odd that commentators have not previously realized the reason why Horace fasts in 7–9; Caelius Aurelianus, *On Chronic Diseases* 4.22 (ed. I. E. Drabkin, University of Chicago Press 1950, p. 828) recommends fasting and rest for those suffering from dysentery or other intestinal ailments, and experience with the water of southern Italy would suggest that Horace was merely following common sense.

19. Cf. his article in *Rendiconti della Academia Napoletana* n. s. 24/25 (1949–1950) 235–55, with the comments by W. S. Anderson in *CW* 49 (1955)57–59.

20. The controversy on whether *optimus* is to be taken with *Maecenas* or with *Cocceius* can only, in my view, be decided by suggesting that Horace deliberately wrote the line so that the adjective could be taken with both.

21. The transmission of the text of the satire is in general very good. But the frequency of abrupt changes may suggest that Horace had shortened his text after reciting it.

CHAPTER NINE

1. See the discussion in G. Bagnani, *Arbiter of Elegance*: *A Study of the Life and Works of C. Petronius* (*The Phoenix*, suppl. vol. 2, Toronto, 1954) 3 ff., with the bibliography cited.

2. For the text I have departed somewhat from A. Riese, *Anth. lat.*, pars prior, fasc. 2 (Leipzig 1870)651, in order to reflect the MS tradition more closely. See also F. Buecheler, *Petronii Saturae et liber Priapeorum*[6] (cur. W. Heraeus, Berlin 1922) frag. 30, 121.

3. For the literature in general, see H. Kenner, *Pauly–Wissowa* 18 (1939) 448–459, *s. v.* 'Oneiros.' For the Epicurean view, see Lucretius 4.962–1036, with the commentary of C. Bailey (Oxford 1947)3.1295ff. On Artemidorus of Daldis, who flourished about A. D. 170, see Nilsson, *Gesch. griech. Rel.* 1 (Munich 1950)499. Cf. also R. Pack, "Lexical and Textual Notes on Artemidorus," *Trans. of the Amer. Philol. Assoc.* 90 (1959) 180–84, with bibliography. It is interesting to note that Sigmund Freud in his *Traumdeutung*, ch. ii, pointed out that his own theory ultimately went back to the principles of Artemidorus, based on the association of ideas. If one may be allowed to oversimplify, however, the difference in Freudian dream–analysis primarily consists in the fact that (a) the analyst is to draw the associations from the dreamer himself, and (b) Freudian dream–symbolism is almost wholly sexual.

4. For a discussion of the influence of Stoic dream theory on Philo, see H. A. Wolfson, *Philo* (Cambridge, 1948) 2.55ff.

5. See Lucr. 4.987ff., with Bailey's commentary *ad loc.*, 1297ff.

CHAPTER TEN

1. For an account of Juvenal's influence upon later literature, see G. Highet, *Juvenal the Satirist: A Study* (Oxford 1954) 180ff. For a general study of the power of literature in its effect upon men's behavior, see Gottfried Benn, "Können Dichter die Welt ändern?" in his collection *Provoziertes Leben: Eine Auswall aus den Prosaschriften* (Ullstein Bücher: Wiesbaden 1956) 25-34.

2. For an outline and commentary, see L. Friedlaender, *D. Juni Juvenalis Saturarum Libri V* (Leipzig 1895)128ff.; J. E. B. Mayor, *Thirteen Satires of Juvenal* (2 vols., London 1900)1.89ff.; Helmbold, "The Structure of Juvenal I," *University of California Publications in Class. Philology* 14 (1951) no 2. 47-60; and Highet, *Juvenal*, 47-58, with the notes 245-49.

3. On the various attempts to construct a logical outline of the poem, see Highet's comments, p. 246. All seem unconvincing—as any rhetorical outline of a poem must be. Apart from the introduction and the conclusion, the satire seems to be constructed of rapid-fire bursts of rage, which come to rest, as it were, in various images.

4. It is because Juvenal's poetic world had been fully constructed before the beneficent influence of Trajan had made itself felt. Apart from the distorting nature of satire as such, we must always be aware, in Juvenal, of the polarity between poetry and history. Highet, in his article on Juvenal in the *Oxford Classical Dictionary* (1949)474, may well be right when he suggests that Juvenal's sense of bitterness was "focused on Domitian's principate," and that "it gradually faded in intensity with advancing years." Cf. also his remarks in his *Juvenal* 54-57. Highet's reconstruction of Juvenal's life, however, 4-41, can be accepted only with reservations.

5. A deprecatory reference to his method of composition—and wrongly applied, by some scholars, to the definition of satire in general. It is possible, however, that Harrison is right and we should delete lines 85-86: *quidquid agunt homines....farrago nostri libelli*. The sense of the entire passage would then become much more tidy: "From the time of Deucalion and Pyrrha, when was there more vice than at Rome today?" Surely it is arguable that Juvenal's satires did not have so wide a scope (at least in the first book) as indicated in lines 85-86. "Whatever men do, their prayers, fears, anger, joys, etc." On behalf of those who would retain the lines it may be said that

these lines indicate that Juvenal's canvas will be realistic and not epic or mythological; with Martial, he does inaugurate a new era in poetry, in revolt against the insipid narrative poems of the Silver Age. As Martial said: *hominem pagina nostra sapit* (10.4.10), "my pages smell of man."

6. On the wax-tablets, see the note of Mayor, *Thirteen Satires*, 1.113. Notes were taken thus briefly, to be written down carefully later on. Compare the picture Horace gives of two informers with their note-books in *Sat.* 1.4.65-67:"Keen Sulcius and Caprius walk along with their books, both rather hoarse, both a great threat to bandits." Horace's reply to his critics is that he only mentions minor faults, and that his *Sermones* were not meant for publication. Juvenal, however, is aware that the crimes he pillories are serious; hence, he protests that he will mention only the names of the dead. That he was neither consistent here, nor completely free from insincerity in using cover-names is adequately shown by Highet, *Juvenal*, 290-94. But Juvenal's evasion on the use of names achieves two purposes. First, he will not then be liable to the delict of *diffamatio*, under the *lex Cornelia de iniuriis* or similar legislation; see the discussion of the legal aspect in W. W. Buckland and A. D. McNair, *Roman Law and Common Law: A Comparison in Outline* (Cambridge 1936) 297-299; and A. Berger, *Encyclopaedic Dictionary of Roman Law* (Trans. Amer. Philosophical Assoc. vol. 43, 1953) 381, 562. In the second place, using the names of the dead is Juvenal's way of suggesting the permanence of the faults, a point first made by A. T. Christ, *Über die Art und Tendenz der Juvenalischen Personenkritik* (Landskron 1881). On Juvenal, see also W. S. Anderson, "Imagery in the Satires of Horace and Juvenal," *Amer. Journ. of Philol.* 81 (1960) 225-60.

7. If the name Umbricius had any significance it escapes us. An *haruspex* named Umbricius is mentioned in Pliny, *Nat. Hist.* 10.6.19, but this cannot have been Juvenal's friend who confesses he "never inspected a toad's entrails." The name is fairly common in Latin inscriptions, and Friedlaender, *op. cit.* 193, mentions a man of this name from an inscription found near Pozzuoli. It had occurred to me to suggest a connection with *umbra*="shadow," as though Umbricius were Juvenal's shadow-self; but this would seem to push coincidence too far.

8. For a discussion of the poem's structure, see Highet, *Juvenal*, 254.

9. For the latest discussion of Juvenal's Aquinum, see Highet, *Poets in a Landscape* 202-12, with the bibliography and notes, 264. See

also his discussion of the lost Juvenal–inscription (apparently from an altar to Ceres) see *ibid.*, 210, and cf. his *Juvenal*, 32, with commentary and notes.

10. Otto Ribbeck, *Der echte und der unechte Iuvenal: Eine kritische Untersuchung* (Berlin 1865). See the bibliography on the controversy in Highet, *Juvenal*, 265, n. 3.

11 Highet has thoroughly grasped the religious aspect of the poem; see *Juvenal*, 125 and 275. On Juvenal's debt to earlier literature, see Friedlaender, 451ff.

12. The lines are not to be deleted with U. Knoche, *D. Iunius Iuvenalis Saturae* (Munich 1950) *ad loc.* The *ergo* is resumptive, and goes back to the theme first suggested in lines 5–9, ending with *nocitura petuntur/ militia*, "we pray for our own destruction both in war and in peace." I read the lines as a question with Buecheler and others; see the note by Highet, Juvenal, 278.

13. Following a suggestion of Friedrich Leo; see the edition of Knoche, *ad loc.*

14. Seneca, *Moral Epistles* 10.4. On the various parallel passages see Friedlaender, *op. cit.* 487; Mayor, *op. cit.* 2.174.

15. Petronius, *Satyricon* 61.1.; cf. also *ibid.* 88.8 for its use as a prayer formula.

INDEX I

PASSAGES OF ANCIENT AUTHORS TREATED

GENERAL INDEX